BEF

By the same author:

Away to Sea

Captain Martha MN *(fiction)*

BEFORE THE BOX BOATS

The story of a merchantman

Captain A.W. Kinghorn

© A W Kinghorn 1999

All rights reserved. No part of this publication may be reproduced, stored in a retreval system, or transmitted in any form or by any means, electronic, mechanical, photocopying, recording or otherwise, without the prior permission of the copyright owner.

British Library, Cataloguing in Publication Data.
Kinghorn, A.W.
    Before The Box Boats
    1.   Kinghorn, A.W.   2.   Shipmasters - Great Britain
    - Biography
    1.   Title
    387.5'092'4   VK 140.K/

ISBN 0 9536406 0 4

Published by Captain A.W. Kinghorn, 15 Kendal Avenue, Cullercoats, North Shields, Tyne & Wear NE30 3AQ

Produced by JASPRINT, 12 Tower Road, Glover, District 11, Washington, Tyne & Wear NE37 2SH ENGLAND

Cover picture; TSMV English Star, the author's first command photographed in the English Channel by SKYFOTOS.

**This is a reprint of the book, exactly the same format except for laminated paper cover with different design from hardback original, which was published in 1983 by Kenneth Mason, Emsworth, Hants.
ISBN 0 85937 297 9**

Contents

Prologue — page 6
Acknowledgements — page 9
Chapter 1 *The Falklands 1982* — page 11
Chapter 2 *Away to sea! 1949-1954* — page 15
Chapter 3 *Up for Second Mate's 1954* — page 39
Chapter 4 *A voyage in the Booth Line 1954-55* — page 47
Chapter 5 *Third Mate 1955-1957* — page 61
Chapter 6 *Second Mate 1957-1960* — page 75
Chapter 7 *The Mate 1960-1961* — page 87
Chapter 8 *Heavy lifters, heavy ships 1962-1968* — page 103
Chapter 9 *On the lake 1968* — page 125
Chapter 10 *The finishing school 1969-1971* — page 135
Chapter 11 *Command at last! 1971* — page 143
Chapter 12 *Old ships on new trades 1971-1973* — page 157
Chapter 13 *Family Odyssey 1973-1974* — page 169
Chapter 14 *Adelaide's last voyage 1974-1975* — page 177
Chapter 15 *Last of an era 1976-1977* — page 191
Chapter 16 *Survival* — page 203
Index — page 209

Prologue

THIS IS ONE MARINER'S STORY of his time at sea — mostly before the advent of those odd-shaped box boats, the container ships. Hence the title. Seafarers wax indignant when shoresiders call ships 'boats' because a ship can carry a boat, but not so the reverse — and that is the difference between the two. Nevertheless, seafarers between themselves talk 'boats' all the time; Star Boats, P & O Boats (and a few of these latter are still, to the modern seaman, Pazzy Boats, ie passenger liners.) They tell of Cross Channel Boats and older hands speak nostalgically of the Port Boats, the Cunard Meddy Boats, and the old Shaw Savill Boats.

But today it's all Box Boats. The seafarer's box boat is described in maritime circles as a Cellular Container Ship, a vessel designed to carry her cargo in the 20ft and 40ft containers now so much a part of the motorway scene. There are no shelter decks or tween decks, and containers are stacked directly over one another in the holds, held in place by skeletal steel guides. Cargo hatchways at the top of the hold must be big enough to accommodate the largest container and can frequently take three. This means container ships need large hatches close together, leaving very little deck space around the coamings. On top of the hatch covers, containers are stacked from stem to stern, as many as five high and 13 across. To allow space for as much cargo as possible her accommodation house must be short — over the engine room but not over the holds — and her navigation bridge must be high to afford a clear view all round, especially over the containers stowed on deck forward of the bridge. Stability is provided by water ballast tanks, the contents adjusted as required to keep the vessel upright in a gale. The large surface exposed to the wind by a high deckload can cause a container ship to heel over like a sailing vessel if not counteracted by ballasting.

Early container ships had the accommodation and engines right aft but at 20 knots or so vibration on the bridge made it impossible to write up the logbook in anything but a shaky scrawl, so to reduce rattle the modern ocean-going container ship has her engines, bridge and accommodation about two thirds of the distance aft from forward, where vibration is markedly less. This makes life pleasanter for her crew simultaneously reducing wear and tear on delicate bridge equipment such as radar, steering console and satellite navigator.

Some box boats have their own deck cranes for working cargo in and out, enabling them to visit ports where there are as yet no shoreside cranes. But deck cranes require costly maintenance and take up valuable cargo space, for a ship must be able to carry as much cargo as possible; this is what pays the bills and leaves her owner with something for himself, and for his ship's eventual replacement.

Because of her cargo a box boat must be almost box-shaped herself, with flat, sheerless deckline, devoid of curve or camber, with flat sides and flat transom. These, with her tall, square accommodation, absence of masts, rigging, streamlining and 'style', have made her the ocean's ugly duckling, a large, self propelled barge. But, ugly duckling or not, she carries the cargo and carries it well, and that has been the sole purpose of every merchant ship since time began.

Is it necessary to carry all cargo in containers? The answer is no. Cargo, after all, was carried in ships for thousands of years before containers appeared. But when containerisation spread from America in the late '60s it was realised that here was a through-cargo transport system better than any other, particularly when cargo was damaged by frequent handling or could easily be pilfered. Containerisation has changed ocean transport as dramatically as Steam outdated Sail a century ago. Because ships now spend nearly all their time at sea, where before they spent over half their lives in port, life for the seafarer has altered. Despite modern communications, he is as cut off from the land as he ever was. Although he has his own cabin now, often with private bathroom, life is still communal, his only company for months on end that of his shipmates.

But before the box boats, life had a quality now sadly missing. We had time, in those days, for a run ashore in port to see something of the country, time to get to know the people. I was a boy during the Second World War, but before it had ended I had decided on a life at sea. Thus I found myself one of those who were the last generation — before the box boats.

Dedication   To my Wife, Brenda

Acknowledgements

I wish to express my thanks to Mr J G Payne of Blue Star Line; Mr Ron Russell, editor of the Blue Star House magazine *Gangway*; Mr Leo Madigan of the Marine Society; The Hydrographer of the Navy for permission to use extracts from Admiralty Pilot Books; Skyfotos Limited, New Romney, Kent, for permission to use their splendid aerial ship portraits used throughout, and to Mr A Duncan of Gravesend, Kent for a shot of the *Auckland Star*; The *Nautical Magazine* for permission to reprint material from my article, *The Great Bitter Lakers*, which appeared in the December, 1969 issue; and to my shipmates (especially Graham White, John Porter and Colin Elms who read and vetted the manuscript), my family and friends for all their help and encouragement.

Front cover picture of English Star and other SKYFOTO illustrations are reprinted here by kind permission of FotoFlite, Ashford, Kent TN23 4FB England

Illustrations

Avelona Star Royal Navy page 13
HMS Conway Skyfotos page 17
Columbia Star Skyfotos page 23
Saxon Star George Heron page 35
Dominic Skyfotos page 48
Uruguay Star Skyfotos page 63
Melbourne Star page 65
English Star Skyfotos page 67
Imperial Star Skyfotos page 69
Penwith SS Co dividend warrant pages 72-3
Sydney Star Skyfotos page 77
Wellington Star Skyfotos page 85
London docks a century ago ILN page 88
Dunedin Star Skyfotos page 93
South Africa Star Skyfotos page 105
Australia Star Skyfotos page 119
California Star W H Askew page 122
Scottish Star Skyfotos page 126
The Suez stamps page 131
Malaysia page 136
Australasia, artist's impression page 138
Caledonia Star page 147
Caledonia's crew page 154
Brasilia Star, C B Mulholland page 159
Montreal Star Skyfotos page 160
Tasmania Star Skyfotos page 170
Tasmania Star's deck cargo author page 172
Pitcairn's schoolhouse author page 173
Adelaide Star page 178
ACT 5 page 192-193
Auckland Star A Duncan page 193
New Zealand Star BSL page 205

All cartoons are by the author

The Falklands 1982

A LOW LINE of snowswept hills along a grey horizon gave the North Sea ferry her landfall. Right on time, she eased speed and headed towards the black and white lighthouse on a low headland. No harbour pilot was offered or expected as the master took his ship in past a line of anchored tankers and cargo vessels, to swing hard a'port through the narrow entrance leading to the inner harbour. Off the little town she came to anchor near three other ferries, two of them old friends from the North Sea, the third in the livery of New Zealand's Union Steamship Company.

Eagerly the new arrival's passengers crowded the rails, many of us seeing for the first time those hills which had become so familiar on television: Two Sisters over there, and Mount Longdon; there is Tumbledown Mountain and here behind the town is Sapper Hill. Neat little white houses with coloured roofs and the dark brick cathedral confirm that this is indeed Port Stanley. The union flag of Great Britain has flown proudly in the Falkland Islands for four months now, after six weeks under the blue and white banner of Argentina. Six weeks which rocked the world.

Merchant Service passengers in the now anchored *Norland* were instructed by public address system to muster with their effects at the starboard shipside door, and soon the tug *Rollicker* had us aboard, crowding her wide afterdeck. In their camouflaged Can't See Me Suits her crew looked bewilderingly like squaddies — as this war's tommies are called. Even before *Rollicker* had left *Norland*'s side, helicopters were busy taking other passengers and equipment ashore. Never had I seen so many helicopters; in every direction they came and went, many with slings of cargo dangling beneath their dragonfly bodies.

Our tug headed out between Navy and Engineers Points to Port

William, the outer harbour, to call first at the pillar-box red *Stena Inspector*, fleet repair ship. She then crossed the green, curdled water, to my own ship, lying grey and white against a grey and white landscape. Her bright Blue Star funnel had long been painted an all-concealing white, as it was found in another war recently fought in the Middle East that the conspicuous funnel star made a convenient line-marker for aerial bombing runs!

As we closed, my ship's stained and battered sides told of months of craft coming alongside and a crew too busy unloading cargo to maintain her appearance. Not that the weather was conducive to painting, anyway. A rising wind splashed seawater over the tug as we climbed up the rope pilot ladder.

Captain H K Dyer, who took the *Avelona Star* out from Portsmouth when war still raged in the South Atlantic, was due to proceed home on leave after a normal tour of abnormal duty. The ship, chartered by the Ministry of Defence as a STUFT — Ship Taken Up From Trade — had become a floating supermarket to the Task Force, a familiar sight on San Carlos Water and Barclay Sound by the time I joined in Port William.

The weather was kind for our trip on the open afterdeck of *Rollicker* — blowing cold and fresh but not snowing. Next night I began to understand what Falklands weather can do. A westerly gale shrieked off Two Sisters, backing slowly and hurling snow before it in a horizontal blizzard. Surrounding hills and ships loomed close a quarter mile distant as we cautiously walked out more chain to prevent our anchor dragging. The blizzard eased briefly to reveal one ship in trouble. Our next door neighbour was dragging her anchors, and even as we watched she went ashore, slowly and inexorably, until another snow squall blinded us. Fortunately she grounded on a rising tide and came off several hours later with tugs' assistance. She was not the first to go ashore in those narrow waters, nor yet the last, and her distress kept us alert, checking position and swing continuously, engines always at the ready to claw us out of danger.

As the long South Atlantic swell drove up the narrow harbour the ships rolled 30 degrees and more to each side, but our cargo was needed by the troops and work discharging it proceeded regardless of weather. Calmly our crew drove the deck cranes, swinging loads of frozen meat, beer, Mars Bars and toiletries from the holds to the snow-covered deck, and then into craft alongside, hooking onto 80 foot strops dangling below helicopters. Revelling

Blue Star's *Avelona Star*

in the excitement, our lads resembled cheerful Eskimos.

Sunrise mirrored in a tranquil harbour could become a shrieking gale by breakfast time, blowing hurricane force at noon, fitful and capricious by nightfall. Anticipating hopes of a quiet night, a new wind screamed suddenly from the opposite direction, an Antarctic blast to penetrate thermal clothing until a warm cabin and cosy bunk seemed a memory of happier times from long ago.

Compared with normal seafaring this was traumatic. Compared with life ashore as lived by our troops in the hills, it was a piece of cake. Not only must *they* cope with the weather as best they could, but also with vast areas of boggy terrain over which Argentine helicopters had sown mines indiscriminately, and where still lay bodies of Argentine soldiers, booby-trapped instead of buried. Life ashore in the aftermath of Galtieri's occupation can be grim, but the sombre hills have their own beauty; clumps of daffodils and gorse flowers brighten the gardens of the pretty little houses, and the warmth of the inhabitants with their British way of life make us realise that they are no more Argentineans than we. As they have long known, and as now we know, the Argentineans would never colonise these islands themselves — *they* will not even farm similar land in their own Patagonia (the only people who work there are the descendants of the Welsh Utopians, and Chileans from over the border). What would happen if the British relinquished control would be an initial show of razzmatazz, then a rapid depopulation, replaced by a Russian Naval base.

Why?

Well, the Falklands control not only the Cape Horn route, increasingly important as the efficiency of the Panama Canal declines, but also next century's continent — Antarctica.

But then I am a seaman, not a politician.

Away to sea!
Chapter 2
1949-1954

I BLAME MY GRANDFATHER. It was he who was mainly responsible for directing my thoughts towards the sea as a career. He, too, had lived his boyhood on the banks of the coaly Tyne during the 1870s and 1880s when, despite the growing popularity of steam, tall ships still crowded into the river assisted by paddle tugs known as Tyne Flappers. Keels, the sailing barges which had for centuries carried coals from up-river spouts to brigs anchored in Shields Harbour, had by then been made redundant by the Tyne Improvement Commission's dredging. Now, the deepened channel enabled the brigs — and the steamers — to navigate the river themselves. Stately battle cruisers from Armstrong's at Elswick put to sea in growing numbers for the world's navies. Order books for liners and freighters were full from Shields to Scotswood, and the fish quay was thronged with tall masts and tanned sails drying, outnumbering, for the time being, the new-fangled steam trawlers.

As quay berths were forever occupied, many vessels lay to buoys in the river, working cargo in and out of wherries. Ferries and steam launches plied continuously, and clinker-built foy boats, traditionally painted green inboard, black and white out, tended mooring lines. Slowly a diminuendo of caulking mallets gave place to a staccato of rivetting as the art of building in wood succumbed to the science of steel. King Coal settled himself firmly on his iron throne.

When my grandfather discovered I shared his love of the sea he quietly aided and abetted me with, I suspect, my father's approval. From the age of five I was taken for purposeful walks around the docks . . . to watch the cruiser *HMS Edinburgh* slide down the ways into a sunlit river while the Royal Marines played *Rule Britannia* to a

15

backing of cheers . . . to linger over ship models in the local museums . . . discuss the rigs of sailing vessels, and together make model boats to sail upon the park lake. I was hooked. Grandfather's recollection of a barque furling sail by sail as she entered the river was so vivid that I could see her myself; clearly the only way to go to sea was in sail. Technically this was still possible thanks to the persistence of the old Finnish shipowner Gustav Erikson who was running sailing ships profitably long after the rest had given up and still owned the four-masted barques *Viking*, *Pommern* and *Passat*. South Africa ought soon to return his *Lawhill* and New Zealand the *Pamir* (both war prizes used as training ships throughout hostilities). *Moshulu* was around somewhere and a seventh, the *Archibald Russell,* was in the Humber. Yes, there was still time to go to sea properly!

My parents slowly came to share my enthusiasm. Though not so full of ships as it had been 60 years earlier, the Tyne was still a busy river in the late '40s. For the first time since pre-war, ships were creeping in as grey, rusting wraiths, to leave several months later in peacetime colours, decks scrubbed, doors and ladders varnished, brasswork agleam. To eyes long accustomed to wartime grey the transformations were startling, like colour television after black and white. Almost unnoticed, in October 1946, one was towed in which aroused more longing in our young hearts than all the lordly liners. The four-masted barque *Archibald Russell*, rigged down to lower masts and bowsprit, came from Goole where she had lain since she was interned for the duration when Finland entered the war. Now she was to be refitted and put back into the Australian grain trade. With luck we would join her! Following her progress with avid interest we were relieved when a drydock survey revealed her 42-year-old hull as sound. Then Captain Erikson died and with him our hopes, for his fleet dispersed and the *Archibald Russell* was broken up. Now, there was no alternative but to 'go into steam'.

The three ways to sea as an apprentice or cadet had remained unchanged for generations. You could simply leave school — with or without a school certificate — and join a shipping company. Some companies had cadets, some apprentices. Blue Funnel Line had midshipmen. Parents or guardians paid a £50 premium for traditionally-worded indentures: the apprentice 'must not enter ale houses or taverns or play at unlawful games'. A cadetship was less categorical although the basis was the same, but usually without premium or indentures. Wages were low: a cadet began at £6 15s a month, rising to £10 in his second year, £12 in his third and £15 in his last year. But few lads who went to sea gave much thought to the financial side of their career. Apprentices never *had* been paid much, either at sea or ashore, and once you got the old man's job, or even the mate's, you'd be rolling in it, of course! Some companies actually paid overtime — 1s 3d (6p) per hour — and there was more discussion about this than salaries. But by the late '40s few companies took lads direct from school without pre-sea training.

The second method of becoming an embryo deck officer was through a sea school. Various courses were offered, some residential, varying from a few weeks to several years, which saw the lad off to a better start. At least he knew port from starboard, could tie a few knots, pull an oar, sail a lifeboat, use a fire extinguisher and box the compass. He might not know all the answers but at least he was learning the questions. Sea time was remitted *pro rata* for time at school, which was valuable, as you had to spend the equivalent of four fifths of four years actually on ships' foreign-going articles before attempting examination for the

HMS Conway **(built in 1839 as** *HMS Nile*) **was Cadet Kinghorn's training ship**

Second Mate's Certificate — the first step up the professional ladder.

More prestigious companies required new entrants to have attended one of the four so-called leading establishments, which provided residential courses of up to two years' duration, earning up to one year's remission. Pangbourne, because of its situation on the idyllic upper reaches of the Thames was perhaps too land-minded. Warsash, near Southampton, founded in the '30s by Captain 'Wally' Wakeford who still ran it with an iron hand, was very much a sea school. It provided shore-based nautical training with a considerable amount of boatwork and coastal sailing in their big ketch *Moyana*. Warsash was a tough school, attended for three terms which earned nine months' remission. The Thames Nautical Training College ran *HMS Worcester*, a steel three-masted three-decker moored at Greenhithe, Kent, with the rigged-down *Cutty Sark* alongside, also used for training before being restored as a tea clipper enshrined at Greenwich. A tough, two-year course was provided.

But the oldest of the four schools was *HMS Conway*. She was third to bear the name since the first was hired from the Admiralty in 1859 by the Mercantile Marine Service Association, which was (and still is) the British shipmaster's trade union, to improve the education and conditions of future British shipmasters. Launched as *HMS Nile* in 1839, she was a wooden, two-deck sailing battleship of 92 guns, fitted during construction with a steam engine driving a screw propeller, while retaining her full rig. She fought against the Russians during the Crimean War and saw service in the West Indies before becoming a schoolship in 1875. Like her predecessors she was moored in the Sloyne off Rockferry in the Mersey, but during the Second World War she was evacuated to Bangor in the Menai Straits, North Wales. In 1949 she was towed to her final anchorage off Plas Newydd, the Marquis of Anglesey's stately home, part of which was adapted to supplement shipboard training.

The *Worcester* had the best site, but the *Conway* had the best ship, so Mike Hatton and I, friends from childhood, applied for scholarship entry at the suggestion of our headmaster. Before interview we met the resident cadets, seemingly a tough lot of hoary old seadogs who advised us to return home forthwith; at the same time recommending that if we were still foolishly determined we should tell our interviewers that we were keen scouts who played rugby, enjoyed mountaineering and appreciated good music.

I was first in to a low beamed white room under the poop, decked with polished planks each a foot wide. The gunport window in the ship's side opened onto the shining straits, beyond which the rolling green hills of North Wales gradually rose to Snowdon's peak, clearly visible in the distance. It was a Nelsonian setting: at one end of a long polished table sat the Captain Superintendent, resplendent as a Captain, Royal Naval Reserve. Silver-haired and fresh-faced, Captain Goddard had the keenest blue eyes I have ever seen. To his left sat the black-gowned headmaster, and on his right were the staff captain, also with the four gold-lace rings of a Captain, RNR; the chief officer (three gold stripes on each cuff) and the senior master, bespectacled and gowned. Daunting!

Why, asked Captain Goddard, did I want to go to sea?
I was interested in ships, sir, particularly sailing ships.
Ah yes, he replied, but not many of those left now are there, Kinghorn? Obviously the *Archibald Russell* would do me no good here. Was I interested in music, asked the headmaster? Yes sir, came the dutiful reply. Could I, he wondered, play any musical instrument? I answered truthfully,
'Well sir, I can play the tin whistle.'
The board laughed. I was also a scout, I added, thinking I may as well lay my best cards on the table.
'A King's Scout?'
Not actually a King's Scout, though I had most of the first class badge, I said, hinting that in our troop's opinion there was more to life than badges.
So, raised eyebrows asked, what *did* they go in for then, if not badges?
'Well, scouting sir. Camping, canoeing, abseiling down the cliffs of Tynemouth. . .'
No, I regretted, I did not play rugby.
'Oh?' barked the frosty-eyed staff captain, then what *did* I do, when not camping, canoeing or abseiling? I replied that my friends and I spent most of our spare time walking round the riverside quays and docks looking at ships.
Didn't I think rugby was more healthy than just hanging round the docks?
I replied politely that I found ships more interesting than organised

games. This interview was not going well.

Right, what *did* I know about ships, the captain asked, not unkindly. Perhaps a fanatical interest in ships was not too bad a start after all. Could I tell him, please, the colours of the Cunard White Star liners? I could, and did, including the number of black lines round the funnels. The staff captain asked if I knew the colours of P and O and I got that right too, with details, and suddenly this became a nautical Master Mind with five Magnus Magnussons.

'How about Union Castle?' asked the chief officer, grinning through his beard. Fortunately I knew that one too but hoped they would not ask too many more.

'Royal Mail Line?', asked the senior master, determined to be on a par with the captains, and when I gave the right answer he changed the subject.

'Do you, Kinghorn, think 10 shillings is a lot of money?'

'It is to me, sir!'

They grinned.

'Thank you Kinghorn, that is all.'

Next day Hatton and I were told we were both 'in', with MMSA scholarships. Those hard years at the *Conway* were two of the best

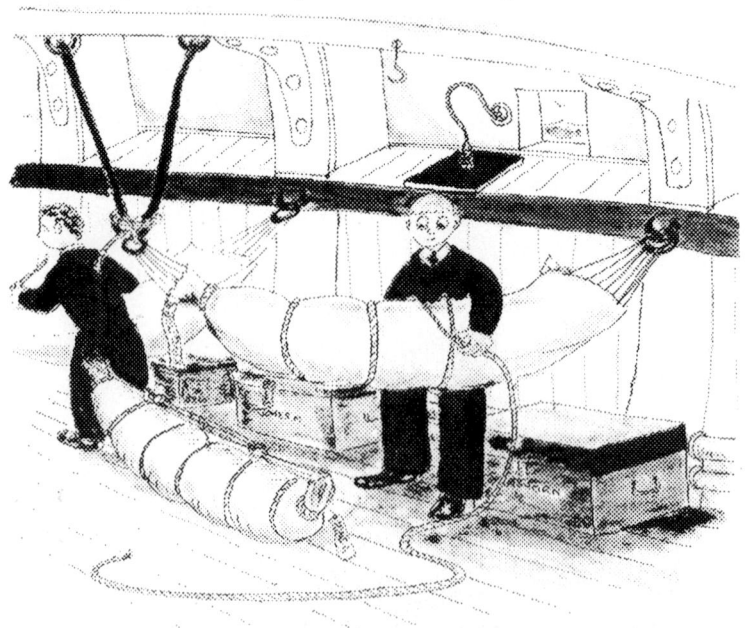

in my life, weaning us from our sheltered lives to the ways of the old sailing navy where seamanship was absorbed as well as learned. The rope's end, or 'teaser', was applied by cadet captains for seemingly trivial misdemeanours during the first and second terms. Not lashing your hammock up properly could qualify for six of the best. Harsh, undoubtedly, but then the sea is a harsh mistress, for your hammock was also your lifebelt, and if the ship went down you had a better chance of staying afloat with it tightly lashed. It was all part of the *Conway* message, 'do the job properly first time, or you'll suffer for it, that's life!' That's life at sea anyway, even today, when sloppy work may cost lives.

The *Conway* was tended by her cadet-manned boats, chief among which was the pinnace, a German boat with powerful diesel and kitchen rudder which made her highly manoeuverable. Water was brought to the ship in the 'juice barge' — a miniature tanker which loaded daily from the hydrant at Port Dinorwic, a little Welsh slate town two miles west of the ship. On a falling tide the waterboat frequently took the ground but was always refloated, even if she had to be pumped out with jigger pumps and hauled off with blocks and tackles for if she went out of service we went without water! Back at the ship, a steam pump transferred water into her domestic tanks. Occasionally the end of the hose dropped into the sea while the pump was still operating — early lessons in contamination! On one occasion as the waterboat lay alongside, a gale blew up on a turning tide — always guaranteed to raise a steep swell quickly. I was in charge of the hose, transferring it from tank to tank, alone aboard the waterboat. As the boat began to rise and fall I made the cardinal error of tightening rather than easing her mooring lines, which parted in rapid succession with a series of pistol shots, and away we went. I could not start the engine and the sea was so rough by now that the motor boat sent after us could only partly check our wild career towards Caernarvon. A grass line was floated down-wind to us with a lifebuoy whereupon we were slowly hauled back by all hands laying on the line. Thus did the *Conway* teach.

Numbers one and two motorboats, together with the 10- and 12-oared cutters were maids of all work. The motorboats had regular crews of four cadets each — coxswain, engineer, bow and sternman, replaced during school hours by a practical-seamanship class crew, so that every cadet learned boatwork. Pulling an oar in a cutter was hard work especially in heavy weather, but we soon got the hang of it. Staff, cadets, visitors, storés and coal were all ferried to the ship so that boat-handling became second nature to us. There were other boats — a skiff, emergency boat, three gigs, sailing dinghies and a couple of De Horsey-rigged sailing cutters. Most were hoisted each night by long lines of the 200 cadets aboard stamping along the deck while heaving on the heavy rope falls. This way we learned the strength of applied muscle and the importance of teamwork.

The *Conway*, in fact, had four decks together with raised poop and forecastle, and a hold which had been her engine room. The decks were called upper; main and lower (both formerly gun decks); and orlop, where we kept our seachests. The gun ports in main and lower decks were still there, now glazed as windows, with securing lugs for gun tackles at either side and concave recesses in the deck to house cannon balls. Headroom was some seven feet, more spacious than in most men o'war of that era. A feature of *Conway*'s construction were Sepping's famous diagonal bracing frames, visible at all levels.

We ate, attended church, and went to school on the main deck. On the lower deck we had divisions (assembly) morning and evening. The main gangway entered here from a permanent wooden staircase on the ship's starboard side. Washbasins (cold water only) and bathrooms were forward, between the anchor chains where they led inboard from the ever-open hawse holes. We washed twice daily and bathed weekly, water permitting, with extra baths after coaling, nice and hot.

Nelson's figurehead stared bleakly from beneath the bowsprit: and although much reduced from her seagoing days, three square-rigged masts towered above. Climbing aloft soon overcame any horror of heights.

On our first ship's tour, conducted by Brooky, the famous Lieutenant J Brooke-Smith, RNR, we learned of her history and construction. Each massive beam and frame had been an oak tree, and her deck planks were huge slabs of teak, oak or pine, the seam nearest the ship's side being called the 'devil'. At sea this would tend to open up in heavy weather, and then there was 'the devil to pay and no pitch hot!' — to use the full original expression. Her magazines were still *in situ*, now used for suitcase stowage, and down the forestore on a wooden pillar was some long-ago sailor's painting of a jack tar with *HMS Nile* on his hat ribbon. Around the ship were trophies, roll of honour boards beautifully engraved and painted, old pictures of nautical scenes, fancy ropework —

polished copper, steel and brass. Rope boat falls and outhauls ran across the deckheads, belayed around enormous wooden cleats, and coiled neatly in wooden troughs.

At school, for which portable bulkheads were lowered from the deckhead to make classrooms, nautical subjects were taught in depth along with maths and English. Interestingly, the only foreign language taught was Spanish. Part of our fourth term was spent at Aberdovey Outward Bound sea school, which provided a happy combination of seamanship, athletics and hill climbing. At that time (1950) Aberdovey had two large ketches, *Garibaldi* and *Warspite*, in which we made short trips across Cardigan Bay to Abersoch. Food was excellent and plentiful, and somehow tasted more interesting eaten off the swastika-badged plates which, with the *Conway* pinnace, had come from the Germans as war reparations.

Conway was no museum but a working ship, teaching young men how to become seamen who could take charge of ships, to stand up to life, and smile at adversity. 'Quit ye like men, be strong!' was her motto, and 'Carry on till the last day's done!' was her song. Hers was an ambience which imbued us with pride and loyalty to ship and shipmates, her charisma to remain with us for the rest of our lives.

Some of the smartest vessels visiting the Tyne then belonged to the Blue Star Line of London, which traded to South Africa, Australasia, the east coast of South America and the west coast of North America — all of which appealed. In my fifth term at *Conway* I applied to join Blue Star and was accepted after a day of interviews in which it was stressed that although the line carried

First love, first ship, first seasickness . . . *Columbia Star* **built in Denmark, 1939. Her two sister ships,** *Canadian Star* **and** *California Star,* **were war losses**

many passengers, my main concern would be the safe carriage of cargo, especially refrigerated cargo. The fleet had been sadly depleted during the war, but was being rebuilt. I would have to wait for a ship. After six weeks at home a telegram arrived, on May 16, 1951. 'Join *Columbia Star* with all seagoing effects 24 shed Royal Albert Dock London am 18th for voyage to South America.'

The *Columbia Star* was the sole survivor of a class of three built in Denmark in 1939. Of 8293 tons gross she was a beautiful five-hatch 12-passenger cargo liner. It was still only six in the morning as I climbed the sleeping ship's gangway, so I tiptoed onto the bridge. In one long glance I beheld more ships than I had ever seen: cargo liners of the Port Line and Shaw Savill, Union Castle, Brocklebank and Royal Mail, Ben Line and Ellerman City, New Zealand Shipping Company and Federal Line, P and O and British India, Clan Line and Glen Line, with a sprinkling of Blue Stars in the hazy distance. Dumb barges were everywhere, alongside the ships or floating, apparently aimlessly, across the dock. Piled high with reels of newsprint, deep laden with steel, they lay at all angles. Unaccustomed to the Thames I had not realised that there were still so many sailing barges, but here they were as well, their tall russet sails loosely furled and limp in the morning sunshine. The dock roads were thronged with lorries and cargo was everywhere, for the Royal Docks were then the centre of world trade.

Today they are vast stretches of empty water, and grass grows knee high between the rusting cranes while foxes and rabbits roam the deserted roads. Militant attitudes, alas, have done nothing to halt the inevitable, but the marvel is that the docks lasted so long, with their locks and swing bridges, their numerous cuttings and hopelessly congested outlet roads. Built in the sailing ship era, the system had become inefficient long before it died. Containerisation has made the conventional cargo liner and her dock systems redundant the world over, a process undoubtedly exacerbated by the deepening of the longest recession the world has ever suffered.

But that Festival of Britain May morning long ago the docks had an air of permanence. This was ever how it would be . . . My reverie was broken by the fourth mate asking if I were the new cadet, and if so would I kindly stop mooning around the bridge and hoist the flags! Another cadet, Peter, also a first tripper, joined from Warsash after breakfast. Our cabin was a pleasant room with three portholes situated at the starboard forward corner of the accommodation midships on the upper or main deck as it was called here. Apart from our two bunks we had a desk, a small table, two chairs and a settee. Compared with many cadets' accommodation at that time it was palatial!

Next day the *Columbia Star* sailed for Tenerife and South America. I was amazed at the speed with which order came out of chaos as the ship prepared for sea. Hatches were covered with tarpaulins and battened down, derricks lowered in their crutches, their guy ropes coiled neatly on cleats. Rubbish vanished. Peter and I finished scrubbing decks and polishing brass on the bridge in time to change into uniform before the dock pilot boarded at 1700. Mr Carr, known to all as Fred, appeared in a charcoal-grey overcoat, dark suit, white silk scarf and black homburg. Tall, silver-haired, distinguished, he could have passed for a prosperous doctor.

'New cadet?' he grinned, lighting a long cigar. 'When you make a pot of tea, son, I like two of milk and one of sugar.' The milk of course was condensed, from a tin, 'conny onny'. He and the captain greeted each other like the old friends they were and

gossiped as tugs were made fast and mooring lines taken in. Fred Carr kept up a flow of outrageous stories and jokes, interspersed with laconic commands,

'Half ahead, mate — port a little, Charlie,' from the corner of his mouth.

Putting to sea was not so frightening as I had imagined it after all! Sternfirst we moved slowly down the dock, turned into a cutting and backed into a lock.

'Have a good trip,' said Fred, as he left us in the hands of Mr Dawson, the river pilot, to guide us to Gravesend. Again pilots changed. This time the sea pilot took us past the Nore in the gathering dusk, through the tricky Edinburgh Channel and across the Downs to Dungeness. A grey dawn was breaking as he left and, without fuss or tension (as it seemed to me), we were on our way.

The Bay of Biscay was rough and I was disgracefully seasick unlike Peter who, to my feeble indignation, revelled in the weather. He and I kept bridge watches with the second and third mates to Tenerife; Peter the twelve to four and I the eight to twelve. The fourth mate kept the four to eight with the mate. Despite seasickness I stood my watches — it was better in the fresh air anyway, and the mates kindly assured me that, with seasickness, the first 10 years were the worst. That turned out to be correct!

Three days out we came to Tenerife where mountains sweeping down to the little white town of Santa Cruz in a glorious dawn were all that a landfall should be. Yeoward's elderly fruit ship *Alca* was leaving for Liverpool, sooty smoke drifting from her tall thin funnel as a couple of white schooners tacked into port ahead of us. A smart Spanish passenger vessel, the *Cuidad de Barcelona*, had just arrived and the quay was a-bustle with ancient taxis making their noisy way through the clutter of horse-drawn carts and market stalls. While our passengers went sightseeing, Peter and I remained on deck patrol to dissuade stowaways, as diesel oil bunkers gurgled into our tanks through a fat black hose.

After Tenerife we went onto daywork and toiled from six in the morning to ten at night. Our first task each day was to clean the bridge under the second mate's eagle eye, polish the brass and copper, wash the windows, scrub the wooden deck. We took turns at straightening our cabin, made the bunks and changed into uniform for meals in the officers' messroom. (The passengers ate with the captain and senior officers in the saloon.) Often we worked with the bosun and sailors called, collectively, 'the crowd'.

Occasionally we worked with Chippy, the carpenter, and sometimes with old Charlie the lamptrimmer in his store under the forecastle head, splicing rope and stitching canvas covers. We checked stores and changed drinking water in the four wooden lifeboats, chipped and scraped rust, washed, cleaned and painted, helped overhaul the cargo gear, and rigged awnings, and when the great day came — sure sign that we were now in the fine weather — helped the bosun, carpenter and crowd to rig the swimming pool. The work, I suppose, was mundane, but we enjoyed it, and it was necessary; the only way to learn how it should be done was to do it over and over again until it became second nature. A ship needs constant maintenance and a future mate must know what has to be seen to and how to do it properly. After evening dinner we again donned overalls and worked with the sailors cleaning and painting empty cargo spaces. These included two tween-deck lockers in number 5 that voyage — each one some 30ft long, 20ft wide at the fore end narrowing to 15ft aft, seven feet high. These lockers were used for carrying deep freeze cargo and we painted them with white insulation varnish — heady stuff with a powerful smell. The bosun looked in from time to time to see how we fared, our squad consisting of lamptrimmer Charlie, a gnarled and ancient Finn who had gone to sea at the age of nine in 'de barque *Hudson*', an ordinary seaman called Jack, Peter and myself. Work proceeded with a swing and soon Charlie's high, cracked voice burst into Finnish songs of long ago. We joined in with our own, and collapsed in a heap, roaring with laughter. Never had songs seemed so hilarious! Unable to stand we lurched around like drunks, making such a din that the bosun was alerted. Sizing up the situation at once he ordered us on deck where I wandered off to my bunk while Peter fell asleep under the stars on the hatch top. Horrible hangovers next morning taught us our first lesson in toxic fumes!

From London to Santos Peter and I looked after a Jersey bull called Burderop Joker, housed in a wooden stall on deck, where he lived up to his name by butting us with his stubby little horns when we mucked him out. He had a sense of humour though, and when he knocked us down in a corner he licked our faces to show it was just a game. Entering Rio de Janeiro we saw where the Royal Mail liner *Magdalena* was wrecked on her maiden voyage, to learn another lesson; the most modern ship, fitted with all the latest navigational equipment, is only as safe as the men in charge make her. We mourned her loss. She was a fine ship.

After Santos, where the Joker left us none the worse for his voyage, we approached Montevideo breakwater on which we spotted the rusted plates, twisted and distorted, of what had once been a ship, the German pocket battleship *Graf Spee*. We gazed with interest, none more so than old Charlie the lamptrimmer who had been in the *Doric Star* when she became a victim of the *Graf Spee*. It was her SOS which enabled Commodore Harwood to bring his light cruisers *Ajax, Exeter* and *Achilles* to bear upon the raider. Captain Langsdorf, the *Graf Spee*'s commander, nevertheless congratulated the British radio officer on risking his life to transmit in defiance of German orders. Charlie was one of that select band rescued in a Norwegian fjord from the *Altmark, Graf Spee*'s storeship, by *HMS Cossack*, which boosted British morale in despairing 1940. The monument erected on the Montevideo seafront in memory of British seamen who lost their lives in the action now includes tribute to the German dead also, an amendment few would question. No British merchant seaman was killed in Langsdorf's raids upon our ships.

Before us lay Santa Maria de los Buenos Aires, Saint Mary of the Fair Winds, Argentina's capital, BA to those who know her. The chief officer gave Peter and me a separate day off each, as work was light. Before setting out for the big city in civilian rig, I was strictly admonished not to get into trouble. As though I would! Strolling from South Dock's grime through the pleasant streets of the Boca, I wandered up the long, straight Almirante Brown, and fell at once for the charms of the faded, crumbling old buildings and cobbled streets.

Feeling hungry (cadets are always hungry) I eventually entered a shady little restaurant and ordered steak, eggs and chips in my best *Conway* Spanish. Would I like wine? asked the waiter, flourishing a large bottle of red. Why not? It was so ridiculously cheap it had to be pretty weak stuff. The meal — my first in a foreign country — was delicious and the wine washed it down to perfection. Back on the sunbaked streets I began to feel that perhaps that wine had not been so weak after all: I'd better return to the ship. For some reason kerbside trees kept getting in my way and it became increasingly difficult to steer a straight course. No, I wouldn't take a taxi, the walk would be beneficial. I ascended the gangway with difficulty as the ship seemed to be rolling. Hoping no one would see me (what a hope!) I found my bunk — to awake next morning still fully clad and more shore leave stopped. Not for nothing is the red stuff known as 'Vino Collapso'!

At Buenos Aires we completed unloading and set off for Tierra del Fuego to load frozen lamb for the British Ministry of Food. Battling south through stormy seas in the depths of the southern winter — July — we eventually came to San Sebastian Bay on the east coast. A desolate landscape afforded little shelter but it was the practice for ships to anchor here and load from coasters called *luchos* which brought meat from Rio Grande, 40 miles nearer Cape Horn to the south. For the next couple of days we cleaned and cooled holds and were buzzed by an Argentine navy plane until we hoisted their national flag as courtesy ensign as well as our own. Rather than waste good flags in the Antarctic blast we had been flying none: who says courtesy costs nothing?

Then the first coaster brought us not only frozen lamb but a gang of swarthy dockers to load it who made themselves at home on our afterdeck by building rude shelters in which they lived throughout the ship's 10-day visit. On the strength of my alleged knowledge of Spanish I was appointed tallyman and accompanied the third mate to Rio Grande in the coaster when she returned for her second load. My *Conway* Spanish in no way resembled the rapid dialect spoken by our new friends, most of whom came from across the nearby Chilean border, but we were soon conversing in a cheerful mixture of Liverpool-Geordie Spanish, smoking their powerful cigarettes and swigging yerba maté as to the manner born. They drank wine from gourds, but of this I was wary.

When we arrived, by night in a snowstorm, the little town resembled a Siberian camp. Next day, in the melting snow, its wide, unsurfaced streets, boarded sidewalks and false-fronted wooden buildings with hitching rails mimicked a Hollywood western. Most of the horses had been replaced by Fords and Chevs, some with right-hand drive some with left. Ten years earlier Argentina had changed from driving on the left to driving on the right which, we were assured, had been done gradually to avoid confusion! Five minutes walk from the frigorifico was our hotel — small and frugal but adequately warm. There were no trees in this windswept landscape, only sparse, stunted bushes, and no cattle, no fresh milk.

We presented ourselves at the counting house, an outer hall of the frigorifico: a large inner door swung open emitting a cloud of steam and a tiny open-sided truck stacked high with muslin-wrapped frozen 'lamps' trundled through the fog towards us, stopping while we checked its contents. Figure agreed, the truck was sent to the quay where the carcases were loaded into the coaster. A few days of this and you automatically counted the buttons on a man's coat, or the posts in a fence. The coasters were unrefrigerated, the lambs frozen rock hard and so remaining until loaded eight hours later in the *Columbia Star*.

Our co-workers were a wild-looking lot, but friendly and much given to laughter, singing and the dancing of elaborate tangoes with each other at the drop of a hat. In the cook house they regaled us with huge helpings of mutton and lamb cooked varyingly with rice, turnips, peas, currants and garlic. When the cold store was empty it was time to go, and all our friends turned out to see us off in the last *lucho*. We promised to return the following year, but I have never been back.

Next port was Deseado on the Patagonian mainland, whither we went through freezing fog. The wharf was carved out of the river bank bedrock and the ship overhung at both ends when we came alongside. There were no tugs and as the river ran swiftly with many a swirl and eddy, it called for all the skill of pilot, master and wheelman. The cold store was only a few miles up the road so the third mate and I — expert counters by now — were able to return to the ship at night. In Deseado we met some of the descendants of the Welsh colonists who had hoped to find Utopia there. They still spoke Welsh and when they found I had lived in Wales, Anglo-Argentinean relations peaked. After Deseado we returned to Buenos Aires to load bone meal, dried blood, horns, hooves and bundles of willows used, it was said, to make the new-fangled plastics.

When we reached England we were more than welcome. Each of us had been given a frozen lamb by the frigorifico, and meat was

still rationed in Britain! We were no longer first-trippers.

Our next two voyages in the *Columbia Star* were from the Bristol Channel to the west coast of North America, the run for which the ship had been designed in 1939. In Newport, Monmouthshire, we loaded general cargo including steel pipes for the Alberta oilfields: on the third voyage we called at Barry to pick up 250 aerial bombs for the Canadian naval base at Esquimalt, Vancouver Island. They were hoisted carefully from a wooden barge into a specially-contructed wood magazine in number 2 tweendeck where Peter and I tallied them in. He made it 251, I made it 247 so we settled for 249 and I went to tell the mate who sat in his room with a senior-looking RAF officer.

'You're *sure* there aren't 250?'

I nodded.

The RAF demanded a recount.

This would have meant unloading and reloading. We had to sail on the tide in an hour's time, but a missing bomb was a serious matter. I thought it might help if I explained how we arrived at our figure. The RAF looked doubtful until the mate poured him an enormous gin, whereupon he cheered up. I was dismissed and we sailed.

In the Bristol Channel we swept through the swan song of Masefield's *Dirty British coaster with a salt-caked smoke stack*, battling at eight or nine knots into a rising westerly, woodbine funnel aft, open bridge amidships, two or three stumpy masts and coaly smoke streaking astern from the galley chimney as they pitched into the gale. Dozens put to sea on the tide — the high rise and fall in the Bristol Channel has always made ships leave there in groups. We passed the three-masted schooner *Result* under sail and power, and clean, squat little motor vessels known to seamen as 'skoots' (from the Dutch *schuyt*) carrying coal, steel, slates, building materials, general cargo and even passengers around the narrow seas. Soon we left them astern and by sunset the distant sky was a pale wash of lemon beneath a grey, stormy rack. Silhouetted on the horizon was a destroyer, and a heavily listing ship accompanied by a tug, the *Turmoil*, towing Captain Carlson's *Flying Enterprise* which was to sink the next day, fortunately without loss of life, while trying to reach Falmouth. Occasionally we came across a French or British weather ship; usually a converted corvette; rolling gunwales under and hardly visible in the steep Atlantic swell.

At Curacao the Dutch authorities took a keen interest in our bombs. An armed soldier was posted at the gangway and another on deck patrol. The latter decided to take a look and climbed down number two — after I had given him the key. When he came out, his face was a study in chalk: he had missed his step and tumbled into the tween deck, landing among the bombs.

We embarked our Panama Canal pilot inside Cristobal breakwaters, and once through headed for Esquimalt to deliver the bombs. Fortunately the RCAF tallyman made the total precisely 250!

Vancouver harbour is one of the world's beauties, surrounded by forested hills redolent with the scent of pine tinged with woodsmoke. The transcontinental railroad passed close to the ship's berth so we were lulled to sleep by the clang of locomotive bells as the engines rolled past.

Outward cargo discharged we 'cleaned and cooled', ready for apples. The holds were first floored with billets of zinc and aluminium — good bottom cargo over which apples were loaded, filling the ship with their scent. Most ships acquire a recognisable fragrance over the years — probably the result of the cooking — but apples nullify all this. After Vancouver, Seattle — gateway to the Golden West — for more apples and timber, stowed mostly on deck, then up the Columbia River to Portland, Oregon, a memorable run through the countryside past pine-topped cliffs and racing rapids, lush green pastures, towns on the edge of the woods — always with the pilot giving laconic orders in a totally unflappable manner. Then, there were echo boards, like hoardings, at turns. As a ship approached a bend in the river in fog, the pilot would sound the ship's whistle: when the echo was heard, it was time to alter course! This, of course, was before radar made it all easy!

Off San Francisco bar the pilot swooped upon us in one of the last genuine pilot schooners to take us in through the Golden Gate, past Alcatraz, then still a grim island penitentiary, to berth at one of the many wooden finger piers crammed with shipping beneath elegant white sky scrapers. Those piers are empty now, broken and dilapidated like so many of the world's old ports; business has moved across the bay to vast container terminals whose efficiency has cost the ports their individual charm. After a week in San Francisco we headed up the Sacramento River through a wide, flat region not unlike the Norfolk Broads, to Stockton, California, for dried fruit.

In port, Peter and I worked alternate days on gangway and cargo watch. The gangway cadet (in his best uniform) answered the telephone, took visitors to the senior officers, ensured that each mooring rope had on its rat guard, hoisted flags in the morning and lowered them at night. We learned the hard way that the Stars and Stripes had to be treated with respect. If accidentally it trailed on deck during lowering (these flags were three yarders) the nearest winchdriver would leap from his perch and deliver a stern lecture — usually in thick mid-European accents — on the necessity of preserving the dignities. We could do what we liked with our own flag (he even went so far as to offer suggestions) but not with Old Glory. Quite right too.

Above all, gangway watch entailed keeping the gangway at the right height. Those magnificent varnished teak gangways with brassbound self-levelling steps took a lot of looking after, unlike today's automatic aluminium turntable jobs whose wheels rest on the quay. The old ones had to be lowered as the tide rose and raised with a small two-fold purchase, a handy-billy, as the tide fell. A sailor tended it by night. Cargo watch was more interesting as we watched all that was unloaded and loaded, noting the times in a book, and keeping a plan book to show where cargo was stowed which the second mate scrutinised daily along with those of the third and fourth officers, entering the information on his master cargo plan. This showed every piece of cargo and its weight. A well-made cargo plan can be read by a stevedore at a glance; from it he orders his labour gangs and advises consignees and transport when to collect. The cargo watch cadet, however junior, must be alert to any damage caused to ship or cargo by the dockers. The safe carriage of merchandise, and protection of the ship, is the name of the game.

After a wet, wintry passage down the Californian coast we came on the tail of a Santa Anna, a local dust storm, to Los Angeles where we loaded sacks of borax, soft, white and silent, and bales of cotton, high fire risk. Then, fully laden, we headed back through the Panama Canal for home. Shortly after clearing Cristobal we took our first year examinations set by the Merchant Navy Training

Board (after a hard day's work, of course!) Our papers were returned marked within a month or so: a cadet doing badly was told either to pull his socks up or quit.

Clearing Mona Passage homeward we struck the most abominable weather I have ever experienced. The wind shrieked from the east causing sea and sky to melt in a welter of foam and spray, a reeling world of grey and white. Even hove to, we still took heavy seas aboard: around us unseen vessels transmitted not-under-command signals. Seas crashing over the bow attacked the face of the deck timber stow until eventually heavy planks were loosened, tossed like matchsticks downwind and lost. Sailors and cadets were sent to tighten the lashing chains with bottle screws and marlin spikes, clinging for life as sea after sea crashed aboard in a chilling, body-battering cascade. Exhilarating work and the closest we had ever come to life in a windjammer.

Our cabin porthole was stove in by a sea one night, fortunately while we were on watch. Stilettoes of glass showered the soft furnishings, ribboned the curtains, smashed the light, and embedded themselves in furniture and bulkheads. The cabin was awash. The sea so strained our bulkhead that for the rest of the trip we moved to spare and dryer accommodation. Our 12 elderly passengers took the storm in their stride and, like us, actually seemed to enjoy it. Fortunately there were no injuries. After 10 days of such buffeting we were glad to creep quietly into the Clyde, licking our wounds. Those bonny banks and braes never looked more beautiful.

After a fortnight's leave I received a telegram to join the motor vessel *Saxon Star* in Salford Dock, Manchester. Slightly smaller than the *Columbia*, she was Belfast-built in 1942, without frills, as the *Empire Strength*. A five-hatch motorship, almost fully refrigerated, she could carry four male passengers in cabins originally used by the extra officers borne in wartime. My mate in the *Saxon Star* — Ted — was an old *Conway*, slightly senior to me, and together we pitched into all life had to offer. We had cargo for Capetown, Port Elizabeth (where kind relatives looked after me), East London, Durban, Lourenco Marques and Beira. In each port we worked by day and played by night, or vice versa, and learned to live on five hours' sleep. Some of our time was spent at the Missions to Seamen, those excellent establishments run to make us feel at home. Entertainment at 'the mish' was free and wages low, so the fleshpots saw little of us, to the relief of our seniors.

After four trips in the motor vessel *Saxon Star*, **built in 1942 as the** *Empire Strength*, **Senior Cadet Kinghorn steps on to the promotion ladder as Fourth Mate at the princely salary of £360 pa**

In Lourenco Marques, swinging forlornly round her anchor a few miles above the town was Erikson's favourite four-masted barque *Lawhill* — the last of her generation. *Pamir* and *Passat* sailed longer but by then both had auxiliary engines. (*Lawhill*, built 1892, never had an engine). We tried to go aboard but looters had caused trouble in the past and watchmen prevented us. In Beira we loaded Rhodesian tobacco, ostrich feathers and copper in refined ingots called cigars, for Port Kembla, New South Wales, and then skirted the southern tip of Madagascar and headed for Melbourne which as a city was impressive and hospitable, if as a port not spectacularly beautiful. But the back-drop of open marsh had its own attractions including the two varieties of black swan which frequented the muddy waters of the Yarra: the winged specimen and the coal hulks which toted bunkers to the coal-burning steamers. Formerly sailing ships, most had lower masts still standing, yards serving as derricks to hoist and lower coal tubs. A conspicuous vertical donkey boiler provided steam for the winches. Beneath layers of grime, tyre fenders and broken rubbing strakes were the sweet lines of real sailing ships as they lay moored among the broken wharves and jetties of a previous time, down river at Rotten Row. Their names painted crudely on their graceful if grubby counters evoked memories of faded sepia photographs— *Shandon, Marjorie, Rathlin Island, Rona* . . . Only *Rona* has survived,

35

exquisitely restored by a band of Melbourne enthusiasts who have called her the name with which she first left Belfast — *Polly Woodside*.

After Melbourne, Sydney where, we were told, there were 26 hours each day.

'Twenty six?'

'Twenty four on the clock, our 'arbour and our bridge. Twenty six!' We berthed at Glebe Island, now a wide, concrete container terminal but then a narrow wooden quay backed by quaint wooden sheds and offices, the perfect backdrop for a musical play of the kind we enjoyed seeing at Sydney's Theatre Royal. Once our copper was unloaded we headed for the Land of the Long White Cloud. New Zealand is a lovely land and its people are hospitality personified. Getting to know folk overseas is half the fun of seafaring and friendships often last for life. Even now, in a box boat, I can visit old friends while the ship stays briefly in port. How will the modern mariner break out of the container terminal's concrete jungles 30 years hence?

I was two years, two months, two weeks and two days in that happy little *Saxon Star* — four voyages, each one memorable, loading in Liverpool for South and East Africa before proceeding to Australia or New Zealand. Ted obtained Second Mate's after two voyages, and another *Conway* cadet called Harris, somewhat junior to me, joined. One afternoon in Beira, Portuguese East Africa, I walked past the mangrove swamps to the wreck of a three-masted barque. The *Charles Racine*, of Sandefjord, was one of the latter-day sailing work horses, never a clipper, but touched with dignity even utilised as a groin, a fishing village nestling in her lee. The round, thatched huts of rusted steel plates were fitted with teak doors, brass ringed portholes, and ship's ladders. There was no-one about until I began operating my Brownie box camera when several spear-carrying natives chased me off. As fast as I could I raced over the soft sand to the sound of hysterical laughter at my terror.

Our second voyage took us to the small ports of Queensland, loading beef and butter, after which we rounded the north of

Australia, inside the Great Barrier Reef. We spent nearly a month in Gladstone and acted as the finishing post for the annual Brisbane-Gladstone yacht race. People seemed delighted to be invited to the ship — many never having boarded a deep sea vessel. There was no television and no cassette tapes in North Queensland then, so we made our own music; what it lacked in quality it made up for in enthusiasm. People invited us home for musical evenings at which piano, concertina, tin whistle and fiddle provided accompaniment, and each night we were taken back to the ship with a splendid supper inside us. This, we felt, was seafaring as it was meant to be! My last voyage in the *Saxon Star* early in 1954 was as senior cadet of three which meant that for the first time I had my own cabin.

After Africa and Australia we sailed for Tasmania, the Land of the ABC. A was for apples, for which the island state was justly famous. B was for beer, from the celebrated Cascade brewery, and C was for Cheer, of which there was always plenty! We called first at Beauty Point, a hamlet on the Tamar River which runs into Bass Strait, and loaded from lorries bringing fruit direct from the orchards. The apple growers packed them into the colourful wooden crates that used to be a feature of every greengrocer's shop in Britain, drove them to the ship, and helped load them onboard, all very friendly and personal. It was in Beauty Point that I first heard Local Radio, entranced by a sweet-voiced sheila retailing the local news between records, and where to buy our next tractor. At Hobart, a roaring metropolis compared with Beauty Point, my three-year cadetship ended. I 'came out of my time' and was promoted to fourth mate at the exalted salary of £30 per month. Never since have I felt so rich!

Our first night at sea I stood the eight to twelve watch as sole watchkeeping officer for the first time, heading south from Hobart, out of Storm Bay, around the southern tip of Tasmania. The Maatsuyker light flashed on the starboard bow as we made our course westwards at almost 11 knots across a gently heaving starlit sea. Joe O'Malley was at the wheel, a senior ordinary seaman of my own age, 21. The *Saxon Star* had no gyro so we steered by magnetic

compass. She had no radar either and I kept a sharp lookout. No ships were in sight, only the Maatsuyker's double flash every 30 seconds out of the blackness of the land. Suddenly the light began to swing, slowly, towards our bow, until in a couple of minutes it was ahead. Then it drifted slowly to port — which meant that *we* were now heading straight towards the rocks!
I careered into the wheelhouse.
'Where d'you think you're going, Joe?' I exploded, thinking he had fallen asleep, feasible after 12 days in a port like Hobart!
But according to the compass, dimly lit in its brass binnacle, Joe was dead on course.

He thought *I* thought he was playing some trick on me my first watch as an officer, and was quite hurt. Between us we settled her back on course — to find that the compass card had stuck under the rim of the compass bowl, unique in my experience before or since. At midnight we changed over to the spare compass and had no further trouble. Without the Maatsuyker my first watch could have been my last! Clear of Aden, heading for the mouth of the Red Sea, traffic increased. When first in charge of a watch (and hence the ship) approaching vessels take on a new and sinister significance, to be watched warily. Here is one five miles off, coming from ahead with a bone in her teeth — must be a flyer! She'll be doing 19 and with our 11 it means we are approaching each other at 30 knots. She will be upon us in 10 minutes.
TEN MINUTES!
I glance sideways at the wheelman who steers on unconcerned, the old brassbound steering wheel moving easily in his confident grip. The ship is now much closer.
'Starboard five degrees' I try to sound calm.
'Starboard five', he replies and puts the rudder over that amount. We swing to starboard. When the other ship is well out on our port bow I say,
'Amidships.'
Amidships comes the rudder, and when I say 'Steady' he repeats the order and puts the rudder to port to counteract her swing. After the other ship has cleared, a mile to port, we resume course. Her wake shows that she, too, had altered to avoid us, precisely as required by the Rules. After the first few times it came easily and the shaky feeling did not return. By the time we reached London I felt I was a seasoned watchkeeper, and, after a short spell at school, ready to try for Second Mate's.

Chapter 3

Up for Second Mate's

1954

THERE WERE TWO NAUTICAL SCHOOLS on Tyneside: South Shields Marine School and Nellist's. South Shields was old-established but rapidly expanding with state finance and for an all-in fee a student could remain there for as long as he felt necessary. The second mate's course, lasting nine weeks, was so arranged that you could begin at any time and work until ready to attempt the examination. Thus the class included men at different stages, an advantage for those behind who were able to learn from those ahead. Nowadays the sea schools operate like shore schools — convenient for the teachers, perhaps, but not for seamen whose homecomings rarely coincide with the beginning of term. Most shipping companies in 1954 allowed a couple of months' paid leave, less National Assistance which had to be collected each Friday at the dole office, a time-consuming ritual which bit deeply into lectures. Nowadays, courses are longer, bookwork harder, and fees higher — especially now that subsidies have been so drastically reduced. The company pays the fees, salary is continuous, and candidates are no longer required to register as unemployed.

The other school was in Newcastle itself, run by two middle-aged brothers who had never been to sea. Their father, the late Captain Nellist, had set up his school when most nautical colleges were just such small, privately-owned establishments as this. The brothers had become interested at an early age in teaching in their father's school, and carried on after the old man died. Nellist's was expensive; for Second Mate's the joining fee was a pound, and 10 shillings weekly thereafter. But Nellist's was on my side of the river and thus easier to reach, and they actually advertised a 90 percent pass rate. The school was in Summerhill Terrace, overlooking a

39

private park which, like the houses, had seen better days. The gardens' iron railings and those around the park had been sent for scrap back in 1940, since when dogs and children had roamed freely. A tarnished brass plate alongside the open front door announced that this was indeed Nellist's Nautical School.

A shabby green door opening off an uncarpeted hall bore a card inscribed *Office*. I knocked and a rasping voice bade me enter. Threadbare carpet partly covered dusty floorboards while bulging bookcases lined the walls of a high, square room. Near the window sat an ancient lady hunched over what was surely Mr Remington's original typewriter. A high, black fireplace held just enough flickering coals to constitute a fire — even in July the house felt cold — and standing with his back to the hearth was a tall, severe-looking man, thumbs firmly hooked in the waistcoat of his navy-blue suit. Beneath wavy greying hair and beetling brows, belligerence stared. I rightly took him to be Mr Billy Nellist, the school's principal. He seemed little pleased to see me.

'I've come to join, sir,' I announced engagingly. By the look of the place they needed every penny they could get.

'Come to join have you? And what, may I ask, makes you think we'll have you?'

I was taken aback. I had been expecting, if not a welcome, at least a civil greeting. Perhaps I should have chosen South Shields.

'Er, I would like to join please. Second Mate's course.'

'Aye, I didn't think you'd come for Extra Master's. Got your money?'

I eagerly proffered my 30 shillings, which Billy regarded disdainfully.

'You've got to *work* here.' (He pronounced the word in the Tyneside idiom to sound like 'walk'.) 'No going off to the *King Billy* at lunchtime!' I assured him I was there to work.

He sniffed, clearly unimpressed, and turned to the secretary.

'Give him his receipt.'

I was in!

Jacky, the other Nellist brother, was much less fearsome: a mustard sports jacket and dark trousers gave him an almost casual air, and his gleaming bald pate seemed to accentuate the intelligence shining behind his spectacles.

They were a quaint pair, who ran their school magnificently, knowing all the answers and all the short cuts. They could make the traverse tables seem beautiful, knew the *Nautical Almanac* backwards, made the ABC tables as simple as their name, and even knew logarithms to five decimal places by heart.

For rule of the road they would push model ships around the table at the front of the class, asking each student a question, in turn. 'What's this one's fog signal?'

'If the next buoy to this in the channel is missing, what *should* the missing buoy look like at night?' And so on, round the class. A retired shipmaster taught us the finer points of practical seamanship; how to rig a jury rudder, or a heavy derrick. A retired Royal Navy yeoman of signals came weekly to explain and teach morse code, semaphore, and the international code of signals.

For an extra half crown each he would turn out on Saturday mornings to give us Extra Signals, as he called it. It paid to take the signals examination first, and concentrate thereafter on the other subjects. The examinations for masters and mates were taken in three equally testing parts, signals, writtens and orals. All three had to be passed within six calendar months of taking the first part. If not, all three had to be retaken.

After a couple of weeks at Nellist's I felt I knew signals backwards and cheerfully applied to SS Westgate Road, as the local examination centre was jocularly called.

'I'll just get signals,' I said.

I failed.

Whereas I had indeed learned the morse code and semaphore, I had spent insufficient time on the international code in which there is a different flag for every letter of the alphabet, each numeral, and other besides. It was essential to know the meanings of the individual flags and how to use the codebook to send and decode messages consisting of various hoists of flags, a system much used in wartime convoys when to break radio silence might mean attracting U-boats, surface raiders, or Condors. The examiner was a fierce old captain of international repute who did not suffer fools gladly. When I made a mistake in decoding he did not beat about the bush.

'Out!' he said, and Out I went, sadder but little wiser. But, I thought, with a little more attention to the flags, I'd be through! I put in my re-application at once, paying the appropriate 10 shillings for the privilege.

This time I reached the last hurdle. Morse code, semaphore, international code were behind me, all I had to do now was demonstrate to the examiner my skill at transmitting morse: the

41

standard message which includes every letter in the alphabet, 'the quick brown fox jumps over the lazy dog.' I had reached 'fox' when the examiner protested.
'No Kinghorn, you haven't got it. Out!'
I looked at him with dismay. His frosty glare softened a little.
'I can't read what you're sending,' he barked. 'Practise the wrist action, and come back when you've got it!'
Back at Nellist's the humorists composed a rhyme,
It was Christmas Day at Nellist's,
Called Jacky down the halls,
Did Kinghorn pass in signals?
Came the answer, did he . . . but I digress.
At my third go I passed.

Now to solve the mysteries of the haversine formula, the ex-meridians and the ABC — to learn how to rig this jury rudder in a gale, smooth the sea by running oil down your forecastle toilets, and construct a sheer legs out of three spare spars.
'Spare spars, sir?'
'Well, spare derricks then!'
'We don't carry spare derricks.'
'Well, unship three of the derricks your parish-rigged ship *has* got and use those. A seaman must be resourceful!'
Spare derricks indeed! Our examiners had been at sea a generation earlier and their seamanship was of a bygone era when, presumably, spare derricks abounded.

To satisfy the requirements of these august gentlemen we learned about long-outdated reciprocating steam engines which ran off coal-fired scotch boilers in ships with upright bar stems, counter sterns, single-plate rudders and rod-and-chain steering. We were taught to cope with fire in our coal bunkers and to find our way around the English Channel by the smell of the mud on the bottom. Sneer we might but this was what the examiners required us to know. As the Nellist brothers pointed out, they were not in business to teach us our trade, but to make us learn the rules of a game called Passing Examinations. As Jacky Nellist, the more patient of the two, explained, our examinations were not a test of what we knew so much as a test of our ability to think, to come to grips with problems and solve them. The oral examination, he said, was mainly to detect an agility of mind, to see what was required and do it, the essence of good seamanship. The man who could learn a set of rules and apply them, he argued, could easily pick up another, and, eventually, devise his own. This was the quality examiners sought. It was what lay behind the examinations which the Brothers Nellist were so good at explaining, as well as the seamanship itself. Though they claimed not to teach us our trade, they inculcated a philosophy which was to stand us in good stead for the rest of our seafaring lives.

One summer's morning, as Jacky drew the navigation class to a close, he announced,

'Well, gentlemen, as you may have heard, the Second Mate's class will be moving to new premises this afternoon. Transport will be here at one o'clock. If any of you would like to help us shift the desks and other equipment, we would be most grateful!'

Over lunch in Carrick's Cafe where pleasant waitresses, dressed traditionally in black, with white aprons and lace bonnets, served scotch broth for fourpence, and a three course meal for only 1s 3d (6p), we pondered the move. Which contractor, we wondered, would have landed the lucrative job of moving Nellist's Nautical Academy across the square to Winchester Terrace? Lunch over, we rounded the corner into Summerhill Terrace, stopped dead in our tracks, then fell about with mirth. The transport had arrived. There, outside the school, was the coalman's cart and horse, contentedly into its nosebag. Jacky and the coalman were at the front door deep in discussion. When he saw us, Jacky's eyes lit up.

'I knew I could rely on you, gentlemen,' he beamed, and gave two of us brooms to sweep the layer of coal dust off the cart, while the remainder staggered under the weight of cobweb-covered desks, tables, forms and teaching equipment new when Captain Noah himself was second mate. We lashed down our load in a seamanlike manner and leapt aboard. The coalman gave a flick of the whip, we cheered, and the horse, carried away with our excitement, galloped off up the hill. Another couple of trips, equally hilarious, followed. As we humped the equipment into our school's new home, a beaming Billy awaited us, thumbs, as usual, in waistcoat.

Most mornings, Billy was dour and crusty, as on the day I joined. By afternoon, however, it was a much more cheerful Billy, a Billy who radiated bonhomie from behind his smiling spectacles. His last lecture of the day would hold us spellbound. On this occasion he thanked us for our loyal efforts and, as a special treat, rounded off the afternoon with his famous talk on tropical revolving storms, one of his best lectures. Much of it remains etched in my mind today, and has often been recalled when avoiding them at sea. Nellist's, we felt, was not just a school, it was an experience and one I have relived with Old Boys all over the world. In 1945, the newly elected Labour Government's Ministry of Education wished to expand Nellist's School with Billy as principal. Billy, a staunch old tory, stated flatly that he wanted nothing to do with 'socialist money'. So that was that! The subsidy, instead, went to South Shields Marine School which prospered accordingly. Nellist's School died with the brothers less than a decade later.

At Nellist's, the callow student at first felt he already knew it all, that going to school was merely a formality to learn the examiners' idiosyncrasies, and that there was little to absorb in the way of knowledge from two old duffers who had never even been to sea themselves! The first seamanship class, however, opened his eyes to the gaps in his knowledge. The other students seemed to know far more. Such expertise was often offputting to beginners, who felt unable to grasp so much information but after a week or two, as other students came along knowing even less, you felt better, and confidence — with knowledge — slowly grew.

Once a week a group of us would have Private Discussion in the snug. The tanker men among us would detail the precautions needed when loading crude oil, and the mysteries of tank-washing and gas-freeing were revealed. Chaps from Baron Line and Runciman's would explain how to carry coal and how to prepare the bilges before switching to bulk wheat or barley. Aristocratic types from the British India Steam Navigation Company would describe the loading of jute, tea, and deck passengers on the Indian coast, and a rugged Yorkshireman from Ropner's gave an excellent description of the way to carry Australian iron ore. Those of us who came from Blue Star, Royal Mail and Port Line were able to clear up a few matters about refrigerated (reefer) cargoes, the subtle differences between carrying apples, lamb, chilled beef and oranges. The examiner was likely to ask a tanker man how frozen lamb should be carried and an iron ore man about a cargo of crude oil or sugar, so these sessions were vital to our education.

Eventually I felt I knew enough myself to try my luck, and consulted Jacky who reckoned my chances were even. He detailed my weaknesses and gave me some old examination papers to work over. According to his system, these papers were likely to reappear soon for the brothers had been quick to spot the order in which the written papers came round and their forecasts were right more often than not. Feeling exceptionally brave, I took my seaman's discharge book (as proof of seatime), my company's reference, birth certificate, eyesight test certificate and completed application form along to SS Westgate Road for the clerk to scrutinise. This was no mere formality as many a candidate who thought he had sufficient seatime had been sent back to sea for another few weeks before being allowed to sit the examinations. However, I was told to present myself on the following Monday at nine sharp.

The written examinations took all Monday, Tuesday and most of Wednesday, after which I was told to return on Friday morning for Orals. Cautiously optimistic so far and with signals under my belt, orals constituted the last hurdle, as much a personal examination as a test of knowledge, we were warned. To look smart, and answer smartly, without giving the impression of being a smart alec, was the advice given. The technique of one of the two examiners was to panic the candidate and watch his reactions, on the premise that when things begin to go wrong on the bridge an element of panic is likely to prevail. If you could keep your head while all around you were losing theirs, you'd get your certificate of competency. If you couldn't, you wouldn't.

One examiner was known to be friendly, helpful and patient, and the other (who had taken me for signals) was not. No one knew until the time came which examiner he would face. I relaxed in the waiting room by gazing out across the railways where I saw to my delight an express from Edinburgh hauled by the old LNER streamliner *Mallard*, holder of the world steam traction record of 126 miles per hour in 1938 and never beaten. In her British Railways livery of blue and black with red wheels she looked

45

immaculate. I could see the plume of smoke of another express across the river and strained to catch a glimpse of her as she roared onto the bridge, when the door behind me was flung open violently and I shivered back to the maritime world. The examiner stood glowering. It wasn't the friendly one.

'All right, Kinghorn,' he barked testily, 'Come on in!'

He took an ancient sextant from its box and slid it across the table towards me, a known opening gambit. The trick was to catch it before it fell off. My mind began to formulate the principle of the marine sextant, including the three corrections.

'Tell me,' he rasped, 'the principle of the marine barometer!'

'The principles of the marine sextant er, sorry, barometer, are . . .' and so the morning passed. While I recited the articles of the rule of the road he read the *Daily Telegraph*. When I had reached the end of Rule 9 — in those days that was the long one about fishing vessels — he folded his paper and nodded.

'That's enough.' Then he placed some model ships on the table to see if I really did know. Slowly we worked our way through the syllabus. After two hours I had not been thrown out.

He then produced two white lights, placed them at an angle, one slightly higher than the other.

'What is this?'

I reeled off all the ships I thought it could be.

'What else?' he demanded, beginning to pace the floor.

My brain seized up. He leaned his elbows on the high mantelpiece and glared, sighing deep sighs as his face reddened. I gave a couple of answers, neither acceptable, and had to admit I did not know. His agonised gasp would have done justice to one of the steam locomotives across the road.

'Could it be,' he asked with withering scorn, 'could it just be, a steam trawler on the quarter?'

'Of course it could,' I agreed.

'Right,' he said, business-like once more, and scribbled on a pad of forms, tore off the top one and handed it to me.

'Give this to the clerk,' he snapped, thrusting the slip into my hand. In blue pencil was the magical word, PASSED.

'Thank you very much, sir!'

'See you get mate's first time also, Kinghorn!', and he actually smiled as he shook my hand.

Chapter 4
A voyage in the Booth Line
1954-1955

TEN DAYS RELIEVING as fourth mate in London's Royal Docks followed my leave. All 40 ships of the Company's fleet voyaged to and from Britain in those days and at any time there would be eight or nine in UK ports. To enable their officers to take leave a permanent relieving staff was employed, supplemented by those awaiting deep-sea appointments. This 'suitcase gang' was an occasional part of everyone's life. The regulars were often elderly, retired masters from other companies, quite happy now to work as second or third mates in dock or around the coast. A junior officer finding himself with these old boys could learn a lot of sea lore — often with a wealth of hilarious anecdote — useful knowledge of the kind not found in seamanship manuals. Relief work in summer could be pleasant: in winter it was one long round of draughty docking stations — hours spend on cold bridges, freezing poops and coldest of all forecastle heads where there was no shelter, as the ship moved slowly along the docks from berth to berth.

I spent a week in the *Uruguay Star*, one of the four passenger ships (whose people appeared to consider themselves on a different plane from mere mortals), then a few days aboard the *Tasmania Star*, when one wet morning I was summoned by the marine superintendent. Captain Dickers was a large, beetle-browed man with a burly manner, but to my surprise he was all smiles. Booth Line, an associated company, urgently needed a second mate, and Blue Star Line had been asked to supply one today. I thought he'd made a mistake; I was a fourth mate. Second mates were senior fellows, often with master's tickets, and I had never even sailed as *third* mate! But I gladly accepted his invitation. 'Ring your mum,' said Captain Dickers kindly, sliding his desk telephone towards me. 'Tell her you're off to the Amazon in the

Aboard *Dominic* here seen in Lamport and Holt colours (her Booth Line funnel was black) Second Mate Kinghorn learns how close you can skirt Wolf Rock

Dominic, tonight!'

It was almost dark and still raining when a taxi deposited me alongside. Several evil-looking sailors in oilskins silently carried my gear aboard. Later I was to learn that they were all from Belem, in the Amazon, a hardworking and cheerful crew who had been years in the ship. A man would do one voyage as able seaman and another trip as steward, reverting later to engineroom greaser with equal facility. Since the first Portuguese conquerors married local Indian girls Brazil had seen a great admixture of the races, enriched by the negro blood of African slaves. Some of the most sinister had black faces and oriental features but after the initial impact I found that appearance was of little consequence when the man behind the face emerged as a person. *Dominic's* master, Captain G G Roberts RD, RNR — a kindly gentleman of the old school — concealed what must have been dismay at his new second mate's tender years and limited qualifications. Most second mates had at least a first mate's ticket. But he shook hands cordially and said we would not be sailing that night after all as the second engineer had not arrived. He suggested I start the gyro compass. Gyro compass? I had never seen one, but this was no time to display ignorance. Eventually I discovered it under the bridge. It was a Sperry, but I had no idea how to start it until the mate came to my assistance. 'Simple', he said, 'just switch this and wait 10 minutes.'

We smoked in silence.

'Then remove the locking snecks and cut this switch — see?'
Like all gyro compasses it was basically a heavy steel wheel revolving on a horizontal axle. Given a little help, a wheel so turning will eventually line up its axle in a north-south direction because of the earth's rotation. I made a mental note to read the instruction manual when at sea.

The cargo was aboard and hatches battened down, so there was little to do once I had plotted our courses on the charts. Whilst in London I had renewed the aquaintance of an old school friend, now a teacher in Tottenham. That last night I took her to a show at the Coliseum which pleasantly rounded off four and a half months of life 'ashore'. In 1981 we celebrated our silver wedding.

Next afternoon the *Dominic* sailed for La Guira, in Venezuela. I kept the twelve to fours. We carried no cadets and my only watchmate was a Brazilian sailor who spoke little English but made excellent coffee. As we headed down Channel into a rising westerly I perceived the *Dominic* was not a fast ship; four knots was all we managed in my first watch. We covered the first 1000 miles at an average of 7.82 knots and, once the swell moderated, built up to a steady 10. Captain Roberts and the mate were keen navigators and had me taking sights with them whenever a clear sky and sharp horizon made this possible. We even took Venus by day, when she appears as a pin-point of white light in your sextant telescope.

I explored the ship from top to bottom and from stem to stern. Built in Wilmington, California in 1945 as the *Hickory Stream* for the US Maritime Commission, she was designed for an assault which never took place thanks to the collapse of Japan. She was a splendid little ship barely 3,000 tons whose engine and accommodation aft gave her a profile more like today's vessels than those of her own era. Her diesel engine, though low-powered, was ample for wartime requirements. Even by 1954 many ships still went around the world at less than 10 knots. She had good generators and all her auxiliaries were electric. The echo sounder was a 'Supersonic Depth Indicator' and an automatic pilot ran off the gyro compass. She was a well-designed, comfortable little vessel and I spent the next six and a half months in her extremely happily. Captain Robers had been a midshipman in the Battle of Jutland, and, for many years, was with Booth Line during the palmy days of the passenger liners. He ran the little *Dominic* on classic lines. There was accommodation for six passengers and she had 35 crew — generous manning even by the standards of the day.

New Year's Day found us on passage to Willemstad and I relieved the third mate (a 19-year-old senior cadet) on the bridge shortly before midnight. We shook hands and wished each other a happy new year. It was traditional for the youngest aboard to strike 16 bells — eight for the old year and eight for the new. He then went off to his bunk leaving me to 1955 with a wet night. Next morning there was no doubt that Willemstad had celebrated; even the dogs seemed drunk, and how the linesmen took our mooring ropes without falling into the water defied gravity. Our slow speed did not worry us, 'more days, more dollars', and the fishing was good. Lines trailed from the ship for barracuda which, when hauled aboard with snapping jaws and flailing tails, were soon committed to the pot. The Brazilians, like the Portuguese, are great fish eaters. The pilot boarded off Salinas, at the Amazon's southern mouth, the Rio Para, and guided us 100 miles up the muddy waters to Belem where we anchored for the night. Customs and Port Officials on what is called The Visit, cleared the ship for entry. For our crowd, Belem was Home. They had grown increasingly cheerful over recent weeks and now went ashore so elegantly dressed that they were hardly recogniseable. Natty suits, silken shirts and bow ties, snappy hats and black and white pointed shoes made an exotic change from the dungarees and singlets of shipboard life.

Booth Line was a big name on the river. We navigated by special Booth Line charts, 'with soundings taken from *RMS Hilary* in 1936'. Booth Line tugs berthed us and towed Booth Line barges with sliding steel hoods, the need for which became apparent every afternoon when the heavens opened. On sailing day we signed on a gang of labourers to clean our two rusty deeptanks, in preparation to receive castor oil which also lubricates aero engines. Each cleaner was paid the equivalent of 25p an hour. They slept in hammocks in the grimy tweendecks, preserving personal dignity and a sense of humour. The constant tap-tap-tap of their chipping hammers was an inescapable background lullaby.

Next port was Sao Luiz do Maranho, 20 miles up an estuary south of the Amazon. There was no quay so we moored to two anchors. The port anchor was let go and paid out as we steamed slowly ahead against the current. When six shackles (90 fathoms) of chain were out, the starboard anchor was let go and the engine first stopped, then put astern. The starboard anchor was paid out and the port chain hove in until there were three shackles (45 fathoms or 270 feet) on each anchor, leading in opposite directions. This enabled the ship to swing to the tide in a narrow space without running too close inshore. The harbour was silting and depths uncertain so the captain and I sounded round with a hand leadline at low water to see if we still floated. As expected, we were sitting on soft mud, which meant we had to sail the following high water to avoid being neaped (trapped by the low high water of the quarter moon.) Bound along the coast to Fortaleza during the afternoon watch I was alone temporarily on the bridge, when I saw men standing in groups on the surface of the sea! Closer examination revealed that these were fishermen on balsa wood rafts, the famous *jangadas*, each manned by four or five men. When the time came to return they stepped the mast with its large triangular sail and raced shorewards. Their rafts had dagger centreboards for windward work but before a wind they performed like sailing hydroplanes. Driving in towards the beach their momentum carried them up the sand, their crews shouting and laughing as they came to rest outside their primitive thatched homes.

The Fortaleza quay was partly protected by a low breakwater. Vessels secured with one anchor forward, another aft, and head and sternlines to the shore. These held the ship 10 feet off, continuously surging up and down along the quay without damage but at the cost of mooring ropes. As at all ports since London we used our own derricks to work cargo, the local dockers driving the winches. In Fortaleza however were steam cranes built in Leeds in 1917 from Consett iron, each with its own clattering engine and wood-fired boiler belching clouds of smoke and steam as it unloaded timber from a coaster next to us. The wharf was the centre of social life. Families squatted round little fires, eating and laughing alongside their goats, pigs, hens and donkeys. Those higher up the social scale made Sunday afternoon the occasion for a visit to the port, and cruised up and down in large American cars or strolled hand in hand. A trio of pretty girls called from the quay. The third mate and I, recalling happy days in Australia and New Zealand, invited them aboard but the Customs officer on our gangway said no. Why not? Brazilian ladies were not allowed aboard foreign ships. We explained that we were British, not foreign, but he was adamant: the girls blew us kisses and strolled on.

After four days in this fascinating place we sailed for Tutoya. The second mate's docking station was aft with half the sailors. Having been warned to get in the kedge anchor quickly we first took in the mooring lines. Close astern, stern to, was the ss *Navem Hembury*, built by Swan Hunter in 1915. She was only 4,974 tons but riding light, her high black counter stern was well above ours. Our heavy kedge was out on a wire rope and as it was being hove in the rope jumped the winch barrel whereupon the anchor plunged back into the water. We drifted closer to the *Navem Hembury*. Our propeller could not be turned for fear of its fouling the wire so we tried again. As the anchor cleared the water, a nimble sailor, without being told, leapt over the rail to secure it with a length of rope. Had he slipped from the muddy anchor he would have been killed. I shouted to the captain when we were secure and he, no doubt thinking dark thoughts about inexperienced second mates, put the telegraph to Full Ahead and we cleared with inches to spare. Whenever we saw the *Navem Hembury* in port afterwards, her crew made dramatic gestures of pushing us away.

At anchor off Tutoya Bay we caught a shark, only six feet long, small as sharks go, but it looked enormous when strung by the tail to an awning spar. Pale grey and white, it seemed to die quickly. A couple of hours later the cook poked its face with a broom. With one snap of its mighty jaws the shark bit the broomstick into three neat pieces, then went to sleep again. The sea was clear and warm, but nobody went swimming.

We returned to the Amazon and anchored off Belem, ready to start work next morning. We loaded bales of japorandy leaves and sacks of gum — oddly-shaped bales of rubber, carved with the marks of the family who had gleaned it from the forest which came down the river in canoes — bags of wax, drums of balsam and rosewood oil, Brazil nuts and cocoa, skins of the otter, deer, alligator, jaguar, and wild boar. At last we set off to Manaus, 1,000 miles up river, with two pilots to guide us. For the next five days one of them was always on the bridge while we were underway. The first 500 miles are tidal. In the narrows we could almost touch the trees as we passed, and Indians put off from the banks in dugout canoes to pick up jars and bottles thrown from the ship. Against the current our best speed was eight knots. Some parts were so wide that both banks were almost out of sight, shimmering beneath the daily build-up of towering cumulus cloud which condensed in a shattering thunderstorm each evening. Occasionally we passed the ruins of mansions built by the rubber barons before their plants were smuggled to Kew Gardens a century ago. When, as a result, Malay rubber became established, the demand for native rubber declined and the barons left. Now, families of Indians lived in the crumbling ruins, stringing their washing on poles out of the empty windows. In 60 feet of water the colour of brown ale, we secured to buoys off Manaus. Near us lay the old sailing ship *Senator*, her wings clipped to lower masts, used as a coal hulk to bunker the coal-burning steamers trading along the Brazil coast. One of the oldest of these was the 55-year-old *Raul Soares*, built in 1900, still carrying passengers.

To me Manaus looked like a city which, left untended for a month or two, would disappear into the jungle. Even new buildings seemed ancient. Electric trams lurched as their tracks dipped on the rough cobbled surface, cambered steeply to carry off the rain. A magnificent opera house with mosaic dome and crystal chandeliers stood unused, its air of decay enhanced by vultures feeding in the street outside. Manaus is now a booming city, but in 1955 it gave me the creeps, and I was glad when we moved downstream to load kapok logs (from the pods of which came the stuffing for our lifejackets). Each log weighed several tons and, waterlogged, stank. A gang came to load them, nimble fellows who leapt around as though it were the easiest thing in the world to work a wet, slippery, 10-ton log into a ship's deep lower hold where one slip could have meant serious injury or death. When the holds were full we loaded another 42 logs on deck in threes, positioned with wire ropes led through snatch blocks to the winches and lashed with wire. The height of the log stow meant that the derricks could not lower into their crutches so they, too, were secured for sea with wire rope.

We came downriver fast, and sailed for New York from Belem on February 18, hugging the Brazilian coast to make the most of the north-sweeping current. To reduce sweat and consequent damage to the cargo the hatch corners were kept open for ventilation until one night a fierce gale sprang up. Deeply laden, our little ship pitched and rolled and began to take water over the decks. At the change of the watches at four in the morning the deck floodlights were switched on and hatches were battened down before water penetrated below. In the screaming wind and rain, it was exacting work which, left too late, could have resulted in the ship foundering. When we left the Gulf Stream two days later the temperature dropped 40 degrees. Long forgotten duffle coats, mildewed in the folds through hanging overlong in the Amazon damp, woolly scarves and hats, boots and gansies (Guernsey jersies!) were broken out. And still we shivered.

The friendly beam of Ambrose Lightship through the thick drizzle of a winter's evening welcomed us into New York Harbour, just as the SS *America* steamed out, a blaze of lights. At that time she was running mate to the *United States*, holder of the Blue Riband. Built in 1940, SS *America* saw war service as the trooper *West Point* and, many name changes later, is afloat today. Next morning we weighed anchor and moved slowly through the murk to Pier 20, Staten Island with two McAllister's tugs in attendance. Longshoremen promptly swarmed aboard to unload. A surveyor sampling our castor oil proclaimed it first class whereupon it was pumped into road tankers by an ancient Smith and Waile steam pump which contrasted strangely with the brand new diesel used in Fortaleza to pump it aboard. So not everything in New York was up to date! But there was nothing old-fashioned about the television set put aboard to give most of us our first glimpse of the magic box which entranced us for hours on end, even the commercials.

Life here in Stapleton was pleasant but it wasn't New York City. Thanks to the poor visibility we could have been a hundred miles from Manhattan for all we could see of skyscrapers. But the night we moved to Carteret the air was crystal clear, so cold that when I dropped a damp glove it froze to the steel deck. As I rose the ship was backing out into the Bay, and there, across the water, lay the most beautiful city I had ever seen. The Statue of Liberty, pale green in her floodlights, stood to the left of that multicoloured mass of skyscraper land which is Lower Manhattan. Calm water reflected a million coloured lights. To the right, up East River, cars and trains made their way over the Brooklyn and Manhattan Bridges but all else was still as we steamed slowly round the north of Staten Island through the narrow Kill Van Kull into the windswept wilds of New Jersey.

Carteret was little more than a wooden wharf and a saw mill. Our kapok log cargo had dried, though still powerfully smelly, and was much easier to handle now than when we loaded. Late in the afternoon I went down the hold to see how many logs remained, and dropped my torch between them to the bottom of the hold. I mentioned this to the longshoremen working there and said if they found a torch when they reached the bottom it was mine.
'What's a torch, mister?'
I described a torch.
'What you mean's a flashlight, mister. Trouble wit' you limeys, you cain't speak de Queen's English!'
But by the time they found it a clumsy log had eradicated any resemblance either to a torch or flashlight. Riding high and light we moved across the Bay in the gathering dusk, to tie up alongside a floating drydock at Bethlehem Steel Corporation's Brooklyn yard, where we were to refit.

The third mate and I had plotted to see the bright lights of the big city together. So far during the voyage the mate had insisted upon one or other of us being aboard whether cargo was working or not. He summed it up for us in his thin Welsh voice,
'I'm onboard on duty all day. I'm not keeping nights as well!'
Just one 'night aboard' would do him no harm we thought, and by preventing his wasting his money on the fleshpots surely we were doing him a favour? Naturally we did not mention this to him, but went to docking stations in go-ashore gear under oilskins. In the

dark nobody noticed that we were ready to abandon ship. The third mate's station was on the bridge, mine down aft. While the mate was on the forecastle head. We made sure that we finished our work before him. He caught sight of us as we scurried along the dockside.

'Here! Where do you think you're going?' he shouted.

'We're off to see the Great White Way, sir! Thanks for doing the night aboard. Good night!'

'Come back here! I've told you before I'm not keeping any blasted nights aboard . . .' His voice faded as we headed out of the dock gates into the streets of Brooklyn. A subway train rushed us to Times Square with its glowing, flashing signs where the crowds, human and automotive, promptly engendered a carnival mood. An advertisement for Camel cigarettes consisted of a huge face puffing real smoke rings. Flashing news headlines declared,

'Princess Meg gets her Man!'

The man was Townsend and the poor girl never did get him, but it seemed then that she would and we were happy for her. Our destination was the Sheraton Astor Hotel where the British Merchant Navy Officers' Club made us welcome and charming young ladies offered to show us the city sights. We dined in pleasant little restaurants and visited Broadway theatres, at one of which we saw a new English musical play about the roaring 20s, Sandy Wilson's *The Boy Friend*, with an up and coming young lady called Julie Andrews in the lead.

Our refit lasted only a week, much of which I seemed to spend late at night getting lost on the subway system. But I was never accosted and saw no unpleasant behaviour. Those abroad at that time of night were most helpful in giving directions and in bars people were cheerful and friendly. Not a few had been Over There during the war which seemed to help my cause. I had heard that Brooklyn was not a place to wander round alone late at night, but such tales are told about most waterfronts.

We moved to Pier 33, the regular Booth Line loading berth to start lifting cargo for North Brazil. We were to take part of an oil refinery being built on the river below Manaus, the first time I had seen a ship taken apart to get the cargo aboard! Much of the refinery consisted of 100 ft steel cylinders, too large and cumbersome to stow on deck. Never mind! Take off a ventilator here, remove a winch there, unbolt a couple of ladders and burn off a section of the bulwarks, and there you are!

Last aboard and bound for Recife were four stalls of cattle, two bulls and two cows. We then set off via Norfolk, Virginia, where we loaded barrels of United Nations powdered milk. Longshoremen here were negroes speaking the rich, fruity accent of Virginia, so different from the clipped Brooklyn twang. We came alongside Newport News to load 2,000 tons of coal in a cloud of dust. When secure we left Chesapeake Bay and headed south for Recife, formerly Pernambuco, between North and South Brazil where a long coral spit protects the lagoon which has been widened and deepened to make a harbour. We moored inside the reef (the meaning of Recife) with anchors fore and aft and lines ashore. The cattle were offloaded in good order so, taking advantage of the mate's consequent good humour, the third mate and I set off ashore in search of fun.

Next afternoon a young Customs officer came aboard with two plain clothes men and a burly fellow equipped with a bag of tools. The Customs officer, smart in his sky blue uniform and white peaked cap, came to see me, the only officer aboard. He would like to look round the ship, he said, and would I accompany him? He was pleasant and spoke good English. After a perfunctory search of the cabins he turned to the engine room where our old Brazilian donkeyman followed us round, answering technical questions put to him in Portuguese by our visitors. We came to a large cube-shaped tank at shoulder height which the donkeyman claimed was full of water. As in many American ships there was no glass gauge, only a vertical line of small taps or cocks on the tank side. The Customs officer opened the taps one by one, but no water came out. Whereupon he ordered the removal of the manhole cover from the tank's side. Even when the nuts were removed no water flowed.

Obviously the donkeyman, at best, was mistaken, but he remained impassive, stepping to one side as though contemplating swift departure. The plain clothes men grabbed him, pinioning his arms — when there was a sudden noise like tearing cloth, and the manhole cover ripped its perished gasket, cascading water over us all. To his eternal credit, the Customs officer burst out laughing, when we moved on to examine first the steering gear and then, on deck, the oil refinery deck cargo and forecastle. Aft was cargo space, while the fore part had the windlass contactor room on one side and the rope store on the other, connected by a narrow alleyway, partly blocked by a pile of old tarpaulins.

57

Shifting these the strong-arm man revealed a manhole cover (which I didn't even know about) looking as though it had not been unbolted in years. Strong Arm took it off, with difficulty, to reveal a narrow, dark space containing tarpaulins green and mildewed with age, looking and smelling as though they had been there since the ship was built 10 years earlier. Below them Strong Arm discovered a small parcel wrapped in green canvas neatly tied with marline twine. Inside were 12 new Swiss watches. The Customs officer smiled sadly and took them ashore. I reported the incident later to Captain Roberts who was much concerned since such contraband invariably meant a heavy fine for the ship's master. But there was no fine, no recrimination, and we heard no more.

From Recife we sailed to tiny Cabadelo where we unloaded UN milkpowder. One afternoon the third mate and I strolled up to the ruins of a deserted fort looking as though no one had visited it in centuries. A massive outer stone wall flanked a grassy courtyard in the centre of which stood a ruined chapel. The ramparts were covered with springy turf and half a dozen iron cannon lay among their rotting carriages, still pointing out to sea. One gun bore the letters GR and the English crown, perhaps from a British ship — Portugal is still Britain's oldest ally. A dark doorway led into the wall, and we made to enter, intending to illuminate our way with cigarette lighters, only to stop dead in our tracks for there, walking towards us, was the most fearsome spider we had ever seen, its body the size of a soup-plate, covered with dense black fur. We backed away and sought refuge by the chapel where we threw stones as it came steadily towards us. When one stone missed narrowly the spider froze, then shot back to its lair like black lightning. Somehow, 'Tarantula Castle' never attracted us after that.

Up river we anchored off the site of the new oil refinery to unload and then in Belem we loaded Brazil nuts, rosewood oil, mahogany, cocoa, six Brazilian nut trimmers and five Dutch passengers, before leaving the river on May 18 bound for Liverpool, Rotterdam and Antwerp. But Liverpool was on strike so we diverted to Rotterdam. Huge barges with families living aboard in neat little houses aft came alongside to take out our Liverpool cargo temporarily so that the Rotterdam cargo could be discharged. After reloading we set off for Antwerp up the Schelde, half a day's steaming away. This was my first visit to the continent and I marvelled at the horse-drawn sleds, onto which our cargo was loaded, moving easily over the cobbles. Gangs of women stitched up rents in the bags made by dockers' hooks. When the English strikes ended we sped along the Channel into dense fog off the Isle of Wight. November is the foggiest month in the English Channel but this was June, which is almost as bad. In 1955 there was no routeing, no traffic separation as now, and you lumbered on as best you could at 'moderate speed', blowing your whistle at intervals not exceeding two minutes and staring into the fog. Some ships had radar but not the *Dominic*. The 'supersonic depth' indicator broke down, so we used the hand sounding machine, studying the colour and smell of the mud which came up on the lead, as taught by the Brothers Nellist.

Channel tides have a powerful effect on a slow ship and before we reached Land's End our position was in some doubt. Had we been heading across the Atlantic we would have carried on until the weather cleared, but bound for Liverpool you *have* to turn right somewhere. We guessed we were a few miles east by north from Wolf Rock, that lonely lighthouse which stands seven miles off Land's End. To my surprise Captain Roberts put a pencil mark on the chart where we thought we were, drew a line from there through Wolf Rock, and used that direction as the course to steer. He stood in the starboard wing of our little bridge, I in the port wing with a lookout man forward. We all knew what we were looking for, and that Wolf Rock's foghorn had been reported out of action. After an hour's steaming at eight knots straining our eyes into the gloom we saw it together. There, almost under our bow, was a cluster of sullen breakers, eerily white against the uniform grey of sea and fog, the lighthouse towering above us, frighteningly large and close.

'Hard a'starboard,' Captain Roberts ordered calmly. After what seemed an age the ship's head came round and we cleared the breakers by 100 yards. My face must have been a study for the captain looked at me and said kindly,

'Plenty of water here, Mr Kinghorn!'

Third Mate

Chapter 5

1955-1957

TOWARDS THE END of my voyage in the *Dominic* I occasionally pondered my future. Although I had enjoyed the Booth Line experience I wanted to return to Blue Star Line. But what of the future? I still wanted to command a cargo carrier, which interested me more and more, so I decided to remain in the Blue Star Line. Although I did not want to revert to fourth mate I realised that the job of second mate in Blue Star was far more complex than it had been in the *Dominic*. Instead of Booth Line's three and a half hatches most Blue Star vessels had five, six, or even seven, sub-divided into many compartments for the carriage of refrigerated produce. The second mate made the cargo plans and was responsible for much of the cargo work, and also calculated the ship's stability. I felt I had better spend some time as third mate who not only understudied the second mate but was responsible for much of the ship's safety and fire-fighting equipment and helped the master with wages. He was also the unofficial medicine man who dispensed aspirins, black draught and sticking plaster and, in the absence of a doctor, injected penicillin. There was a lot to learn and to miss it would not be in my own interest. So, towards the end of my leave I went to see Mr Cox in West Smithfield. After five years of phone calls, letters and telegrams, this was our first meeting.

'What were you thinking of sailing as, old boy?' he asked.

'Third Mate, sir.'

'Third Mate? Just what I had in mind!' He was beaming. I was appointed to the *Brasil Star,* one of the four passenger ships on the South American run known as A Boats because their pre-war predecessors' names all began with A. They were said to impart a social polish to those sailing in them who tended to look down on their lowly brothers in what *they* called the 'Colonial Boats'. The lowly brothers, of course, shared no such illusions of inferiority and in turn sneeringly referred to the A Boats as the Chay Boats, from the habit of those sailing in them of calling each other *Chay* — an Argentinian word roughly equivalent to 'Dear fellow.'

'I say, Chay, it's a lovely day today, eh!' — was how they were supposed to speak in the *Brasil Star* and her sisters. And now I was to join them!

I knew I was only in the *Brasil* while she refitted in the Royal Albert drydock. I tested fire extinguishers, counted hoses, checked the leather washers on deck hydrants and followed the piping of the CO_2 fire detection system. The carbon dioxide bottles had to be weighed on a spring balance to see if they needed recharging. Getting dozens of these large steel bottles from their racks and weighing them, always in a confined space, was warm work. Interesting though. The lifeboats, too, came in for my attention. After I had examined a boat thoroughly, noting all defects, along would come the Ministry of Transport surveyor (whose word, unlike mine, carried the weight of law) who would point out much I had not noticed — here a cracked rib, there a split gunwale; down there, rot in the keelson! The lifeboats' equipment was laid out in the wheelhouse by the fourth mate and me. (There were no cadets in those ships. Cadets did not need social polish.) There were tins of condensed milk, barley sugar and ship's biscuit (one pound per person). Boat lamps, compasses, torches, heliographs, balers, buckets, heaving lines, jacknives, water dippers, drinking cups, whistles, plugs, crutches, hand flares, smoke floats, parachute flares — all were inspected meticulously. There were life jackets and lifebuoys, oil navigation lights for emergencies, anchor balls and not under command balls. Not under command balls? Yes. When a vessel is broken down and unable to get out of the way she must indicate this by displaying two red lights by night, and by day, in a vertical line, two black balls. I had worked on life-saving equipment as a cadet of course, but as third mate it became that much more important. In the evenings when the ship was quiet I worked on the accounts. There were 80 people or so onboard, even in dry dock, and it was my job to assess how much each man, including officers, should be paid after deductions for income tax, pension fund, national health, etc. I drew the cash from the office and paid it out on Friday afternoons. In London help was given by the wages department, but sometimes they were away on another ship, signing her on or paying her off, so the third mate had to know how to do it himself. On voyage the writer did this work, but he was on leave. The knowledge gained stood me in good stead later as there were no writers on the Colonial Boats and their work was carried out by the third mate. Sometimes the captain did it all, but most masters insisted (quite rightly, I now feel) that this was all part of the third mate's education. Nowadays most of this clerical work is done ashore by the Wages Department; everyone is on salary, and weekly subs onboard are paid by the purser. Third mates, perhaps, are poorer for missing the experience.

When the *Brasil Star*'s refit was complete I joined the *Argentina Star*, due to refit in Antwerp. This was the first time I had been to sea in a turbine steamer which, I was told, was silent and free of the vibration of a motor ship. But the *Argentina Star* rattled all the way over the North Sea. I mentioned this to the third engineer.
'Ah,' he said, 'It's not the engine vibrating, it's the ship!'
Although the turbines ran smoothly, the propeller, half out of the water, set up vibrations through the steelwork which rose to a crescendo, centred on the third mate's bunk. As the engineer kindly pointed out, if I ever did any real work I'd be so tired at the end of the day that a little vibration wouldn't keep me awake!

In drydock again the mate took me round examining the wooden insulation in the cargo spaces, noting damage or rot. We also looked for damage caused by slings of cargo hitting the brine pipes which ran through the hatches. We explored bilges for traces of oil leaking from the fuel tanks and studied the shell plating for dents caused by coming alongside heavily. When the *Argentina* returned, I transferred to the *Uruguay Star*, refitting in London, and I was told to remain aboard for the forthcoming voyage. This

A spell in the *Uruguay Star* one of Blue Star's four cargo-passenger liners on the South American service in 1956

surprised me as I thought by now everyone realised that I was not really a passenger ship type. As well as 65 first class passengers she carried cargo and mail to ports between Rio de Janeiro and the River Plate. Outward we called at Brest to load seed potatoes, Lisbon, Las Palmas for bunkers, Rio, Ilheus (an anchorage port, for bagged cocoa), Santos, Montevideo and Buenos Aires, where we spent two weeks.

The cargo spaces were thoroughly cleaned, those allocated to carry chilled beef being fumigated with formaldehyde 'bombs' to kill traces of fungus lurking in the woodwork. Chilled beef was carried as fore and hind quarters hung on sterilised hooks, at $29°$ F with only half a degree of tolerance either way. It commanded a better price than frozen meat carried at 15 degrees, as freezing bursts the tiny blood vessels which bleed when thawed. Increasing quantities of chilled beef were being carried from the Argentine, somewhat less from Australia and New Zealand, because the length of time which chilled beef remains in perfect condition is limited. We also carried frozen lamb, tins of hearts and kidneys, and general cargo. The deck officers were kept on their toes as loading, especially at the Anglo Frigorifico in South Dock, proceeded with incredible speed. Dunnage had to be laid carefully to ensure correct air flow and when a deck completed it was important to ship all the insulated hatch plugs (as the covers are called) properly. It was equally important to watch the quality of the meat loaded; the ship's chief refrigeration engineer would be on the quay in a spotless white boilersuit, spearing carcases with a spiked thermometer as they came out of the trucks. He used a hand drill to get the thermometer into the bone to ensure that the meat was thoroughly frozen. If a ship accepts cargo as being in good condition then unloads in a lesser condition, the deterioration 'must' be the ship's fault, so officers have to be constantly alert. An insulated truck may leave the cold store with its load and be delayed beneath a burning sun en route to the ship. If loaded into the ship soft it will soon freeze hard again but may become mis-shapen. It is also unhygienic to refreeze thawed meat.

The nearest town to South Dock was the Boca, half a mile away past a line of shanty bars. The Boca itself was quite pleasant with good shops and pleasant restaurants, but adjacent was an appalling shanty town where people lived in squalor, especially in wet weather. Despite their poverty, the Argentine dockers were a cheerful crowd. Their sustained interest in our dealings with the local ladies caused some officers to invent stories of incredible sexual exploits, appreciated by teller and listener alike, if believed by neither.

I would have been happy to remain in the *Uruguay Star*, after that voyage. The run was interesting, the people not bad when you came to know them, and — important to a young man contemplating matrimony — you could forecast when you would be home months in advance and so arrange holidays, a rare privilege for seafarers. But Mr Cox had other ideas. The A boats were considered senior ships, where officers polished their social style before promotion in lesser vessels. Thus I was transferred to the *Melbourne Star*, loading at Tilbury for Australia.

The *Melbourne*, and her twin sister *Imperial Star*, were built by Harland and Wolff on the Clyde in 1947/8 to replace war losses and were equipped with double-acting Burmeister and Wain engines easily able to maintain their service speed of 17½ knots. The master, radio officer, four mates and two cadets lived abaft the bridge, above the 12 passengers. Across number three cargo hatch the engineer officers lived on the port side and the catering staff on the starboard. Deck and engineroom ratings were housed in the raised poop, above which lived the petty officers (bosun,

'Demoted' to Third Mate of the *Melbourne Star* **— passing under Sydney Bridge — Kinghorn prepares for marriage, after attending a Defence Course**

carpenter, engineroom storekeeper, donkeyman and lamp-trimmer). They were happy ships which ran well. We loaded endless cars from Dagenham, machinery, huge rolls of Bowater's newsprint, steel, chemicals, toys, paint, cement, carpets, pianos, glass sheet and glassware, crockery, cutlery, whisky, gin and beer; and sailed on Christmas Eve, 1955.

After bunkering at Tenerife we called for one night at Capetown, where I kept the night aboard while most went ashore. We had a crew of 73, mostly Scots from the islands, on deck, and the gaelic was their mother tongue. They were splendid fellows, hard workers — but hard drinkers also and the cheap brandy known as Cape Smoke had done its work as they returned in twos and threes. A 19-year-old seaman tried to climb up the after mooring ropes and fell into the dock where his wild cries for help were heard coming from the black water. By the time I was summoned, a middle-aged Liverpool greaser had dived overboard into the cold waters and borne him to the quayside where willing hands hauled them out. By this time he was deeply unconscious and blue with cold, his heartbeat nearly gone and we thought we had lost our shipmate when he was rushed to hospital. Sadly we turned in, though sleep did not come easily. In the early hours the phone woke me from a doze. It was the night sister. Would I please come and collect my sailor? He had made such a dramatic recovery that he was chasing the nurses round the ward with gaelic ardour!

The Great Southern Ocean did not seem so large in the *Melbourne Star* at 17½ knots as it had in the little *Saxon* at 11. Before arriving in Adelaide we heard that dock strikes had broken out and that we would have to anchor off, and I had a wedding arranged for the end of April! As the strike dragged on I sent word home to postpone the wedding until May . . . and then again, to the end of June. No sooner was the June date fixed than the strike ended and we raced round Australia in record time. Our progress meant that we would now be home in May, but I did not dare ask for yet another alteration in the wedding date.

An old lady passenger who had joined in Melbourne died peacefully as we cleared the Australian Bight. Her burial at sea, conducted by the captain, was the only sea funeral I have seen. The ship was stopped just before sunset, with the ensign at half mast. All hands were assembled at the starboard side of number three hatch, between bridge and funnel. The body, sewn neatly in canvas and weighted with iron, lay on a hatchboard under a new red ensign. At the captain's words, 'We commit our sister to the deep,' the hatchboard was tilted and the canvas-covered body slid from under the flag into the sea. It was a simple but moving ceremony and, I felt, a good way to go, if you died at sea.

As far as I was concerned we arrived home too soon. Had I taken my leave then I would have been back to sea long before my wedding! Mr Cox would not allow this however and sent me relieving for a while in the old *SS Vancouver Star* — a bit of a comedown professionally, but the pay was the same. Then I was sent on a Defence Course, a huge joke according to the family who believed it to be a course in self defence before taking a wife. In fact it was to show us how to defend our ship in war. After the wedding Mr Cox let us down lightly by appointing me third mate of the *English Star* at Palmer's Yard, Hebburn on Tyne, where shelter decks were being converted to carry bananas, which involved insulating the steel with cork, fibreglass and timber, and installing more refrigeration machinery. I was able to commute daily. The *English Star* and her sister *Scottish Star* were built at Fairfield's on the Clyde in 1950. They were handsome ships, well suited for world-wide refrigerated trading as it was in those days.

The beloved *English Star* **in which the author serves as Third Mate, Chief Officer and, his first command, Master under God in 1971**

After several weeks, conversion completed, we sailed out of the Tyne — the first time I had done so — adjusted compasses off the river, and headed for Rosario, up the Plate from Buenos Aires, to load meat. I spent the next three voyages in that ship, on the South American service. On the second we approached South Dock to see the masts and yards of the four-masted barque *Pamir* towering over the dockside sheds. The Germans now ran her and her sister *Passat* as cargo-carrying cadet ships — out to the Plate with coke from Bremen, home with grain to Hamburg. She was in magnificent condition, as one might expect of a vessel with 90 cadets one of whom showed me round. His name was Vinnen, a relative of the famous shipowner; I have long hoped that he was one of the few who survived when she foundered in a North Atlantic hurricane a year later.

The *English Star* carried pineapples from Recife to Buenos Aires in season, and there loaded meat for London, lifting bananas in Santos, Brazil. They were carried by the bunch, each bunch about four feet long and containing many 'hands'. They came covered in straw wrapping, often with thin green snakes and tarantulas hidden beneath which caused consternation when they came out to explore their new surroundings. Nowadays bananas are carried in hygienic cartons and the snakes and spiders stay at home. The *English* and *Scottish Stars* supplemented the four A boats on this run but did not usually carry passengers, although each had comfortable accommodation for 12.

After three voyages I had sufficient seatime to attempt my First Mate's certificate and returned to Nellists to find many of my old friends from the Second Mates' class. The brothers were in fine form, and the examiner who took me for orals — the other one — cocooned the ordeal in sensible conversation. On passing, my ticket stated, in gold letters upon its handsome, hard black cover, that it was a First Mate's Certificate (Steamship). Engineer friends asked if I also received an endorsement for motor ships, as they did. And why did a mere mate need to know the difference anyway? They were informed loftily that the difference was not between steam and motor but between steam and sail!

Third mates with mate's tickets were fairly common and Mr Cox appointed me third mate of the *Imperial Star*, the *Melbourne's* twin sister. We loaded general cargo down to our marks, in Gladstone Dock, Liverpool, and sailed with 12 passengers one sunny day in June, 1957. Such ships then were in their heyday: the poits of

Imperial Star **in the English Channel**

Britain, Australia and New Zealand were full of the splendid cargo liners of Blue Star Line, Shaw Savill, Federal, New Zealand Shipping Company, British India, P and O, Clan Line, Blue Funnel, Port Line, and others, each loading up to 13,000 tons of cargo — general outwards — primary produce homeward. Now these cargoes are carried in a boxful of container ships.

We berthed in Fremantle on a Saturday at first light. The wharfies took most of the forenoon opening the old-fashioned hatches. As they opened number two, a pungent chemical smell rose, emanating from a stack of 40-gallon steel drums in the corner of the shelter deck. The wharfies would have none of it and for once we did not blame them, especially when an industrial chemist declared the gas toxic. The gang transferred to another hatch and a large, electric wheat-blowing fan with canvas trunking was hired to extract the fumes.

I was night aboard and made my last rounds at midnight. A cold

wind blew in from Gage Roads and an elderly gentleman, muffled with warm clothes, stood at the head of the gangway. I wished him good evening to which he replied with a frosty gaze and a grunt. When I returned from inspecting the moorings and checking that the canvas hatch tents were secure over the open hatches, he was still there. As duty officer I was supposed to know the identities of those onboard at night, so asked if he was the night watchman.
'I am not!'
'Pardon me, sir, but who *are* you?'
The owner of the electric fan we had hired, he had come to keep an eye on it himself. So he *was* a sort of night watchman, and did not seem to relish the experience. I asked him if he'd like a cup of tea. 'Now you're talking, young man!' he replied with warmth, and his weatherbeaten face even cracked into a grin. We adjourned to my cabin where, in addition to a pot of tea, I just happened to have a bottle of rum in the way of further hospitality. He eyed a model sailing ship I was making with the hope of eventually putting it into a bottle. The bowsprit, he said, was too long, and I hadn't rigged the mainmast quite right. But his criticism was kindly: it transpired he was a retired captain who had served his apprenticeship in sailing ships. As the night wore on and the teapot was refilled he tacked four-masted barques across my tiny cabin in the teeth of a Cape Horn gale and then, after another nightcap, decided his fan was old enough to look after itself and went home to bed. Next day his family came down to thank me. They had been sure he would catch his death of cold but he would not be put off. We have been friends ever since.

In our first port, Dunkirk, I joined a crowd eagerly awaiting the finish of a long-distance cycle race and seized an opportunity to visit one of those public places for which the French are justly famous. The ornately-filigreed iron screen, painted blue, was at shoulder height, and in the distance I saw three of my engineering shipmates. Just then my trouser zip parted — the only way to deal with it was to remove the garment and wrestle the zipper back onto its track, a task requiring total concentration. While thus employed I had not realised that the leader of the cycle race approached, to much cheering. Looking up, I saw our three engineers, who also spotted me.
'Hallo Sandy, what's up?'
I was foolish enough to tell them.
'This is a job for engineering brains. Let's have a look,' said the

third, all concern for my problem.
I handed him my trousers.
With a cheer, which suddenly made me realise they had been drinking, they made off, and disappeared into the crowd, waving my trousers like a banner. We Kinghorns are not often embarrassed as unfortunately I had stressed once or twice during the voyage. They were soon back.
'Is Kinghorn embarrassed?' they enquired eagerly.
'Well, yes, I suppose I am. Chilly, too!'
With a delighted yell they flung my trousers at me and disappeared once more into the crowd. They had fixed the zip.

In London, discharge completed, we were sent to Smith's Docks, North Shields, for a refit. I was kept on, working by, carrying out fire patrols throughout the night, watching with amazement as my ship was steadily dismantled piece by oily piece. When off duty I was able to go home, but I was aboard the afternoon our first-born arrived — a splendid baby girl. It was then that Mr Cox, realising that Kinghorn had another mouth to feed, decided that I should be promoted to second mate.

Penwith Steamship Company, Ltd.

———•▶•◀•———

Truro, July 9th, 1903.

Dear Sir,

  I beg to hand you the Audited Statement of Accounts for the Sixty-second Voyage of the S.S. "PENWITH," showing a profit of £198 4s. 8d. After debiting £9 7s. 0d. brought forward, the Directors have declared a Dividend of £187 10s. 0d., being 7s. 6d. per share, and carried forward the balance of £1 7s. 8d. to the next Account.

  The Boat is now at Cardiff.

  I beg to enclose a cheque for £ — : /5/- :   being the Dividend of 7s. 6d. per share on *two* shares.

Yours truly,

        RICHARD B. CHELLEW,
           Managing Director.

Capt. N. J. Tregaskes

Penwith SS Co Dividend Warrant

Penwith Steamship Co., Ltd.

SIXTY-SECOND VOYAGE.

Cardiff to Porto Empedocle with Fuel, and Achtary to Bristol with Barley.

APRIL 12TH TO JUNE 17TH, 1903.

DISBURSEMENTS.		£	s.	d.	£	s.	d.
1903.							
Apl. 12.	Cardiff............	325	2	8			
,, 29.	Porto Empedocle	207	3	6			
,, 16.	Achtary	102	11	0			
,. 27.	Kertch	24	10	9			
,, 30.	Constantinople.	51	4	1			
June 10.	Gibraltar.........	2	11	6			
,, 17.	Bristol............	198	4	9			
					911	8	3
	Wages				278	0	6
	Victualling				97	2	2
	Coals				312	12	0
	Insurance				224	17	3
	Incidentals				18	18	2
	Commissions				52	6	6
					1,895	4	10
	Balance				198	4	8
					£2,093	9	6

RECEIPTS.	£	s.	d.
Freight :—			
On 2,131 $\frac{800}{1000}$ tons of Fuel, Cardiff to Porto Empedocle, at 8/6 per ton	906	0	4
On 2713 $\frac{411}{1050}$ units of Barley, Achtary to Bristol, at 8/9 per unit	1,187	0	6
	2,093	0	10
Sundry Credits	0	8	8
	£2,093	9	6

	£	s.	d.		£	s.	d.
Balance brought forward	9	7	0	Balance	198	4	8
Dividend of 7/6 per share	187	10	0				
Balance carried forward	1	7	8				
	£198	4	8		£198	4	8

RICHARD B. CHELLEW, *Managing Director.*
JOHN DOIDGE, *Secretary.*

Examined with Vouchers and found correct,
N. B. Bullen F.S.A.A., Auditor.

The shareholders of shipping lines at the turn of the century did not exactly make a fortune as Captain Tregaskes' dividend statement reveals

Second Mate

Chapter 6

1957-1960

SHORTLY BEFORE CHRISTMAS 1957 I was appointed second mate of the twin-screw motor vessel *Sydney Star*, a prewar prototype of the *Melbourne* and *Imperial Stars*. She was in Antwerp and Mr Cox had economical ways of changing officers abroad. I was first to join the *Timaru Star* in Liverpool and proceed in her to Glasgow, Cardiff and Antwerp, where her second mate and I would swap ships. The *Timaru Star* (built 1945 as *Empire Clarendon*) was a pleasant little ship but a poor substitute for Christmas at Home. There were few of us onboard and the miserable weather matched our mood until the captain said I could have weekend leave from Glasgow.

We berthed at five in the morning and when all was secure I stepped down the gangway and walked rapidly through the cold, dark streets towards the two main stations. Both offered journeys to Newcastle — one via Carlisle, the other via Edinburgh which I chose. Edinburgh was crowded and I found to my dismay that the train I hoped to catch was an All Seats Booked Special. Reservations were being checked at the barrier and the queue for cancellations was so long that to join it seemed futile. I wandered the length of Waverley station: a man must be mad to go to sea! He should be at home with his wife and baby daughter, not wandering around Scottish railway stations unable to get onto trains!

My spirits lifted a little when I came abreast the steam locomotive which would haul the train. It was *Sir Nigel Gresley*, first of the LNER Pacifics, an engine famous in its day. Now, fresh from the sheds in her gleaming livery of green, red and black, she simmered gently, the embodiment of steam locomotive power. When was she built? By climbing round this barrier — there was nobody about — I would be close enough to read her builder's

75

plate. Having read it I realised with guilty surprise that I was now on the platform. I could step aboard, hide in a toilet until the train left, and then nonchalantly stroll down the corridor to claim an unoccupied seat — there was sure to be at least one! I was as good as home! All went according to plan until I emerged from my retreat and strolled along the swaying corridor. Panic gripped me when I saw the guard approaching, sliding open compartment doors, inspecting tickets. But of course he would not want to see a seat reservation, and I *had* a rail ticket.

Pleasantly he studied my ticket, and looked up. He was an elderly man, smart in his navy blue uniform.
'Are you going to Newcastle?' he asked with a grin.
'I am.'
'It's a funny thing,' he said, 'but our first stop's London!'
London is 280 miles past Newcastle!
'You must have boarded without a reservation? Hide in the toilet, did you? That's the oldest trick in the game!'

He shook his head sadly. I began to see the weekend stretching bleakly ahead on British Rail. I'd be lucky to get back to Glasgow by Monday at this rate!
'Do you by any chance go to sea?' asked the guard.
Although I was not in uniform, my blue gaberdine raincoat and white shirt were indications.
I nodded.
'Going home for the weekend?'
I nodded again.
'My son went to sea. *He* used to come home whenever he could, for weekends. He was killed when his ship blew up off the Dutch coast in 1945.'
My heart warmed to this sad, kindly man. I told him I was trying to get home to see my wife and daughter.
'Look,' he said, 'You know Gateshead?'
I knew Gateshead, across the Tyne from Newcastle.
'Well, we slow down at Gateshead. I'll make sure she slows *right* down, and if you're nippy, you can hop off there. Mind you, I don't know anything about this, understand?'
I understood, and thanked him. It was good to get home. Even in two weeks Jennifer had grown prodigiously and my wife seemed happy and relaxed.

When I picked up the *Sydney Star* in Antwerp she was undergoing repair. Homeward bound with a full cargo and 12

Second Mate in the *Sydney Star*, veteran of a 1941 Malta Convoy

passengers, she was clearing Panama when a Greek Liberty ship had rammed her in way of number two hatch, starboard side. A huge steel patch was made and applied using underwater welding — a superb piece of American ship surgery — and she went to Antwerp for permanent repairs after discharge of her cargo in the UK. The *Sydney Star* seemed jinxed. Her long career had been dogged by incidents — serious in themselves but never so bad that they could not easily have been worse. Damage caused by the collision near Panama was serious but would have been much more so had the Greek struck only 30 feet further aft where passengers were sleeping. In 1938 she had collided in Sydney Harbour with a ship taking a short cut round Bradley Head. Repairs took months. Bound for Malta in one of the convoys (her 13th voyage) she was torpedoed in number three hold (the only one not packed with explosives), narrowly missing the engine room. She struggled into Malta and eventually made her way through Suez to neutral Argentina for permanent repairs. I was her second mate for just over two years — four voyages — and each had its share of nightmarish troubles such as I have experienced on no other ship.

Built and registered in Belfast in 1936, the *Sydney Star* and her sisters entered the southern dominions trade against strong opposition. Shaw Savill, Federal Line, New Zealand Shipping Company and the Commonwealth and Dominion Line (which became Port Line) were not pleased to see the new Blue Stars. But with their huge carrying capacity and 17 knots speed the new ships could not be ignored and were soon an accepted part of the conference. The *Empire, Imperial, Dunedin, Melbourne, Auckland* and *Wellington Stars* were all war losses. With their distinctive profiles and well-known refrigerated cargo capacities they were prime targets for U-boats and other raiders. But *Sydney, Australia, Brisbane* and *New Zealand Stars* survived to become the nucleus of the postwar fleet. They were fine-looking ships, modern in their day. A tall, single mast, nicely proportioned funnel amidships and six hatches gave them a well-balanced appearance. Hard ships to work, especially in the engine rooms during their later years, the huge double-acting engines became a source of constant concern to chief engineers. They were, for everyone, a challenge; good ships for experience!

While lying in Antwerp she became the home of rats, so brazen that they played on deck in broad daylight. So the crew spent a night ashore in a hotel while sinister men in gas masks exploded cyanide bombs aboard. When the air had cleared we returned. Rats were rarely seen thereafter. Many tales are told of the rats in freezer ships. They live in the numerous narrow tunnels which carry cold air around the holds and grow long coats like Persian cats. Because the cargo always contains edibles the rats grow to an enormous size, fat and sleek. So fierce are they that an officer going down a hold to inspect the cargo at night was attacked and eaten. All that was found next morning were the brass buttons off his jacket. (So the tale goes).

Repairs completed, we towed across to the locks which control Antwerp's huge 'Siberia' dock system. A nasty wind blew up as we went, and at the critical moment when tugs let go to allow us to enter the lock, a gust swung the ship against the sharp concrete edge of the wall. There was a crunch and a four-inch gash appeared in the brand-new rivetted plating. Fortunately the damage was well above the waterline and did not delay our departure for London. It was repaired in the West India Dock, where we loaded for South and East Africa. In Lourenco Marques a greaser returned to the ship late at night and slipped from the gangway into the water between ship and quay. We had to abandon our search for him when the tide began to ebb strongly, and never saw him again. A death in the small community of a ship hangs heavy on all and it was with sad hearts that we set off across the Great Southern Ocean towards Bass Strait.

We loaded a full cargo at Lyttelton, Timaru and Auckland and although the pace was leisurely by today's standards of container working, there was plenty to do. We made sure the cargo was stowed properly in its appointed place, noting its position on the cargo plan, separating it where necessary, port by port and mark by mark. The plan showed every item of cargo in the ship, listing weights — lamb carcases, crates of cheese, bales of wool and sheepskins, leather, casks of tallow, bags of milk powder, grass seed — et al. I was very proud of my first cargo plan. The original was landed before we sailed and copies of it sent to our destination ports. Homeward bound I checked all the figures from the tally sheets and made a master plan on tracing paper, from which up to 30 copies were made using special paper, chemicals, a glass frame, and bright sunlight, as in the early days of photography. As each plan and summary measured four feet by two, the wheelhouse resembled a laundry when they were hung up to dry on printing day. They were then coloured with water colours or crayons, port for port — red for London, blue for Liverpool, and so on, so that each port's cargo could be seen at a glance.

Before loading began the mate had worked out the allocations from the booking lists by deciding where each item of cargo should be stowed, by how many gangs of labour. His calculations took into account the order of discharge ports, stability, and draft (no use loading her too deep to get into the next port!) Economical distribution of labour was important and we were required to be able to load and unload the cargo in the shortest possible time. Having done this — and it changed daily as more cargo was booked — he usually left the loading details to the second mate, assisted by the third and fourth mates and the cadets. When eight gangs were loading at six hatches we had to be on our toes all the time. Mistakes were too expensive!

Below, monumental tasks were in hand. The refrigeration machinery had been overhauled outward bound and was now running continuously to maintain the required temperatures. In the main engine room pistons were drawn, liners changed, purifiers, generators, pumps and valves dismantled, overhauled and reassembled. The whole complex arrangement of the ship's machinery was conditioned for the long run home. The passengers had left at our first New Zealand port and now the stewards prepared to receive the 12 who would embark at our final port. Even though air travel was becoming popular, many — especially older people — preferred to treat their voyage as a holiday, and our quiet, unhurried pace suited them better than the organised activity of a passenger liner. By and large they were a pleasure to have aboard, bringing outside interests to our narrow, nautical world; at worst they were someone else to grumble about; at their best they made the voyage memorable — impromptu musical evenings round the grand piano were great fun — and not a few weddings took place as a result of courtships conducted in the starlit tropics. Before seafarers' wives became part of the shipboard scene, lady passengers provided the only spot of feminine colour; it was amazing how a rather plain lady boarding in Auckland became an absolute stunning beauty by the time the ship reached Panama, 17 days later.

Meanwhile the bosun supervised the cleaning and painting of those parts of the ship unreachable at sea. Sailors 'cut in' the red boot topping against the gleaming black topsides, which contrasted handsomely with the white forecastle, centrecastle, and poop. Painting the tall, yellow mast took a day, the funnel usually two. Inboard, paintwork around the passenger deck was completed before the customers arrived. Unlike South America, all this work in New Zealand and Australia was carried out by the ship's crew.

After returning to refit in the Tyne, we loaded in London's Royal Albert Dock for Fiji and New Zealand via Curacao and Panama. Half way across the Atlantic a lady passenger became ill and our doctor needed a second opinion. Our captain made a rendezvous with the Shaw Savill liner *Karamea*, homeward bound from New Zealand and we neared each other that night. The sea had been rough and the swell heavy but both were now moderating when I was told to take the boat away. I soon realised that a 'moderate swell' observed from the bridge, 50 feet above sea level, was not quite so moderate in a ship's boat. Even though we had a good lee she rose and fell alongside excitingly. Then the fore end jammed and the boat almost upended as the next swell surged along the ship's side. Occupants, oars, boathook and boatlamp slithered into the stern, but fortunately she cleared on the next rise. The fourth engineer, a keen young New Zealander, coaxed the old petrol engine to life and off we went into the darkness. Our ship, lying stopped with all her lights on, including the funnel flood lights, was a picture, and when we rose on the swell we could see the lights of the *Karamea* almost a mile distant.

Halfway over the engine cut out, I dropped my torch, and the boatlamp blew out. The ship thought we were gone. I now realised I had not taken enough men to make a full rowing crew, but by taking an oar each and leaving the rudder to look after itself we made fair progress until the fourth restarted the engine. The *Karamea* was rolling, slowly but heavily. First her bilge keel would show, breaking the surface in a welter of foam, then her high, black side towered above like a cliff. A pilot ladder was already rigged, and as we came under her bridge I called out to ask if anyone would care to help us row back in case our engine failed again. As soon as we were alongside six keen lads in blue and orange lifejackets leaped down into the boat. The *Karamea*'s doctor came last, looking terrified, not surprisingly as one minute the boat was at deck level and the next had plunged 15 feet or so. He edged his way down the pilot ladder until we came level with him when I yelled, 'Jump!' He was grabbed by several hands, and off we went. As the lads seemed determined to row the oars were shipped, and singing lustily, we returned to the *Sydney* in fine style.

A medical consultation took place when it was decided not to operate. In due course we returned the *Karamea*'s doctor and his cheerful shipmates to their vessel. Our engine now ran sweetly and the swell so eased that the ride back under the stars was pleasurable. Within three hours of first seeing the *Karamea*'s lights we had made four short boat journeys and were on our way, grateful for their help. Regardless of international or company rivalries which exist normally, seamen will ever cheerfully risk their lives to help each other in time of need.

From Panama to Fiji the route is dotted with low islands customarily given a wide berth at night as they are difficult to detect. The chief officer was a dayworker and I kept the four to eights as senior navigator. Our 1935 vintage Sperry gyro was usually as reliable as the Bank of England but a vital part had worn with no replacement available at Panama: so we crossed the Pacific guided by magnetic compass only. From the Canal onwards overcast skies precluded the taking of sights, and we proceeded day after day by dead reckoning alone, unable even to check the compass error and, I should add, without radar. Then, one morning during my watch, the skies cleared just before dawn. Above a hard blue horizon stars twinkled just when they were needed. Five of them told me we were 35 miles north of our dead reckoning position, and five stars do not lie, so I laid the position on the chart, placing us 20 miles east of the tiny island of Flint, low and uninhabited. Allowing for time elapsed at $16\frac{1}{2}$ knots since I took my sights, we would now be 10 miles off. I stepped out of the chartroom onto the bridge with my binoculars. There on the horizon ahead were several tiny crosses, like kisses at the end of a letter. Palm trees. Entering the wheelhouse I spoke nonchalantly to the helmsman,

'We'll be coming to a little island soon, right ahead. Let's know when you see it please.' I retired to the chartroom. Five minutes later the helmsman cried excitedly;

'Land! Land ahead: it's your island! What navigation!'

On my fourth and last voyage time became of the essence as we left Beira for Melbourne: we had to cross at maximum speed to beat another vessel into port. If we succeeded we would not only secure the berth but also the attendant labour to work the cargo: if we lost we would have to anchor for several days awaiting a berth. Such races with unseen rivals were common and our contestant always seemed to be a Dutch cargo liner — Royal Interocean or Rotterdam Lloyd. It seemed to us as though fleets of Flying Dutchmen lurked in the Tasman, always trying to pip us to the post. Whereas we normally crossed in the roaring 40s, this voyage we ventured south to the screaming 50s to shorten the distance as much as possible without incurring the risk of meeting ice. For once we won the race, and embarked our Port Phillip pilot one hour before our rival.

Off the Cape I had slipped on the bridge deck when coming on watch in a hurry; a teak deck looks superb and lasts for ever, but is extraordinarily slippery when wet. My spectacular fall, legs and arms flailing, was witnessed with great amusement by the mate and Sparks until they realised I had broken a bone in my foot, which caused my lower leg to be encased in plaster. Captain Pitcher would have been quite justified in paying me off but he knew I had almost sufficient seatime in to attempt my master's, so he allowed me to stay on, and helped with my watches. Had he paid me off I would have been sent home as DBS (Distressed British

Seaman. The law required a British ship to take any such seamen home, provided accommodation was available onboard. Nowadays a DBS usually travels by air.) But then I would have needed another voyage to clock up the required seatime — and time was money.

We loaded in the pleasant little Queensland ports of Cairns and Townsville, where ocean yachtsmen congregate having sailed in from the ends of the earth, mostly broke, to live in their boats while working ashore to finance their ventures further. Some, realising that a cargo ship may be a source of goodies like charts, call on the second mate who, if he is not busy — and they are polite — usually offers them cancelled charts, obsolete for big-ship purposes but still useful to yachtsmen.

One Saturday I was visited by two Norwegians whose pretty little red-sailed white ketch I had watched beat slowly up harbour that morning, believing her to be one of the local ketch-rigged pearling 'luggers'. But the *Rondo* was an old Norwegian pilot vessel to whose owners I was able to give a few charts of the Cape of Good Hope. They told me something of their adventures when by way of return they took me aboard. She was a lovely old thing, roomy enough for six pilots and heavily rigged, but I could not help noticing that the sails and gear were showing a lot a mileage. As we sat round her cabin table under the old brass oil lamp drinking mugs of tea, they told me how they were writing a continuous article for a Norwegian magazine to help finance their voyage. As we sat talking long into the night, numerous cockroaches came out of the woodwork and dropped noisily onto the table. The Norwegians took not the slightest notice so I too pretended indifference. Did they keep watch-and-watch at sea? They used to when they first left Norway, but not nowadays. *Rondo* steered herself well, so they hung a lantern in the rigging which had usually blown out by morning. It was then that I realised the risks taken by ocean yachtsmen, as theirs, it appeared, was standard practice. A ship could run them down at night and never know she'd done so. They were heading back to Norway by way of Torres Strait and South Africa. I often wondered how they fared.

We completed loading at Melbourne, taking a considerable quantity of wool on deck. This came in bales which, having been 'dumped' in a screw press, was held tight by steel bands. There were about 27 cubic feet to the bale, six and a half bales to the ton. Each bale was wrapped in hessian, often home-grown flax. Some

New Zealand wools contained chemicals which rendered them liable to spontaneous combustion, so these had to be carried on deck. Australian wool would be carried either above or below deck but great care was needed to stow it, especially on deck. First, a wooden grating was carefully built over the battened down hatch top, and tarpaulin wool covers laid six feet over the grating's outer edges, port and starboard. When the wool was stowed, two or three bales high, covers were tightly drawn over, and their edges stitched down. Tarpaulin was then stretched over all, criss-crossed with tensioned wire rope led to a cargo winch. The stow was then further secured with a rope net lashed down with more wire, tightened with bottle screws. All overlaps were made back to weather as every effort had to be made to keep the wool dry. Salt water could damage the fibres; even rain could cause spontaneous combustion.

In those days there was no substitute for wool, as the advertising poems in London's Underground trains would tell us.
'Lord Nelson was an admiral bold,
Who beat the French, the storms, the cold,
Because in fleecy wool he clad, each jolly pigtailed sailor lad.
And if one tar so much as coughed.
He had this signal run aloft.
Remember men, the Navy's rule,
There is No Substitute for Wool' . . . and so on. A few years later man-made fibres had encroached to such an extent that the whole wool industry was threatened, but a compromise was reached when it was realised that man-made materials on their own lacked longevity. Now wool is an essential ingredient in most high quality mixtures but it travels like everything else — in containers.

Crossing the Indian ocean my plastered leg was so painful that one night I rose from my bunk and removed the plaster with saw and chisel. It was as well I did for it had chafed into my foot, exposing a gleaming white bone. Nobody noticed next day that I was no longer plastered!

Steaming up the Red Sea one of our three cadets developed appendicitis. The doctor hoped to keep it on ice until Suez, where good hospital facilities existed, but it grew worse and he decided to operate. The passengers' card room would be his theatre, where electricians rigged powerful cargo lights. Fortunately the doctor's wife was a nursing sister. The mate acted as anaesthetist. An hour before the operation the patient was given a tranquilliser, and lay in

his bunk trying to relax. His shipmates crowded in, 'to pay their last respects' as they cheerfully put it. The air became thick with cigarette smoke and beer was produced — for the mourners only.
'What's that box Chippy's making?'
'Shut up man, the lad's not dead yet!'
Totally relaxed, no doubt, our victim was carried to the card room. The chloroform was old and took longer than expected to send him to sleep, but no sooner was he off than the doctor and his wife set to work. They made it look easy. Next day the cadet was cheerfully apologising for all the 'trouble' he'd caused, and in three days he was up and about, even wanting to work. At Malta we delivered a

Aboard the *Wellington Star* — the Welly Boot — a seagull scores a direct hit. The author is promoted

part cargo of meat and butter, and bought the doctor and his wife a Queen Anne clock.

After drydocking in Liverpool I went home to study for the last hurdle, master's. This time I went to South Shields Marine School. Sadly, I could no longer afford the luxury of Nellist's. Three months later I became the proud possessor of a Master's Foreign Going Certificate (Steamship) — on which I could command the *Queen Mary* if asked. Instead I was appointed relieving second mate on my old jinxed *Sydney*.

Bound for Glasgow to load we entered the Clyde late one grey afternoon, with the wind freshening to gale force. Light ship, we would be vulnerable in the river, so we anchored for the night close to Rosneath Patch — opposite Greenock — where the best anchorages were already occupied. Ben Line and Clan Line and the black swan of Trinder Anderson snuggled smugly into their anchorages while we found a place on the outer fringe where the holding ground was less. The gale freshened during the night and our starboard anchor began to drag. Out to six shackles (540 ft), the gale had caused the ship to swing and yaw until the anchor had broken clear of the bottom ground, so we let go the port anchor to prevent swing and drag, the engines intermittently running ahead until by daybreak the wind abated. With dawn came a steady drizzle, and the discovery that our anchor chains had eight turns in them! As the ship had not turned more than 180° in the night this could have been caused only by the port anchor dropping into a coil of bights of the starboard chain, laid thus on the bottom by her constant yawing. This fouled hawse (as it is called) took all day to clear, by breaking one chain and passing ends over and under. It could only have happened in the *Sydney*, we felt. I left her in Liverpool and joined the *Wellington Star* which sailed up the Thames one sunny morning in June 1960. Off Southend a seagull scored a direct hit on my head. 'That's a sign of good luck!' laughed the pilot.

And within hours came a letter appointing me chief officer of the *Dunedin Star*.

But first a week's leave.

Chapter 7
The Mate
1960-1961

THE AMERICANS CALL HIM the Chief Mate but in British ships he is the First Mate, the Chief Officer, the Mate or, in rhyming slang, Harry Tate the China Plate.

I was now he.

I enjoyed being second in command. As third mate I had looked after lifeboats and fire extinguishers; as second mate navigation and bridge upkeep; now I had to see to everything (outside the engine room and the steering flat, the domains of the second engineer).

It was a labour of love, I found, for the *Dunedin Star* was a beautiful little vessel, in which we all took pride. Built at Linthouse on the Clyde in 1950 by Alexander Stephens, she was laid down as the *Bolton Castle* for Mollers of Hong Kong to have British officers and Chinese crew, with accommodation for 12 passengers. When Blue Star Line bought her on the stocks she was altered to carry only two passengers, with a British crew housed amidships. The engineer officers would live in the passenger accommodation and space aft intended for the Chinese would house cargo and store rooms. She was propelled by steam turbines with Foster Wheeler boilers driving a single screw, and traded as a general cargo liner until 1956 when number two and three holds and tween decks were insulated for refrigerated cargo, and her passenger cabin was commandeered for the refrigeration engineer.

We were 58 aboard — an enormous crew even by the generous standards of those days. Her profile was conservative, with number three hatch separating bridge from funnel, a raised forecastle and poop, straight raked stem and cruiser stern. Her funnel was so tall that her mainmast steaming light was fixed to it. She had a gyro compass but no automatic helmsman, although electric clocks ran throughout the ship controlled by a master in the chartroom — a time-saving device when clocks were altered with the longitude.

I joined the *Dunedin Star* as she loaded in the Royal Victoria Dock, London. A new company rule had just allowed the wives of chief officers and second engineers to live aboard in UK ports and we made the most of this privilege until the ship sailed to Australia via Suez and back — a typical voyage then of four months. Shortly after I arrived home on leave our daughter Jennifer was presented on her third birthday with a baby brother. She thought Michael a lovely present and, after due reflection, announced that for her birthday the following year she would like a baby sister. She got her wish eventually, but not to schedule. Sisters take a little longer.

My logbook of the next voyage included this entry:
I rejoined in Royal Victoria Dock on November 21, 1960. The London docks are recovering from the recent tally-clerks' strike which caused unprecedented amounts of cargo to pile up. Now they are working as never before and boom conditions prevail.
Rain stops play for much of the day making it difficult to decide whether to stop work and cover hatches, or risk wetting the cargo. The decision in London is the mate's as the dockers are on piecework and will work through all but the heaviest downpour. I have great admiration for the London dockers, who are hard working, tough, skilful — and robustly cheerful.

On Tuesday, November 29 the last sling of cargo was squeezed in, hatches battened down, and loaded to her marks the *Dunedin Star* left for the South Seas. I kept the four to eight watches, as we had only three mates. Without a doubt, this is the best watch of the three, with every sunrise and sunset in the book. Sometimes on a calm, cloudless tropical evening the sun falls below the purple horizon with a flash of green. Then the stars rush out, snapping and twinkling, while you seize your sextant to take sights. Five stars give a good position. By the time you have worked it out and pencilled it in on the chart, the third mate relieves you for dinner! Next morning, still in darkness (unless in high summer latitude), your eyes slowly adjust as you sip the tea provided by a thoughtful second mate. If not in a hurry to go below, he leans against the dodger to chat; when he is about to leave, you inject a new topic into the conversation and there's another 10 minutes of your watch gone.

We have an excellent crowd on this voyage splendidly led by the bosun, Joe, one of the five famous MacAskill brothers. When Joe was a boy on the Hebridean Isle of Eriskay, the second world war was going badly and the island was without its staple nourishment, the whisky, until the Harrison liner Politician went aground there one foggy night. Next morning the islanders examined the wreck, her crew having taken to the boats during the night and been rescued by others. To their delight the boarders, including young Joe, discovered that part of her cargo was whisky, upon which Compton McKenzie based his hilarious novel Whisky Galore. Because of the haste with which it was buried, Politician whisky still occasionally comes to light to this day.

So having taken morning stars and found your position the steward appears with tea and toast, while enticing smells of bacon waft up from the galley. People appear on deck, tea mugs in hand, and the bosun comes to discuss the day's work.

For those not keeping watches the day begins at six o'clock and lasts, with time off for meals and tea breaks, until 10 pm. The carpenter, bosun, cook, second steward and engineroom store-keeper are petty officers; on deck are a lamptrimmer, four daywork ABs and a deck boy, called the peggy, a name which harks back to the days of sail when the sailor with the wooden leg (peg-leg, or peggy) could not go aloft so looked after the others, cleaning the forecastle, washing the dishes, collecting meals from the galley. The three cadets work days at sea, and the watchkeepers turn-to on overtime when required — no wonder the ship looks a yacht!

Anything over eight hours is paid as overtime, 4s 7d (23p) for petty officers, 4s 4d (22p) for adult ratings, 3s 3d (16p) for ordinary seamen, 2s 3d (11p) for boys and cadets. (Cadets' overtime had risen since the 1s 3d - 1s 6d of my day.) My own salary as chief officer — one of the highest in the ship — was then £97 per month.

The bosun and I have decided what's to be done (it often depends on the weather) and the old man ambles out to take the morning air. If you are lucky he will do half an hour of your watch, enabling you to go below for a shave and shower before returning to write up the log book ready to hand over to the third mate at eight bells. The old man, of course, is the captain — often called the owner in the Royal Navy, though never in the merchant service.

When I first went to sea it was still customary to mark the passage of time with bells every half hour. A small bell outside the wheelhouse was struck by the wheelman tugging a lanyard. During the night the prescribed strokes — in pairs for even numbers — were answered by the lookout man on the forecastle head, to prove he was awake. Fifteen minutes before the end of the watch one bell was struck and slumbering mariners would be roused by the standby man calling, 'one bell!' in a manner so cheerful as to be offensive. The advent of the wristwatch ended all this, a passing unmourned by those with cabins beneath the bridge. In the engine room, where nobody sleeps, the habit lingered. The *Sydney Star*'s engine room 'bell' was a four-inch shell case, beautifully polished, with a handsome chime. By mutual consent we did not strike bells in the *Dunedin Star*.

After breakfast the mate gets round in a pair of old shorts or boilersuit, for there is always much to examine and be done. The forepeak tank may need inspection, or a close check of the cargo gear up the masts and sampson posts may be the self-appointed job that day. Holds and bilges must be inspected and if there is room to get down amongst the cargo it is not a bad idea to investigate this from time to time.

That voyage I got lost among the outward cargo. Climbing down the ladder hatch (called the booby), I wormed my way through crates and boxes, between bales and drums, cartons and bags, inspecting as I went, for the mate must have an inquiring mind. I listened to the creaks and groans of the cargo gently working with the movement of the ship; kicked shores and toms to make sure they were tight and made them so if they had worked slack. The shelter deck was full of cars, stowed fore and aft in gear with brakes on, lashed with rope tightened by Spanish windlasses, (a stick twisted in a pair of ropes is a Spanish windlass, said to be named after one of the Inquisition's milder tortures, tightened round the victim's forehead until his eyes extruded).

I worked my way from shelter deck to tween deck, to the lower hold where, in the centre of the stow, I dropped my torch. It rattled down between a crated tractor and a stack of iron pipes, and went out, leaving me in pitch darkness bereft of any sense of direction. Which was starboard? Where was port? Was that forward, or aft? At first I was not even sure which was up and which was down, as I had been crawling horizontally on my side. The creaking and groaning of the cargo now took on a menacing note. Eventually, after many moments of claustrophobic panic, a grey-faced chief officer found his way out on deck, dazzled by the sunlight, chilled by the tropic breeze. Never would I go round alone after that!

On Saturday and Wednesday mornings at eleven, the old man, chief engineer, chief steward and I went on formal inspection, as required by the Merchant Shipping Act. All knew we were coming and everywhere was clean and tidy, with bunks neatly made, decks scrubbed, mirrors and windows polished, brass shining. We inspected the food in the storerooms and the meals cooking on the galley stove — tasted drinking water and found it potable.

Each weekday I took our three cadets for school for an hour and endeavoured to instruct them in the arts of signalling, seamanship and navigation — *au* Nellist. On the bridge, weather reports were compiled every six hours and transmitted by radio to the nearest station. These reports, sent simultaneously by selected ships, form the basis of ocean weather maps and forecasts even today, giving surface patterns which supplement satellite information. We organised fire and boat drill once a week, usually on Friday afternoon. That way, everyone knows that if the alarm sounds at any other time it is for emergency, not drill.

Eleven days out from London we entered the Caribbean and on December 12 arrived at Willemstad, Curacao, for bunkers and fresh water. With a full, heavy cargo we had to keep fresh water to a minimum. Full bunkers were taken and enough water to get us through the Panama Canal. Here, having burned fuel en route, we could take more water. Fuel consumption was 40 tons a day, fresh water 20 tons, so in terms of weight one days' fuel equalled two days' water. On no account must we become overloaded (with Plimsoll Mark submerged) or the master could be heavily fined and the vessel held until no longer overloaded — with all costs to the ship!

At the Canal we flew the new 50-star United States flag as courtesy ensign. For most of my life Old Glory had 13 bars and 48 stars. Then Alaska joined the union and there were 49 stars. No sooner had we grown accustomed to this than along came Hawaii, the 50th state!

The electric locomotives which towed ships through the Panama locks — four each side of a ship our size — were those with which the Canal opened in August 1914. Called 'mules' by seamen, it is an old joke to tell first trippers to save crusts and carrots to feed the mules at the Canal. But the faithful old mules were nearing the end of their days, and two huge yellow locomotives of revolutionary design were being tried experimentally. (These were not a success and the originals were eventually replaced by the Mitsubishi mules in use today.)

Humorists say there are two seasons at the Canal; the wet and the rainy. November is usually the wettest month, February often the driest. We were halfway between the two. In Panama Bay, on the Pacific side, we anchored to allow the tug *Gatun* to come alongside with fresh water to enable us to reach Fiji — and left on December 15, keeping well clear of Flint and other islands as the old man sensibly preferred sea room to scenery.

At sea the mate's work falls into three categories: first the cargo gear. Derricks and their goosenecks, wires, blocks, shackles, pennants, guy ropes, pins and hooks must be overhauled and maintained in first class order and must match their safe working load certificates. The electrical officer looks after the electrical parts of the winches, the mate sees to their lubrication, all under the helpful eye of the chief engineer.

Secondly, all the structures of the ship must be kept clean, free of rust, and well painted, scrubbed, or varnished.

Thirdly, the accommodation must be kept well decorated.

The second and third mates and I, assisted and abetted by the old man, took the Kelvin sounding machine to pieces, overhauled, cleaned and greased it, restoring it to working order. The cadets were not allowed to help as the old man said our language was unsuitable for young ears, but when it was reassembled they were allowed to test it. At 2000 fathoms the ocean was too deep for a real sounding, but they went through the motions and ran out the wire to 50 fathoms, applied the brake, and reeled it in. Then they measured the 'depth' on the boxwood scale — part of their education. You need such machines when the echo sounder fails, usually when you're worried about the ship's position in fog, so practice never comes amiss.

Christmas and Boxing Days were spent pleasantly, in mid Pacific — even when you're homesick Christmas away from the family is better deep-sea than around the coast. New Year came more quickly for us than for most as we crossed the International Date Line on December 30 and went straight to January 1, 1961, the day we arrived in Suva. As the Fiji newspaper proclaims in its title, 'This is where the day begins!' Next day cargo work began and carried on for 22 hours out of every 24 until completed. The third mate and one cadet kept the night watch, from 7 pm until 7 am, while the second mate and another cadet kept days with me. The third cadet stood the gangway watch. This was a flexible arrangement and all managed time ashore. The unloading of a part cargo of mixed general must be watched closely to make sure every item is discharged, and that, in this instance, it is marked SUVA.

In London we had loaded some 32-ton cases of machinery and now unloaded these with our heavy derrick, the 'jumbo'. Heavy lifts are fascinating and present interesting rigging problems — leading the wire ropes correctly to ensure free, safe running at all stages. The shipbuilder's rigging plan has often been lost by the time the ship is 10 years old, so you devise the best rig yourself.

The day the funnel was painted was a sad one. As previously

First Mate in the *Dunedin Star*, **'a little yacht'**

mentioned the *Dunedin Star* had a large funnel — 46 ft high and 70 ft around its oval cross section. It was far too big to paint at sea but Joe and I reckoned it could be done in one day in Suva harbour, with a bit of application. Funnel day dawned bright and clear with hardly a cloud in the sky, and the lads rigged stages before breakfast, hanging them on gantlines from portable hooks over the rim of the funnel top. A few clouds appeared on the horizon as the funnel was washed down, and the clouds began to jostle each other, heaping up as though to see which could become the tallest. But overhead the sky was blue and the sun shone warmly. The funnel top was painted black, then the white band. So far, so good, although clouds were now scudding across the sky, occasionally blotting out the sun. The lower black band was painted to smart effect. Perhaps the clouds would pass over. The lads were coming now to the intricate part — stars half painted, the white discs and surrounding red — when the clouds halted overhead, solid grey, and heaven opened! By the time the sun came out again, black, red, white and blue had run into each other in one horrible mess. But the bosun was unperturbed and with a few skilled dabs here and there soon put matters to rights.

As we sailed for Lautoka a couple of pretty little white schooners crept in — not many of them about these days as the ubiquitous motor coasters of Burns Philp have taken over the islands trade almost entirely. As we cleared the reef the Shaw Savill tourist liner *Southern Cross* came over the horizon, Suva-bound. We hoped the weather would remain fine for her passengers' one-day visit. Mr McDonald, a coastal pilot, guided us through Mbengga Passage, the shortest route to Lautoka. It is deep, though only a mile wide, beset on both sides with jagged coral and tricky in parts. There is not much room for error and blinding rain comes swiftly. We were lucky, and made the passage in beautiful weather with the weirdly contorted hills of Viti Levu always in view on our starboard hand. Before noon we reached the Navula Passage, a narrow opening to Nandi Waters. Some 26 miles along the shore of this lagoon, past the spot where the first Fijians landed, lies the little town of Lautoka with its sugar mill.

The writers of romantic fiction who wax lyrical about blue lagoons have not, I feel, seen many for always their colour is a most amazing shade of turquoise *green*. The deep, deep blue is outside the reef where the water breaks to dazzling white in thundering breakers.

The Queen's Wharf then was only building, and we moored fore and aft to buoys off the town. Our labour force, 50 strong Fijians, came with us from Suva, and lived under the forecastle head. Despite their fearsome appearance many had a flower tucked coyly behind the right ear, their only clothes a lava-lava, or skirt. Barefooted, they worked cheerfully, a bucket of kava nearby from which they supped from time to time, using a half coconut shell as scoop. Kava looks and tastes like dishwater, but has a message when taken in quantity.

We completed Fiji discharge here and loaded a couple of unpacked cars for Lyttelton and 81 drums of honey for London. This, technically, made us homeward-bound, and though we still had a long way to go, our spirits lifted. As the last barge left, bearing our dusky dockers, they broke into a moving song of farewell somehow in complete harmony with the lagoon, the white coral sand and the nodding palm trees. We hauled in mooring lines, rang the telegraph to slow ahead, and steamed round Vio Island towards the sea and Auckland.

However, the aftermath of the London tally-clerk's strike and the resultant congestion preceded us to New Zealand. There were no vacant berths in Auckland so we were redirected to Lyttelton. To beat one of the Flying Dutchman we were urged to proceed at maximum speed, which in our case was 16½ — half a knot faster than usual. We came to Banks Peninsula, which encompasses the little port, on January 10, and next day went alongside. The Flying Dutchman was already there.

Lyttelton, surrounded by green hills, must have seemed like Paradise to the early settlers after months at sea in their four small sailing ships. They were especially selected migrants sent by the Church of England in 1840 — people of good character, each man with a useful trade. Climbing the port hills they would have seen the lush Canterbury plain stretching away to the distant Southern Alps, snow-capped like their northern namesakes. Undaunted those hardy citizens built Lyttelton, the road over the hills, and — at the edge of the plain — Christchurch.

In port with us, as well as our Dutch friend *Straat Malacca* and a few coasters, was the *Ellaroo*, an ancient Australian loading scrap for Hong Kong, after which she too would be scrapped. With her straight stem and counter stern she already looked a relic of the past. Also present were Shaw Savill's magnificent twin-funnelled *Dominion Monarch*, the *City of Birkenhead*, and the *Tasmania Star*.

The Americans, like the ill-fated Captain Scott before them, use Lyttelton as a base for their antarctic expeditions, and soon the icebreaker *Staten Island* arrived, complete with helicopters.

The port hills had their heads in the clouds and drizzle fell steadily. Cargo work was at a standstill except for the red-painted Dane, *Argentinean Reefer*, unloading Californian oranges through her side doors, a hint of things to come. The port filled. Every berth was occupied and four ships were anchored in the stream. We were 17 days in Lyttelton — a happy little port — thanks to rain and a shortage of labour before sailing for Nelson, an even smaller port at the north end of South Island. We anchored in the roads next morning and cleaned hatches, a big job. Holds and tween decks were strewn with rubbish, dirty dunnage, straw, dust, dirty paper and sticky substances. All must be removed and the spaces scrubbed and cooled quickly ready to load, for time is money.

In the evening the pilot came aboard. There was no tug yet at Nelson whose entrance is narrow and beset by strong tidal currents. A fresh, gusty breeze sprang up, making steering of the ship, now riding high out of the water, fraught. Once inside the breakwater the starboard anchor was let go and we dredged down sternfirst to the quay, using engines and rudder to manoeuvre alongside. This interesting evolution had been explained at Nellists, and, like everything else the brothers taught, it was simple, old-fashioned, and practical.

Nearby, on a patent slip, was a hoary old schooner-scow having a refit. Rigged originally as a two-masted topsail schooner, the *Echo* was built in 1910 and though she now had twin-screw diesels, still used sail to help her on her way. She ran regularly across the stormy Cook Strait between Wellington and Blenheim, year in and year out. The third mate and I were shown over by her proud captain. She was massively built of timber, with the heavy centreboard casing an integral part of her construction. Many a time had she bounced over Blenheim bar in heavy surf, an experience which would have spelt the end for a lesser vessel.

Four days later our cargo was discharged, and we left on top of high water. The pilot/harbour master came to see me about taking the anchor in, as we would not need it to sail, and accompanied me forward with Chippy. The windlass was put in gear and for a while the chain clanked in merrily. With 10 fathoms still out it stopped, leading bar taut straight down into the muddy water. We backed up the windlass with a stout wire rope led to a forward cargo winch and tried again, heaving on both at once. Groaning and protesting the cable creaked in, and as the anchor came out of the water we saw with astonishment that it had another anchor and a length of chain hooked over its fluke.

Not often you let go one anchor and haul in two! Our find had been lost by the dredger *John Graham* in 1910, the year *Echo* was built. For another 15 years the old anchor lay rusting and forgotten in the harbour board's boat yard. Then, cleaned and painted, it was mounted on a ceremonial plinth in a place of honour outside Nelson's new civic centre. So, having made a little piece of local history, we cleared away and crossed a smooth Tasman at 15.64 knots in three days, six hours and 24 minutes, to Hobart.

We completed hatch-cleaning at sea, laid dunnage, and cooled number three hold to 15 degrees F. ready to load lamb. We were too early for Tasmanian fresh fruit and in any event were due to load apples in Brisbane, somewhat to the chagrin of our Tasmanian friends. In Hobart I searched for the little sailing ships which I had seen on my first visit seven years earlier. The three-masted schooner *Alma Doepel* was now a motorised hulk carrying carbide, and the ketch *Lenna* was laid up. However, the little ketch *May Queen*, built in 1867, was still going strong. Her topmasts had gone and she had a powerful engine, but she also had a new set of red sails — and was off that morning for another load of sawn timber from one of the tiny outports.

At Hobart the agent brought the first booking list. In London, outward cargo was booked and arranged by Blue Star Line who employed their own stevedoring firm to load. The ship's officers were mainly relieving staff so the deep-sea mates, who returned from their leave to take the ship to sea, did not control the loading from the outset. On the Australian and New Zealand coasts, however, the ship has more say in the loading of cargo, which is booked through Sydney or Wellington, though secured for the ship by local canvassers — those ever vigilant space-sellers who are the backbone of any liner company.

Booking lists detail the commodities with approximate weights and measurements. The measurement per weight of cargo is its stowage factor and although this is a constant figure on paper, the real stowage factor is determined by the tightness of the stow in the ship, the shape of her holds, and the skill of her mates and stevedores. Head office specifies which holds will take which reefer cargo — meat, fruit, butter, cheese and so on — and will stipulate carrying temperatures, but the ship is left to work out details. At this stage it is essential to keep options open as long as possible, especially when you are loading at several ports for a multi-port discharge. Experience of what is likely to be shipped is a help . . . no use flooring off your hold in Hobart with lamb thinking you'll get more lamb in Brisbane, because what you'll get in Brisbane is beef, too heavy to stow over sheep meat! Instead, you load half the hold, forward or aft, in Hobart, bottom to top, leaving a similar stow for Brisbane. It means slower working — one gang at each port in that hatch instead of two, but you can't win them all and you learn! You must be prepared to accept another 100 bales of Antwerp wool in addition to the 40 Hamburg received yesterday; and you must guard against cargo for one port being overstowed by cargo for subsequent ports. First allocations are mental, then you commit yourself to paper. The chief and refrigeration engineers are, of course, advised the proposed stowages of reefer cargo as they will supply its refrigeration. It's a good idea to get the second mate to check your plan before taking it to the captain for approval. If it looks right and he is wise, the captain will leave stowages entirely to the mate. For this, more than anything else, is that officer's job. Finally, the agent is advised, labour ordered and loading begins.

Hobart, Geelong, Newcastle, Sydney and Brisbane were the loading ports that voyage, for Dunkirk, Liverpool, Antwerp, Hamburg and London. 'Cargo comes first in the Blue Star Line' — but appearance, too, is important and while we were in Hobart the sailors chipped and scaled the bridge front — a mammoth task. It is the mark of a young, keen and inexperienced chief officer that he wants, at once, to scale the rust off the whole ship and I was no exception.

The old man retreated ashore to avoid the racket of chipping hammers on the other side of his bulkhead. The chief engineer grumbled away to the engine room and the chief steward claimed he was going to have the vapours. But when the rust and old paint had been removed, the bare steel wire brushed, and four coats of red lead were followed by two undercoats and the final, gleaming coat of shining white completed, all praised her smartness.

From Hobart we sailed to Geelong to pick up bagged barley for London and Hamburg. (In London the same bags were off-loaded into the sailing barge *Cambria* which took her cargo to Rochester.) At Newcastle we loaded wool for Liverpool and Bradford's mills. Painting proceeded — the overside white, blue star on bow, black topsides at bow and stern neared completion, with the name and port of registry — London — in yellow on the black. The midships section was left until last, as it suffered most alongside the wharves. Between Newcastle and Sydney the strength of the Australian east coast current gave her 20 knots! At Pyrmont, one of Sydney's oldest waterfront suburbs, we stowed frozen mutton and beef, tins of frozen egg pulp in cartons, and frozen crated rabbits. The general cargo spaces were loaded with wool, sacks of flour and rice, sheepskins, empty oil drums, wet hides, drums of neatsfoot oil, cartonned canned meats and fruit, and — Australia's oldest export — eucalyptus oil, in drums.

At this time, we were one of many similar vessels in Sydney, all loading or discharging, all painting ship, all vying with each other from hoisting flags in the morning to football matches in the evening. The Bibby cargo liner *Cheshire*, on charter to Ellerman's, was in, and we had become friendly with her officers in Newcastle. Great interest was aroused, during our six days in port, in the 13,587-ton Shaw Savill liner *Runic* which stranded on Middleton Reef while on passage from Brisbane to Auckland. Awash, but difficult to detect, Middleton Reef lies athwart the strong southerly current (which had helped us to Sydney). In the early hours of Sunday, February 19, 1961 she ran hard upon the coral. Being light she proved impossible to refloat, and is there to this day.

On Sunday, February 26 we reached Brisbane, and next day loaded butter and beef at Hamilton cold store. Before the wharfies arrived the following morning we warped along to Hamilton No 1 shed for apples, the first big shipment ever to leave the port — 50,000 cases — to be on the English market a month before the Tasmanian apples. No wonder our Hobart friends had glowered! Two electric fork-lift trucks came aboard to stack the cartons and all went well until noon, when the wharfies struck. One of their number had called the stevedore an unmentionable name and been sacked on the spot. A battle to save face ebbed and flowed for two days when work suddenly resumed, culminating in a superb party on deck to celebrate the shipment, attended by Mr Frank Nicklin, Premier of Queensland, and representatives of all sides of the apple industry.

Gradually the ship filled with cargo. Last aboard were 132 bags of mail for Singapore (enabling us to fly the Royal Mail pennant) and a kelpie border collie cross called Dingo, for Liverpool. 'Bad dog Dingo' was looked after by the senior cadet who placed the kennel on the boat deck and rigged a long wire on which to run his chain. He was walked round the decks every day and generally pampered. A dog so looked after is no trouble onboard, but one whom nobody loves whines and barks fit to keep the whole ship awake. Dogs are like people.

Our old friend the *Cheshire* was in Brisbane with us, bound as we were, for Dunkirk. Although we were sailing a few hours before her, and were a trifle faster, she was sailing direct, whereas we were calling at Singapore, so the odds were even. They were prepared to stake much beer on their berthing in Dunkirk before us and the bet was accepted. The weather held perfect and most nights I slept in my canvas hammock on deck. The pilot disembarked at Thursday Island, taking our mail, and we crossed the Arafura Sea. Leaving Timor to port and Wetar to starboard we entered the Flores Sea. Tales by Conrad came to life as we passed small sailing vessels becalmed on waters as flat as an ornamental lake; we passed the Alor and Solor Islands, Flores and Sumbawa and, leaving Lombok and Bali well to port, we headed up between Java and the Kangeans, across the Java Sea. In Singapore's Eastern Road hundreds of ships were anchored while junks and ketches with high, standing gaffs made slow progress in the light airs.

When the port doctor had given us pratique, we proceeded to an inner anchorage where a barge came alongside for the mail, and numerous Chinese ladies swarmed aboard, the famous Singapore Sew-Sew Girls. They darned socks, sewed on buttons, washed and ironed shirts, but there was no hanky panky with them. The Sew-Sew girls were virtuous ladies. Alas, 20 years later the permissive society has blown in on the wind of change, and Singapore Roads are frequented by ladies less virtuous, who ply their trade from ship to ship under the collective code name

Bumboat Mary.

Clearing Malacca Strait on March 18 we headed west across a calm Indian Ocean, meeting a squadron of British warships led by the cruiser *HMS Belfast*, now preserved in the Pool of London. We passed Dondra Head, the southern tip of Ceylon on March 21, and saw the 'Beautiful Island' as the English translate its modern name 'Sri Lanka', seven miles distant. But of the *Cheshire* we saw no sign. She had to be well ahead!

With considerable interest we reached the Suez Canal to see how it was faring under President Nasser. Since the British and French left en haughty masse in 1956, pilots had been recruited world-wide. Most were from Eastern Europe — USSR, Poland, East Germany, Hungary and Bulgaria — but there were also Americans and Canadians, Swedes and Danes. There were even a few Egyptians. Our pilot from Ismailia to Port Said was a youngish Yugoslav who was not only a good pilot but an entertaining ventriloquist. As our old refrigeration engineer came up for a breath of fresh air he nearly had a coronary when the cat, sunning itself in the corner, remarked that he was getting a bit thin on top! Work on widening and deepening was proceeding well, and gangs of women dressed in voluminius black toiled to build up the banks with stone. Mr Nasser's canal was certainly prospering.

But still no sign of the *Cheshire*.

We had to put into Gibraltar to land our third engineer with an abscess on his eye. Undoubtedly now the *Cheshire* must forge ahead, if she had not already done so. The English Channel was sunny at first but foggy as we stood in towards Dover to embark our pilots and the Decca set. As we steamed up the approach channel to Dunkirk in the golden haze of early morning the silhouette of a ship loomed ahead. At first we thought she was coming out, but no, we were overtaking her. And yes, it was the *Cheshire*!

She went in ahead, through the larger lock while we were directed to the small lock which, because it was small, filled up first, and we were secure in our berth just five minutes before *Cheshire* tied up in hers.

Chapter 8: Heavy lifters, heavy ships

1962-1968

I WAS AT HOME when the telephone rang. It was Mr Cox.
'What do you know about heavy lifts, old boy?'
I answered flippantly, for my leave was going well,
'All there is to know, sir! Er- why?'
'Have you heard about the *South Africa Star*?'
'Not recently,' I said.
'She's in Hamburg to be fitted with a 180-ton derrick,'
'One hundred and eighty tons! (The upper limit of my experience was 60 tons').
'The biggest of its type in the world, old boy. We want you as her chief officer.'

I was flattered, of course, apprehensive, but flattered. That week there was no Blue Star ship heading for the continent so I travelled in style and was met in Hamburg by Asdic Thompson, an elderly and highly respected member of the permanent relieving staff and the only man I ever knew who chewed rather than smoked tobacco. Because he wore a deaf aid he had been known since the war as Asdic (a wartime listening device used for detecting U-boats.)

Asdic told me our ship lay at the Howaldtswerke and that our hotel was the Monopol, on the Reeperbahn. Here I spent the following nine weeks, commuting to and from the ship daily. Hamburg's celebrated Reeperbahn is, by night, a glittering thoroughfare, but at 8 am it is less glamorous as drunks and litter are swept from the doorways of the gin palaces. So it was refreshing to board the clean, green and white ferry to cross the sparkling Elbe where I found that the ship, like every ship in every shipyard, was being taken to pieces and placed on the boatdeck. To make room for oily pieces of machinery the boats themselves had been landed on the quay together with the old mast. The new mast had just been shipped. Of special high tensile steel this remarkable structure stood 100ft above deck and bristled with railed platforms. The longest of these, near the masthead, projected aft for 20ft like a huge gallows arm, but I soon discovered that these platforms were in precisely the right place when rigging her gear. It was the largest unstayed mast afloat. I was impressed.

By 1962 the *South Africa Star* was no youngster, having been built as an aircraft carrier at Tacoma in 1944 and rebuilt to Blue Star specifications at Mobile in 1948 to help satisfy the need for non-refrigerated tonnage. She had huge, deep holds with spacious tween and shelter decks above, and was a splendid cargo carrier. Number two hold was divided into four deep tanks, originally to carry her aeroplanes' fuel, now used for general cargo, bulk grain or wool. For several years she sailed full in both directions, usually on the UK-Australia-New Zealand service via South Africa.

But it is for the carriage of refrigerated cargo that the Blue Star Line is mainly famous and after the boom years of the late '40s and early '50s she spent periods laid up in the Blackwater with her twin sister *Rhodesia Star*. Even in those days of relatively cheap bunkers her fuel bills were high and she had become something of a white elephant. Now there was a need for a heavy lift ship to carry large items of cargo in undivided loads between Britain and the Antipodes. There was no time to build a specialised vessel, but the *South Aftrica Star*, with her stout hull, adequate stability, and abundant electrical power could be converted at a fraction of the cost of a new ship, and quickly. This conversion gave her a new lease of life, as other improvements were built in at the same time. Two of her deep tanks were grit-blasted, painted with pale green epoxy coatings, and fitted with steam heating coils to facilitate the carriage of bulk tallow for soap manufacture as this, too, was in growing demand.

She had three pairs of large sampson posts along the foredeck and when the new, wider, mast was fitted it would be impossible for the wheelman to see ahead clearly. This is less important at sea as he steers by compass (when not in automatic), but in close waters, particularly in the Panama and Suez Canals, the wheelman himself must line up the ship's head with some shore light or beacon. At the captain's suggestion steering wheel and compass were moved to the starboard side of the wheelhouse and the jackstaff (the little flagpole at the stem) similarly moved, giving a clear line ahead. We were told later in both canals that had this alteration not been made we would have had to wait until daylight every time, which would have wasted much money.

Like the *Dunedin Star* she had a crew of 58, but she was a larger ship and needed every one of them. There were 22 cargo derricks to maintain, a complex engineroom, and 12 passengers to care for. In the American manner furniture was steel, but when painted in cheerful colours it looked tasteful, even cosy. Her wooden decks were spacious, offering more square feet per passenger than most ships. Her ungainly, boxy superstructure belied her fine underwater lines. Foster Wheeler boilers and Allis Chalmers turbines drove her single screw at an effortless 16 knots, 18 if pushed. She had many advanced features — gyro compass with repeaters in the bridge wings, auto pilot, large, steel lifeboats in gravity davits, each with its own electric hoisting winch, and an individually-controlled temperature control system in every cabin — almost air conditioning! Outside the wheelhouse was a forward gallery which made window cleaning easy — a great improvement over the smooth bridgefront where you have to perform aerial gymnastics or rig a bosun's chair to remove the salt stains of heavy weather. She was a strong, utilitarian, useful ship in which I spent two happy years.

As in all shipyards, there seemed little sense of urgency or order, but imperceptibly the pace quickened, then with a great rush the derrick's installation was completed, and it was tested to

South Africa Star — **heavy lift ex-aircraft carrier one time white elephant**

198 tons, 10 percent over the Safe Working Load. The ship drydocked and undocked, all the machinery returned from the boatdeck to its proper place, and we were almost ready to sail.

She was not a welcoming sight when our crew arrived from England that December. Her all-steel accommodation was cold, damp and dirty, the heating system worked poorly, lights frequently failed and the galley stove was even more temperamental than the cook. The deck crew was run by a shambling, two-fisted, beady-eyed Liverpool bosun of the old school. Despite his fearsome appearance and no-nonsense attitude, Jim had the dry sense of humour of his race and a gentleness which his brusque manner belied, although a sailor questioned his orders but once. The storekeeper who ran the engineroom crowd was a tall, eagle-faced Irishman and he, the bosun, and Chippy, the Estonian carpenter, became great friends. Like the Ancient Mariner, Chippy would occasionally tell his tale, or part of it, for he was cautious of speech. His father, a university lecturer in Tallinn, had fallen foul of the communist authorities, and was banished with his wife to the virgin lands — Siberia. Chippy had to abandon his ambition of becoming a civil engineer and, instead, became a deckhand on a Baltic fishing vessel. Eventually he stowed away in the coal bunkers of a small tramp steamer, unsure of her destination, but uncaring as long as it was away from the Baltic. In his dark sanctuary he heard the engines throb to life and realised they had reached the open sea when she began to pitch and roll. He lost count of time in the gloom and slept a lot, but awoke to realise the ship was in smooth water. After several hours the engines fell silent and soon there were the sounds of cargo working — hatches being uncovered and winches rattling. This is the safest time to get off a ship unnoticed, and he found himself in a smallish riverside town. By the colourful advertising hoardings and an absence of political slogans he was relieved to find that he was not in a communist state. Then, having seen pictures of them, he spotted an English bobby. Asking haltingly for political asylum, he was taken to the police station — in Gravesend, Kent. Thus had Chippy come to Britain.

The chief engineer was a gigantic New Zealander who had been years in tramp steamers, a hard case and just the man to coax the ship back to life after her hibernation. The master, too, was well chosen. Tall, distinguished, with thick, iron grey hair over twinkling eyes in a craggy face, he was from the Bristol Channel where his father was a pilot in the days when pilots had their own sailing pilot cutters. His seafaring began with his father and developed in his uncles' Irish Sea schooners during school holidays. His formal apprenticeship was with an old London tramp company and he commanded a small coastal tanker at the age of 23. He came to Blue Star Line in the '30s as fourth mate with a master's ticket. Captain Aldridge was a seaman to his finger tips and a fine shipmaster, with the knack of running his ship efficiently and happily. After a ticking off you were left in no doubt, but it was your work he was criticising, not you as a person, and he bore no grudges.

The new crew set to work cleaning and painting the accommodation, which gave them an immediate interest in the ship. Nothing like a fresh coat of paint to cheer up your cabin! Chippy began a long-term programme of cabin improvements, removing surplus steel wardrobes and substituting settees and desks which he constructed with the skill of a cabinet maker. Shortly before Christmas we steamed down the Elbe with an illuminated Christmas tree lashed to the new mast head. On Christmas morn we docked in Newport, in the Bristol Channel, and after the holiday with a fork-lift truck loaded mixed general cargo which included cartons of cellulose wadding stacked in number three tweendeck. We then went round to Liverpool where we used our new derrick to load heavy electrical equipment for a power station in Victoria. It was the beginning of the exceptionally cold winter of 1962/3. Fire broke out one night in number three tweendeck, immediately forward of the bridge as she lay in Gladstone docks. Those onboard turned to with a will and brought hoses to bear on the flickering orange glow amid dense clouds of black smoke. Six fire engines arrived quickly, but by that time we had reduced the flames to a smoulder. Had the fire taken greater hold it could have cost us the ship for even as we worked the water froze in the hoses. Calmly the dockers began to *unload* cargo to get at the seat of the fire, so that the blaze could be properly extinguished and damage assessed. As soon as a sling of cargo was hoisted into the chill morning breeze, it would burst into flames, to be extinguished by the fire brigade on the quay. By breakfast time all were black with smoke, soaked and weary, but satisfied that it was entirely out. Time is of the essence with fires. If you can hit them soon enough you have a chance.

The cause was never proven. It may have been a cigarette but

107

more likely was an electrical fire, caused by a bulkhead conduit being sliced by the fork-lift truck loading the cellulose wadding in Newport. The cable had not come alive until Liverpool, when the fire started. A General Average was declared, which meant that all those owning cargo in the ship would be required to pay a contribution towards the cost of the damage, whether their cargo was actually burned or not. (This law of General Average dates back at least 1,000 years BC when it was inaugurated by the merchants of Rhodes.)

Later we moored one evening in Port Said with both anchors down and sternlines to buoys, awaiting our turn in transit. Bumboatmen swarmed aboard and were allowed to set up shop on number four hatch with the normal proviso that none should enter the accommodation. But during the night a cadet discovered two furtive gentlemen going from cabin to cabin, challenged them and was grabbed. Fortunately the third mate appeared at this juncture and ordered the boatmen outside. As they withdrew sullenly, he came to report the matter to the master, with whom I was sitting discussing the coming transit. The captain ordered me to remove *all* bumboatmen from the ship, an instruction gleefully carried out by the crew, who had tired of the oriental sales talk so late at night. When the bumboatmen refused to leave hoses were turned on them, and they and their wares cascaded along the alleyway and down the gangway in a flurry of screams and salt water. I came in for much abuse from the head boatman, a gentleman called Jock McNab, who claimed the burglars were not his men at all. When he spat at me I saw red and punched his nose. Egyptian blood flowed.

Up to this time there had been commotion, but nothing compared with the uproar which followed. An Egyptian policeman appeared, as did our agent — agitating behind thick spectacles. We all steamed up in an undignified gaggle to the captain who, calm as ever, silk dressing-gowned sat smoking a long-stemmed pipe. What on earth, he wanted to know, was all this noise about? We all tried to tell him at once; when we paused for breath, he looked at me with a sad smile.
'Well,' he said, 'you've certainly stirred things up here, haven't you! Perhaps the quickest way to resume harmonious relationships with our Egyptian friends would be for you to apologise to Mr McNab for punching his nose.'

He was right of course. The heat was off now, anyway. I

apologised. Jock McNab flung his arms around my neck and gave me a smacking kiss, then rushed off to return with a brand new suitcase — real leather! — as a present. The agent's spectacles relaxed and the policeman courteously accepted the cold beer which the captain poured. Peace reigned as day was breaking. It was time to sail.

At Aden we called for bunkers, and embarked our 12th passenger, a dear little old Australian lady who proceeded to charm us all. In mid Indian Ocean we crossed the line in style one overcast evening. The sea was calm and all off watch participated. The swimming pool was rigged on the after deck alongside number four hatch on which was set the throne. Flags and coloured lights were decked around but all was in complete darkness as eight o'clock drew near when people assembled, hard to recognise in their fancy dress and elaborate disguises. Eight bells struck and Sparks, standing above on the boat deck, switched on the green beam of the aldis lamp and flickered its spectral glow over the scene. A strange, wailing lament arose, apparently from the ocean, and a hollow voice called. 'Ship ahoy!'

The captain, whose white uniform contrasted well with the fancy costumes, stood by the throne and bellowed, 'Who's there?'

The Voice from the Deep answered.

'Is that the voice of Giles Aldridge I hear?'

'It is!'

The Voice began, 'There once was a captain called Giles,

'Whose features were all wreathed in smiles . . . '

'That's enough!' barked the captain. 'Come aboard, King Neptune!'

An accordion struck up a lament and under the green floodlight a strange procession climbed 'aboard' from behind the swimming pool led by an ancient, gnarled and bent King Neptune, helped by a voluptuous Queen Nefertitty and followed by an entourage of wailing pirates, whales, barber, barber's mate, bishop, curate, herald and executioner, all carrying flickering torches (old signal flares). Neptune sat upon his throne with ceremony. Suddenly all the lights went on and the trial began.

The herald read out a list of charges against the ship and all who sailed in her. The cook was feeding us too well, so nothing was thrown overboard to feed the hungry little fishes. We were steaming too fast, frightening the baby dolphins. Our engines had not broken down, there was nothing for the sharks to laugh at. We were in deep trouble!

First victim was the cook, an Australian, who had crossed the line many times but had been volunteered to set an example, to reassure the passengers. He was hauled gibbering before the throne and made to kneel to hear the charges against him. He was wasting food by feeding it to common sailors. Proclaimed Guilty, sentenced to be Almost Drowned, he was dragged to the pool side where the bishop and curate administered last rites by pouring foul liquid out of a jug over his head. The barber's mate lathered him and the barber shaved him with an enormous razor. He was pushed into the pool where the whales pushed him out again. Back before the throne he was given his Crossing the Line Certificate and a large brandy by the captain, then helped on his way with three points of a trident.

'Next victim please!'

No one was hurt, it was a splendid night, and the dear old Australian lady joined in the fun as to the manner born, a natural actress. A few days before Fremantle she asked if I thought the Customs would search her bags? She had bought a few presents for her grandchildren in Melbourne and invited me to her cabin to see her array of clocks, watches, transistor radios, toys and jewellery laid out, as in a shop window. She must have a lot of grandchildren! Should she declare 'these few items'?

'Certainly!' I replied.

'What if I don't?' she asked defiantly.

'You couldn't be so silly as to try to smuggle this lot in!'

But no, she didn't declare them. The Customs officer in Fremantle found them of course, and warned that she *must* declare them to the Customs officer before disembarking in Melbourne.

But after Fremantle we called at Adelaide where the wharf was quiet that Saturday afternoon, with not a Customs officer in sight. She received a telegram telling her to return home at once where her two dogs were seriously ill.

'I'll *die* if they do, poor creatures, she declared as a tear crept down her crumpled cheek. We were all sympathy and phoned a taxi to take her to the station. When we arrived at Melbourne a week later the Customs asked especially to see the lady with all the grandchildren. Summoned to the ship from her home address, she came full of wrath and indignation.

'Where are my belongings?' she demanded. 'I left them *here,* in this cabin! Someone must have stolen them. Presents for my dear grandchildren,' and her voice trailed off to a whimper as the Customs officer helped dab her eyes. But her attempt to import 'duty free' goods for sale via a shady shopkeeper friend in Melbourne stood no hope of success from the beginning. The missing articles were recovered and she was charged duty on them although the case was taken no further. After all, she was such a *dear* old lady!

In Sydney one afternoon a couple of sailors were using our small punt, painting round the stern. The big four-bladed propeller was clearly visible below them in the green water. They noticed a large crack in the uppermost blade, and informed the second mate.

'Pull the other one!' said he merrily.

'See for yourself then!'

He went, saw, and reported promptly to me.

'Oh yes?' said I, for whoever heard of cracks in the propeller? But I went to see, too, and told the captain, who studied it from the quayside, in company with the chief engineer. The chief had the propeller turned slowly which revealed that all four blades were cracked — a few feet in from the tip of each blade. Lloyd's surveyor was summoned, and said we must change the propeller before leaving the Australian coast but that in the meantime we should have the cracks drilled and metalocked, a process which stitches the crack with metal inserts. By pumping fuel and ballast water forward the stern was raised sufficiently for this to be done with the propeller partly out of water. Cairncross drydock in Brisbane was the nearest available, so there we went, over Easter, still with several hundred tons of cargo aboard. The dock was built by the Americans during the war to take their capital ships and it was a far cry from European drydocks. Swallows chased after insects between the masts in a rural setting where cocks crowed and cattle lowed. We could step off the ship and be lost in the bush in minutes. The propeller was changed for the spare carried onboard, and the cracked one — something of a showpiece — was carried home on deck. Metal fatigue of some sort must have been the cause, possibly accentuated by Liverpool's icy water.

After this rustic interlude we carried on round the coast, working the heavy derrick at every port. Although it was customary for dockers to drive a ship's cargo winches, we worked the 'big stick' ourselves, as special care and knowledge were needed to prevent accidents. The blocks and tackles were enormous — and plentiful. Depending on the weight of the load, so was the derrick rigged, with 13 men to control it. The wire rope guys were guided by hand onto winches to prevent bunching; the secret being to keep them reasonably tight at all times. As the derrick swung over the quay to land a heavy lift, the ship leaned over with it. When the weight came off the derrick head as the lift was landed, the ship righted and the mate in charge had to watch carefully to ensure that the lift was not dragged sideways. The moorings were tended to keep the ship hard alongside the quay, the gangway being raised as the ship heeled. The engineers had to be careful with fuel and ballast tanks and the cook had to guard against pots and pans shooting off his galley stove. Stewards prevented crockery falling off sideboards; all hands were involved. She heeled never more than 10 degrees but that is sufficient to cause consternation in port if not anticipated.

At one time in Sydney we had seven black eyes aboard. Shore persons would come and marvel, wondering what sort of hellship this was. We had a young passenger *en route* to Australia to make his fortune who had been allowed to stay aboard round the coast. He was pleasant enough most of the time, but one evening he picked a quarrel with the second engineer. The second, too, was normally equable but on this occasion he reacted violently and fists flew. I stepped in to stop the fight — and exchanged black eyes with the passenger. The captain, hearing the din, stopped us all with firm words. That same evening the bosun and lamptrimmer, normally good friends, fell to discussing a convoy in which they had both sailed in 1942. An argument ensued over the name of the escorting battleship. Tempers flared, fists flew, and they ended the discussion with a black eye apiece. Black eye number seven was collected by a tough able seaman recently signed on in South Australia. In an altercation with his girl friend she swung at him with her handbag whose buckle caught him across the eye.

The captain put it all down to the unseasonably hot and humid Sydney weather.

Two weeks later we steamed into Port Kembla one sunny Saturday morning and tied up at the wharf opposite a Scottish tramp. The master went up to the Custom House to 'enter his ship in', and met the Scottish tramp's master,

'Did I see a sailor called McTavish on your ship this morning asked the latter?'.

'Signed him on in Adelaide' said our captain. 'Seems a good seaman.'

'Yes — I paid him off into jail a couple of years ago for leading an armed mutiny!'

The tramp ship, apparently, had been trading to China for 18 months. Drink, heat and boredom had combined to make her crew demand to be paid off when the ship reached Adelaide. The captain had refused as they were on two-year Articles: he would pay them off only when the ship reached Scotland. One evening McTavish came to the master's dayroom brandishing a revolver, and threatening to kill him if he did not sign the crew off immediately.

'At once, Captain, d'ye hear? Ye can get them all lined up here and now. Sign us off and we'll all go home, sir!'

By blandishments and whisky in the right proportions he persuaded McTavish to hand over the gun and the police took him ashore. Strictly speaking it was not mutiny, as that famous word means taking control of a ship from her rightful commander by force, but it was serious enough. To avoid unpleasantness with the unions McTavish had been given a 'good' discharge. (Not 'very good' but not so damning as the more serious 'decline to report'.) When he came out of jail he took odd jobs, before joining us.

He had told me about the odd jobs, but had not mentioned jail, of course. If a man can use a gun once, we argued, he could use one twice, and whereas possession of firearms onboard ship is strictly illegal, it is difficult to detect and prevent if a man is determined. What to do?

Our problem was solved for us by the lady with the handbag. It seemed that the incident had been only a tiff, and they still wanted to wed. He had the offer of a shore job as a rigger; she was a dressmaker with a nice little house and they could marry next weekend by special licence if the captain would only pay him off. How could the captain refuse?

Next voyage we carried the usual load of heavy lifts including several 110-ton steel boilers and then loaded general for home. Containerisation was still in the future in the early '60s and our holds were carefully stowed with cartons of canned fruit and meat, wool, sheepskins, casks of tallow, bundles of wet hides, drums of honey — the usual, plus two tanks of bulk tallow. The other two deep tanks were to carry bulk oats from Sydney. They had been cleaned thoroughly before loading started. When the surveyor arrived to inspect I accompanied him followed by two cadets carrying portable lights. The sides of the tanks were heavily stiffened with steel girders, which made dark corners. The tanks, of course, were spotless — inspecting them a mere formality until, behind the heel of a deep frame, our torchbeams fell on an old corned beef tin, lid curled back, meaty contents long gone. Five pairs of beady eyes looked out. Whiskers quivered. A mouse's nest! As we stared the baby mice scattered and the surveyor laughed aloud. He could hardly pass a tank infested with vermin! To speed the work of demousing, the chief steward's cat was lowered in a sack. She did not take kindly to this at first until she realised the treats in store.

As a tiny kitten she had been rescued from the snow by the steward when he returned to the ship one night in Liverpool (before the fear of rabies put a ban on ships' pets.) Now Suzy was amongst the first ashore and last back aboard at every port. It was as though she could read the sailing times chalked on the gangway noticeboard. The captain had to sign a bond of £50 for every animal aboard when the ship arrived in Australia, a sum to be collected if the animals could not be produced when the ship cleared outwards. The chief steward was happy to cover the £50 bond, but when Suzy produced five kittens she became expensive. He threatened to drown them but hadn't the heart, so his financial stake rose to £300. Then, one of the kittens crawling from its box blind and helpless was stood on by somebody who thought it best to drop the tiny carcase overboard. A body is quite acceptable to Customs, but the chief steward baulked at the thought of paying £50 for a non-existent kitten. The cadets and I thought we could help here, and went ashore one lunchtime in Melbourne to find a black and white kitten in the shed where they were encouraged to keep down rats and mice. But it was a wild kitten we found and, despite wearing leather gloves, we were sorely scratched by the time we had it onboard. Once it had a good meal, though, it soon settled down.

I knew there was another cat onboard, having seen a ginger wraith around the foredeck, usually at night. It had probably joined in Liverpool and never came near our accommodation. But one morning I was sitting at my desk writing the logbook when a piteous yowling began outside my door. Looking round I saw old Ginger, on the point of giving birth. I was quite touched that in need she had come to man for help. I gave her a saucer of warm condensed milk, a bit of fish from the galley, and made her a bed from a cardboard beer box lined with a curtain. The sound of her purring filled the room as she proceeded to give birth to four handsome kittens. But of course the captain had to draw the line somewhere. Ginger and her brood would have to go, so in Sydney I phoned the Port Health Department. He came down next morning, as Ginger tucked in to her Last Supper. I felt like Judas but was assured that she wouldn't feel a thing, as I lured her into a canvas sack. Port Health put the yowling, spitting bag into the boot of his car while I carried the box of kittens. Next day he told me he had opened the car boot at his destination and Ginger had shot out off up the street before he could stop her! So we drank her health: for she was a heavy lifter, too.

Homeward-bound we called at Istanbul with Australian wool. Our captain had been there long ago as second mate of a tramp steamer. Steaming down the Dardanelles after departure a stowaway had emerged from his hiding place in one of the lifeboats to the captain's rage, for the ship's owner meets all costs incurred in returning a stowaway to his port of origin. The second mate (now *our* captain) was ordered to take the stowaway in the jolly boat and land him on the nearest beach, the Aegean shore. Ship's boats did not have engines in the late '20s so four sailors manned the oars while the second mate took the tiller, with the terrified young stowaway alongside him.

'Don't risk the boat, mister,' the captain had ordered. 'If it's too rough to land, throw him overboard and let him swim for it!'
But breakers along the coast made beaching impossible. Although he spoke no English the stowaway gave the second mate to understand that he could not swim. Grim-faced, the second mate edged the boat nearer to the shore until the undertow began to

make her pitch and roll alarmingly. Between boat and beach a welter of breakers was pierced by black, jagged rocks. The second mate looked at the rocks, then at the white face of the boy beside him, and turned the boat around. The sailors suddenly grew cheerful and began to pull towards the ship, now hull-down in the distance, while the stowaway wondered what would happen next. What occurred next was that an afternoon fog descended, white and clammy, blotting out all signs of the shore save for the crash of breaking seas, reducing their world to a few yards around the boat. Nightfall approached and of their ship there was now no sign.

The second mate headed in what he hoped was the right direction, and blew blasts upon his pea whistle. Darkness came and the fog persisted. They had been away four hours, were cold, tired, and hungry. Suddenly they heard a ship's siren and rowed hard in its direction. Then it came again, faintly, as though she were steaming away. She must have been turning in a circle however for next time they heard it she was upon them, a cliff side in the darkness, her lights faint through the swirling mist. After they were hoisted aboard the second mate was given the dressing down of his life. Not only had he disobeyed orders, but he had 'nearly lost a boat and four good seamen!'

This had all happened nearly 40 years earlier but such events are recalled vividly when you return to the scene for the first time.

We entered the Dardanelles on a bright, sunny morning and lowered our ensign to those lying in the well-tended cemeteries — British, French, and Turks who fell there in 1915. The sparkling city of Istanbul was like a backdrop for the Arabian Nights. Minaret and dome glittered against the bright sky and the Golden Horn was crowded with ships, ferries and craft of all kinds. Outside the dock gates cars and lorries honked ceaselessly, day and night, as our wool was unloaded. Shortly after sailing we held boat drill, and there in the port lifeboat was a stowaway, a well-dressed little chap of 18 or so. With a strange feeling of *dèjà vu*, I took him to the bridge. The captain sternly questioned our uninvited guest. He had no dark reason to leave Turkey, no police record. 'No work,' was his reason for leaving. 'Plenty work in England,' he said with a shy grin. And in 1963 so there was.

We nicknamed him Abdul and put him in the spare cabin. He scrubbed alleyways, messrooms, washrooms, and generally made himself useful so cheerfully that everyone liked him. A passenger had bought a phrase book which Abdul borrowed, and soon he was able to say, 'Please porter, carry my valise to number seven platform. I wish to catch the express to Vienna.'

When we docked in Hull two huge policemen came to take him off handcuffed, whereupon our crowd protested to a man. The policemen looked ashamed when Abdul came up smiling to shake hands with them. His head barely reached their chests. When alongside, and after paying off, the crew had a whip-round, leaving Abdul with tears in his eyes and a plastic bucket full of fivers and pound notes. Several days later he was charged in the local court, but a local Turkish family offered to stand security, thus absolving the company of further expense. So Abdul, our little Turkish heavy lifter, had landed on his feet. We were glad.

Commercially, the *South Africa Star* was so successful that a new heavy lift ship was designed, with a 300-ton derrick, a world record-beater. Unfortunately heavy lifts and refrigerated cargo do not carry well together. The insulation and small hatches of a reefer ship are incompatible with the widest possible hatches and uncluttered holds of the heavy lifter, so the new ship had only one reefer hold, aft — number five. She was called *Australia Star* in memory of the previous vessel of that name, herself a pioneer of 1935, recently broken up. The new ship was slightly bigger than the *South Africa*, more powerful and faster. Her Sulzer oil engine gave her 21 knots. She was the first Blue Star ship with a bulbous bow, designed to streamline the vessel's underwater hull, thus increasing fuel economy, and was built by Austin and Pickersgill at their Southwick yard, Sunderland. I stood by her building as mate from March 1965 until she completed in December. It was fascinating work — watching a heap of rusty plates grow into a sweet-lined vessel. She was built under cover, piece by piece, in a large prefabrication shop, the paper-work having been largely calculated by computer. Austin Pickersgill's were well to the fore in shipbuilding technique — one reason for their survival. When a section of the ship was completed it was cut into manageable pieces and trundled to the berth on tractor-drawn trailers. Cranes lifted the sections into position where they were held with spot-welding and wire ropes tightened with bottle screws until welded permanently. The slowly growing ship was grit-blasted nightly, section by section, when the clouds of dust would not interfere with other work. Part of my job was to examine the night's blasting early next morning to ensure that it was ready for its first coat of paint.

The bottle of champagne crashed against the gracefully curved stem on May 11 and our ship gathered momentum down the ways to the river, where tugs towed her to the fitting-out berth. A launch may look easy, but there was tension in the air that morning, as there always is. Sending several thousand tons of steel down a tallow-greased way into a river is never simple: ships have refused to budge, others have slithered sideways off the ways, some have capsized. There is always profound relief when all goes well.

The Sulzer engine was built at Vickers, Barrow-in-Furness, watched by the ship's chief engineer and shipped by coaster to Sunderland to be lifted aboard with the heavy crane at Palmer's Hill. Much of the fitting out was contract work, and co-ordinating the contractors did not always go as planned. One morning, asked where I wanted the spare anchor to be housed, I suggested the starboard side of the break of the forecastle, vertically against the bulkhead. Fine. The place was marked, the anchor would be put aboard the next day. Next morning we found three air pipes sprouting from the deck in that very place. Oh well, put the anchor on the forecastle head — where ever afterwards people would trip over it cursing the fool who put it there!

The 300-ton derrick was a Stulcken, named after the Hamburg firm which designed and developed it during the 1950s, originally for the Hansa Line of Bremen. The derrick was supported by two athwartships masts, sloping up and out. Its advantage was its availability at two hatches, forward or aft of the derrick. Needing little maintenance and easily handled, the *Australia Star*'s derrick lifted 300 tons, served two hatches, and took only three men to handle it, against the *South Africa Star*'s 180 tons serving one hatch and requiring 13 men! Towards the end of August she was ready to be towed across the North Sea for the derrick to be fitted. I accompanied her as a guest — she was still owned by the builders

Australia Star **lifted 300 tons, the world's biggest derrick**

— but my master's ticket helped with the insurance. Each of the two masts stood 70 ft high, 12 ft in diameter at base. The four electric winches — two each for purchase and topping lifts — were installed inside the masts to protect them from the weather, and cabs up the masts housed the derrick's controls. The derrick itself was 87 ft long and weighed nearly 60 tons, a magnificent piece of machinery.

Our first lift was at Newcastle-upon-Tyne where we loaded a 147-ton stator core from Parsons for the Hazelwood power station in Victoria. We loaded another 1,000 tons of general cargo at Newcastle and Middlesborough, completed at London, and on December 31 sailed out into a SW gale, bound for the new port of Dampier, in King Bay, north west Australia. Included in our cargo were three 70-ton diesel generators and other heavy equipment. At that time King Bay was hardly a port at all — just a wooden jetty in a brown, muddy landscape. Iron ore had been discovered in the nearby Hammersley Range and very soon Dampier developed into a major iron ore exporting centre. This trip we felt that we were really helping the pioneers to pioneer.

The *Australia Star* was a fine looking ship with few straight lines in her — only sweet curves, but she was awkward. There was nothing wrong with the derrick — *that* was a poetry of motion, but the ship herself had a terrible motion at sea and vibration increased vertically, at its worst on the bridge deck and in the captain's cabin. In 1965 the problem of vibration in ships had not been resolved. When solidly-built ships had low-powered engines the problem did not exist, but as ships became lighter and engines more powerful, vibration grew proportionately. But the *Australia Star* was like the awkward child its parent could not help loving: she pitched and rolled in any chop, scooping up the ocean like a ship demented. True, the Germans who built her derrick had predicted such a motion for they had constructed a class of ships in the '30s with a lot of weight above stiffened with weight below, about the same size as our baby, and behaving similarly at sea. The British called them pocket battleships.

After experiencing our first bad weather we realised that cargo had to be carefully secured, and then secured again, to make assurance doubly sure. Voyage two saw us sailing from Liverpool early in June 1966, after the seamen's strike, bound through Suez to Fremantle, West Australia. On the foredeck, port and starboard, were steel posts, 10 ft high, each with a vertical sheave at the head. These were to guide wires to the winches as part of the auxiliary hatch-opening gear, used if the hydraulic system did not function. Crossing the Indian Ocean one day we found that the sheave of one had rusted frozen so a seaman, clad only in shorts, shoes, and goggles, stood on a wooden ladder, squirting release oil and hitting the sheave with a hammer. A sliver of metal struck him in the stomach, making a small scratch. A few minutes later the bosun walked by and pointed out that he was bleeding a little. The second mate washed the scratch and applied a sticking plaster. Shortly after mid-day the second mate found the sailor sitting at the foot of the monkey island ladder, looking pale. His temperature rose alarmingly, his abdomen in great pain, and he sweated profusely, shivering and frightened. He recalled that he was number 13 on the Articles and became delirious.

We had no doctor onboard and the *Ship Captain's Medical Guide*, told us little. The captain gave him a penicillin injection to combat infection which, we learned afterwards, probably saved his life. Our radio call for medical advice was answered by the Shaw Savill cargo liner *Afric*, 400 miles astern, also Australia-bound, for whom we turned back to meet next morning. Her doctor decided to take our lad back to the *Afric* where he could keep him under observation. With thanks, we resumed our course. As we were the faster ship of the two *Afric* was soon hull-down astern, but our radio operators kept in touch. At first the patient responded to treatment and made good progress, then, after a couple of days, he relapsed and deteriorated rapidly. The *Afric*'s captain and doctor wondered anxiously what to do for the best. The *Afric*'s fourth mate happened to be in the chartroom when they were talking.

'There's a British air force hospital at Gan, sir.'

'Gan?'

'South end of the Maldives, a staging post for RAF comets. My brother's in the RAF, sir.'

'Thank you very much, to Gan it is!'

And the *Afric* changed course and headed for Gan. Without a chart she made a good approach where a boat took our man ashore. X-rays revealed a sliver of metal in his intestine, removed by immediate operation. He survived. But it was a near thing.

While passing our injured seaman to the *Afric* we had noticed that she had, as deck cargo, a boiler, a long, round ended cylinder with pipes sticking out like quills, its weight painted in white letters — '110 tons'.

In Melbourne we met her again and went across to express our gratitude. By their prompt action, they had undoubtedly saved our lad's life but modestly they brushed aside our thanks, whereupon we fell to discussing cargo. Their big boiler was for Sydney and would be unloaded by floating crane. But in Sydney, the floating crane was in drydock, out of commission. The only two shore cranes big enough were also unavailable. Either the *Afric* would have to take her boiler to Melbourne, or Brisbane — or take it home again — none of which appealed to the consignees or Shaw Savill. Could we help?

For the *Afric* we would move mountains!

She came alongside us in Sydney's Darling Harbour having given herself a slight list towards us, while we listed away from her. As play began, both main decks were level. Wharfies passed the slings and hooked on as our derrick plumbed the boiler. Word had passed round the waterfront of something unusual and a crowd gathered. When all was ready we began to lift, slowly, taking the weight off her deck and causing her to come upright. The fenders between squealed in protest. By the time the boiler

121

was 'afloat' *Afric*'s foredeck was 14 ft above ours, and for a few exquisite moments it looked as though we would not clear her bulwarks because our two purchase blocks had come together, 'two-blocks'. But by cautiously raising the derrick head itself, the boiler floated clear with inches to spare! We landed it temporarily on our hatch while tanks were trimmed to give a slight list away from the quay, during which time the *Afric* let go and departed. Slowly we rehoisted the boiler and swung it over the quay, the critical moment with a Stulcken derrick as with no guys there are only two topping lifts on swivels at the mast heads to check the swing. Stretch out too far and your derrick can collapse. But the boiler was far enough over the quay for the low-loader to be driven under. As it settled into the lorry's cradle, purchase and topping lift wires were paid out swiftly and the ship swung upright. A sigh of relief arose from the spectators — as well as the operators!

Heavy lifting made a change from frozen meat, but it is refrigerated cargo which is the bread and butter, and most of the jam, of the Blue Star Line, so after nearly four years I returned to

Built as the *Empire Clarendon* in 1945 she became in turn *Tuscan Star,* and *Timaru Star* before ending up the *California Star* duly laid up in the Blackwater. Seen here in Los Angeles.

the reefer ships — less glamorous perhaps, but equally satisfying.

My next ship was the *California Star* (biggest derrick 15 tons!) with general cargo and passengers to New Zealand; passengers and apples home — a voyage of three and a half months. New Zealand apples did well in 1967 as two ships carrying the Australian apple crop were trapped in the Suez Canal by the Six Days War between Israel and Egypt. But after unloading there was no work for the old *California* so we took her to the Essex Blackwater — a favourite laying-up place. Not far from Colchester, handy for London, less remote than Fal or Gareloch (the other favourite lay-up waters). Only two other ships were there, both Union Castle intermediate liners up for sale. We hung off an anchor and connected to a permanent swivel mooring using our anchor chain whereupon Captain Askew and all but a skeleton crew went home. The engines, including generators and auxiliaries, shut down and the ship fell silent. Having rigged canvas covers over funnel and ventilators to keep out the rain, packets of silica-gel were placed among the vital parts in the engine room. Inventories were made, what would lock was locked, and after a week I handed over the keys to the local agent, and sent the skeleton crew home.

Until then it was normal to lay up a few refrigerated ships during the late northern summer, then after a couple of months send them out again to New Zealand for lamb. But in the early '70s a more vigorous policy was pursued to keep the ships employed throughout the year. The company began tramping; bananas from Central America to the USA, Europe, or the Persian Gulf; meat from New Zealand to Russia, butter to Bulgaria, oranges from Algeria to Japan, Canadian potatoes to Northern Europe, a policy that has kept us in business in an increasingly competitive world in which, sadly, so many British and continental shipping lines have gone to the wall.

I then joined the *English Star* for two voyages covering familiar ground — to New Zealand with general cargo, home with their apples and meat from Australia. She was a large, complex ship, and work in her was difficult but satisfying. At the voyage end, when we brought her home, full of cargo and pretty as a picture, all onboard felt a sense of achievement. By now I was quite a senior chief officer. As a junior mate I was amused how senior mates always fell to discussing promotion at get-togethers. Made on a combination of seniority and merit, the laws of supply and demand operate, so the last step up the ladder to command is far and away the greatest. It was 20 years since I joined the *Conway* and I was 36 yet to my surprise I found that I, too, was becoming keenly interested in the promotion stakes. I even compiled secret lists of those ahead of me — probables and possibles — and noted the ages and health of senior masters!

Chapter 9
On the lake
1968

HOW WOULD YOU LIKE a voyage to nowhere old boy? said an enigmatic Mr Cox, over the telephone. 'On the other hand, you could just become one of that happy band of brothers destined to sail to Freedom!'

He was talking about the *Scottish Star*, holed up for more than a year in the Great Bitter Lake of the Suez Canal, and whose chief officer I would relieve. The *Scottish Star*, twin to the *English Star*, was one of 14 ships of a northbound convoy trapped by the Six Days War when the Canal was closed at both ends by blockship and mine. It was ironic that a German ship, the *Munsterland*, with part of her refrigerated Australian cargo destined for the British garrison at Aden, was told to miss Aden and get through the Canal before it was too late. Had she made her Aden call she would not have been in the Canal when it closed. There was no question of release while Israeli troops occupied the Canal's east bank when diplomatic negotiations to free the ships were unsuccessful. Anchored nearer Egypt all their dealings were with Egypt, through the little lakeside port of Fenara where faded RAF roundels on some of the buildings spoke of a former occupation.

I flew to Cairo where I had a day to myself. With an air of timeless tranquillity deep laden barges crept along the Nile under huge lateen sails, but sandbagged buildings and air raid shelters were grim reminders that this was a nation at war. Military hardware was Russian and though Soviet troops were not in evidence, their civilian advisers frequented all the best places in increasing numbers — as had the British in their day. The car ride along the dusty road from Cairo to Fenara unfolded scenes from a children's illustrated Bible. In villages of flat, single storey dwellings with tiny windows, the colour of the houses matched the surrounding desert, and under the palms by an oasis an ox, harnessed to a beam, trundled in an everlasting circle, driving an irrigation drill. Women in black swayed gracefully along the road to the well, pitchers balanced on their heads while intent old men in white robes jogged by on donkeys. Wars had passed this way before.

The driver nudged me as we breasted the last hill: below us the Lake, with the faded fleet at anchor reflecting the rays of the evening sun. A launch took me to the ship, where my welcome as a newcomer was exuberantly cordial, and that evening I was taken to each ship and introduced. For the next four and a half months I never went ashore, but time refused to drag. It was a cheerful life, far more interesting than I had expected. Everyone suffered to some extent from dysentery and the dangers of sunburn were ever present but plenty of fresh air and exercise kept us fit. During the first few days of the incarceration several of the ships' crews, moved by compassion for the remnants of the fleeing Egyptian army arriving at the lakeside ahead of the Israelis, ferried the stragglers across the lake in ship's boats to safety. The Egyptian authorities looked benignly upon the vessels thereafter. We were not allowed ashore — except for the very occasional sightseeing trip to Cairo which was not encouraged. After all, how could we look after our ships while dallying at the pyramids? On no account were

Scottish Star **of Suez**

we to approach the Israeli shore although we could move freely by boat within 500 metres of our anchorage.

One night a carelessly tied boat from one of the British ships washed up on the Sinai bank. Next day another was sent to recover it, but while the first boat was being refloated an Israeli craft full of armed soldiers hove alongside and took our men prisoner. After interrogation they were sent home to Britain, not to be allowed back, as in those days the Egyptians would have no truck with anyone who had been to Israel.

Early hopes of a quick release for the ships faded, and as the months rolled by the little floating settlement became more permanent. Away to the north of our anchorage, out of sight, was an abandoned tanker which played no part in our life. The other 14 ships which formed the Great Bitter Lake Association did:

Scottish Star
Port Invercargill
British. Blue Star and Port Line which formed a joint management company while these two ships were in the Canal, lasting until 1972. It was not an ownership merger though sea staff became interchangeable

Melampus
Agapenor
British. Blue Funnel Line. These ships were moored together and manned by one crew, known as the *Agalampus*

Nippon
Killara
Swedish. *Nippon* was a cadet ship of Swedish East Asiatic Company but her cadets had left. *Killara* was Transatlantic Line, a fine, twin-funnel Scandia-type ship, barely a year old when trapped. These two moved together and unofficially became *Nippara*, with one crew

Munsterland
West German. Refrigerated cargo liner of Hamburg America Line

Nordwind
West German. A beautiful little tramp of a type which, even in 1967, was almost extinct

Sindh
French cargo liner of Messageries Maritimes. Served best food on the lake, real French cuisine!

Lednice
Czechoslovakian. Danube Navigation Company, a lovely little ship homeward bound from East Africa with wool on deck

Vassil Levsky
Bulgarian. British-built Merchant Aircraft Carrier (MAC from 1944) Ex-*Empire Mackendrick, Granpond, Condor, Saltersgate*. In ballast

Boleslaw Beirut
Djakarta
Polish Ocean Lines. Cargo liners, one of which had been on her way home from North Vietnam

African Glen
American. Farrell Lines. A C3, the only steamship of the lake fleet; on her way home in ballast from South Vietnam.

The ships carried the big, box-shaped searchlights slung over the stem (hired from the Canal Company, having a split beam to illuminate both banks for use during transit. Regular Canal users carry their own built-in searchlight). The Canal Company mooring boats were on deck as though the ships were just awaiting the passage of the southbound convoy before proceeding to Port Said. The paired ships lay head to tail with fenders between, two anchors leading ahead from both ships.

The single ships each lay to one anchor, swinging to the wind and slightly varying currents in six and a half fathoms (39 ft) of very salt water. They were a typical cross-section of cargo ships of their time, all with predominantly white crews. Complements varied from more than 20 in the refrigerated ships to a mere half-dozen in the *African Glen* — a total of around 220 men when I was there. Individual crews were relieved by their companies at intervals of from four to nine months. Some choice was allowed, and a few stalwarts remained for a second or even third term while others returned to the lake after a spell of leave or normal voyaging. Financial inducement ranged from none at all (though with little chance to spend it was easy to save) to double normal salary in the Swedish ships, with further increases again in the event of nearby warlike action. The Americans were onto such a good thing that they remained forever — the captain had been her third mate when she arrived! In the British ships we were paid £2 per day each, regardless of rank, as hardship/danger money, though we did not really consider ourselves threatened. Even when the Suez oil tanks were hit and burned for days, when manoeuvres on both sides of the lake erupted into a shoot-out once a week (usually on a Saturday night) — and jet fighter bombers roared overhead — we watched with an air of detachment. It is extraordinarily easy to drift into a false sense of security!

The *African Glen* was away from the main fleet, having dragged her anchor towards the Israeli shore during a sandstorm. It was not considered worth raising steam to move her again, and she came under frequent Egyptian suspicion of acting as an Israeli listening post. We saw her small crew less often than the others, but their Captain Jack made us all Great Bitter Lakes Association tee-shirts and luggage labels as his contribution, and he and his black bosun, George Washington, were popular members.

The ships were maintained as well as limited materials allowed. My deck crew consisted of a third mate, bosun, carpenter and two sailors. We turned-to at 6.30 am and scrubbed the wooden decks, invariably ending our pre-breakfast task by hosing down the permanently rigged accommodation ladder. The pitchpine wooden decks, exposed to the sun's rays, deteriorated fast, although those under flimsy canvas awnings did better. The *Port Invercargill*'s decks were of teak and in much better condition. But then she was a much younger ship — a stripling of 10 years compared with our 18. The lake water, strongly salt and rich in bacteria, caused every vessel to foul up along the waterline. Grass a yard long grew over heavy shell and anchor cable links could hardly be distinguished as such, so heavy was encrustation. More serious was the growth of tiny shellfish within the pipes of the vessel's machinery-cooling system: on the reefer ships, reaming pipes was a constant job to give cooling water a chance. Toilet flush valves became so encrusted with salt that those not in regular use were dismantled. Fresh water and diesel oil were supplied occasionally by a motor barge carrying water in its tanks and oil in 40-gallon drums on deck. These were hoisted aboard and the oil pumped either by hand or air pump into the ship's tanks — a laborious process but one which helped to pass the time. The agent came out once a week and the chandler made a fortune. We had no choice but to pay his prices and — as he constantly reminded us — there *was* a war on! But with permission from our companies we dipped deeply into our cargoes. The first Monday of every month was shopping day. Lists of requirements were passed around after church on Sunday for boats next day to collect fish from the *Nippon*, meat and eggs from the *Munsterland*, canned fruit from the

Scottish Star, Tom Piper brand canned meat from *Port Invercargill* and rice from *Agalampus*. *Port Invercargill* and *Scottish Star* had apples as main cargo — still under refrigeration and still edible after more than a year aboard — but they had to be eaten immediately as within half an hour they collapsed into brown mush. Our general cargo included wool, fruit, and personal effects, unharmed. The cartons of currants had weevils but the *Sindh*'s Senegal cook was still able to use them! *Port Invercargill* had casks of Australian red wine which became known as 'steam'. This was dispensed by the bucket to which the Swedes in particular were partial. The *Scottish Star* had 240 cartons of Australian Swan Lager which were released by the consignees in London — a magnificent gesture! We called for a working party to help us dig it out, as it was heavily overstowed with currants and bales of wool. Never have wharfies worked so fast! The temperature was more than 100 degrees F when we got it out, but it cooled beautifully. Five cases were given to each ship as samples, 50 each to the Polish vessels as their supplies had been delayed in Alexandria. Thereafter, while stocks lasted, we supplied beer for all festive occasions.

It is a fact of sea life that if you have nothing to worry about you worry about nothing: most of us felt we were slowly going dotty. One fine day a channel marking buoy from up lake drifted into our midst. It was immediately seized, cleaned, and crowned with a large brass GBLA badge — an anchor with figures one dexter and four sinister (for the 14 ships). It was then painted yellow and moored firmly in the middle of our anchorage to become the start and finish of the monthly sailing regattas. Two classes of boat were raced. Class A were ships' lifeboats rigged with two masts and two sets of sails each. Only a vertical plate keel (made in the engineroom) was needed to make them tack well. Class B were 'any other boats' — mostly Canal boats, similarly fitted. (In those days most ships carried four lifeboats, all equipped with masts and sails. Nowadays the diesel lifeboat needs no sail and ships usually carry but two boats). A different ship organised the race each month. The course of about four miles was announced on the day — a map being given to each ship. The host vessel provided the party at night, made the trophies, and printed the stamps. For the making of postage stamps was another hobby taken seriously. At first the stamps were crudely made, often on gummed paper, but as time passed they became more professional and were sought by philatelists the world over. Production was laborious and materials limited, so the printers made only sufficient of an issue for a couple of sets per man on the lake — say 500. Not many in mint condition were left for international collectors. The best were printed from hand made blocks, etched, carved, and printed in two colours. Less serious efforts were printed on the *Scottish Star*'s duplicator, then hand-painted. Most bore the inscription 'GBLA Postage' and a figure 5, 10 or 50, which you could translate into pence, cents, francs, zlotys, or kroner as you wished. One set produced by a Polish officer to commemorate the Great Bitter Lake Olympiad of 1968 was so good that it was legitimated by the International Postal Union.

As the time for the Mexico City Olympics approached, the Poles

Philatelists the world over look out for the valuable home-made Suez stamps

suggested that we ran our own Olympiad, whereupon a feasibility study was held aboard the *Djakarta*. The Poles, taking their work as organisers seriously, produced bows and arrows, and targets. They padded obstructions on their foredecks to make running and jumping courses, and swung out derricks to support the goals of a water polo pitch (first scraping the barnacles and weed off their waterlines). They made weights for weightlifting, certificates and even winners' medals, gold, silver and bronze. Also stamps, of course. Everyone on the lake pitched in with a will. There were airguns in the *Agalampus'* cargo — so we would have a shooting contest! Whereas weekly football was on a ship to ship basis, the Olympics had to be national. Britain had the strongest team by virtue of numbers, so a Commonwealth team was formed also, to include all those not actually English (such as Geordies). Three of the Canal boats were transformed into racing gigs, for rowing. The *Munsterland* was the venue for table tennis. Swimming was from one Polish ship to another — about the right distance in the super salt water.

To accommodate those lacking sufficient numbers to make a national team, there was the International team. Nobody was left out. The events were football, running, jumping, sailing, rowing, swimming, diving, darts, weightlifting, archery, shooting, water polo, table tennis, and fishing. The lake teemed with fish. Our Sparks came within an inch of his gold when his last catch, a superb mullet, slid down a scupper back into the lake just as 'time' was called!

When it was learned that we were having our own World Cup (football), someone in Germany donated a handsome silver cup, and similar trophies were sent out also by wellwishers for the Olympics. We made our own trophies for the more modest tournaments, such as the monthly regattas — later to be lodged in the Hamburg Mission to Seamen, as representative a place for them as anywhere. The BBC came to see us — assuming that the Olympiad would be a British venture — and seemed quite shocked when we told them it was Polish. But they cheered up when we said we could probably arrange a visa for them to board *Djakarta*!

Church was a meeting held on Sunday mornings aboard the *Nordwind* which most people attended. It wasn't exactly religious — too many denominations were involved for it to be interdenominational and none of us had taken holy orders anyway — but it was a social meeting, held with dignity and respect. We even wore shirts.

One of the Polish ships had our only doctor — a splendid fellow who spent much time repairing the ravages of four-a-side football. He doubled as a dentist upon the *Agalampus'* cook, but as no anaesthetic was available few people suffered from toothache thereafter!

Most of the ships acquired pets, usually dogs or cats, but the *Scottish Star* had a pair of rabbits. The most famous lake animal was Bulbul, a small black and white canine crew member from the *Sindh*. He barked in fluent French, and enjoyed sailing and ship-visiting. He even played football and took part in the Olympics match, standing solemnly on the rostrum to receive his medal afterwards, to the astonishment of the BBC.

Occasionally a ship weighed anchor and steamed around the lake to test her engines. On such occasions she flew such useful international code flag signals as HLN — 'Ice is insufficient to hinder navigation.' (This was in the old code. In the new — 1969 — version it would be VSO).

Onboard every ship lived an Egyptian soldier-policeman who ensured that the radio room remained sealed, by order. But we heard news from the outside world on our cabin transistors. It all seemed far away until we heard one day that Soviet, Bulgarian and Polish troops had rolled into Czechoslovakia to quell the Prague uprising. We were nearest ship to *Lednice* — and that afternoon her whistle began to sound a long, mournful blast. This was a distress signal, and I went to see if they needed help. As we rounded *Lednice*'s stern I noticed her ensign was at half mast. Fearfully I climbed the gangway. Captain Vladimir met me on the poop, and thanked me for coming, near to tears. The whistle and ensign were to mark their grief. Next day the captains of the Polish and Bulgarian ships paid him a long visit to agree that although their countries were fighting each other, peace must prevail here on the lake.

The Great Reopening of the Canal came in 1975, eight years after the ships were trapped by which time most had been abandoned. The only ships to leave under their own power were the *Munsterland* and the *Nordwind*, both of which had been maintained with Teutonic thoroughness: the others were towed to Port Said. *Scottish Star*'s copper piping for the steering gear had been looted after she was abandoned in 1969; the fruit cargo was a write off but the wool had increased in value due to inflation. She was unloaded and sold to Greeks who renamed her *Kavo Yerakas* — her colour scheme unchanged. She spent all her time under the Greek flag laid up in Piraeus waiting for better times which never came. In 1979 — 12 years after making her last voyage — she was towed from Greece to Spain for breaking up, still in Blue Star colours. She had outlived her *English* sister by six years.

The finishing school

Chapter 10

1969-1971

HOW WOULD YOU LIKE TO SAIL as chief officer of a big white liner old boy?' was Mr Cox's next cheerful greeting. 'The *Malaysia.*'

Built as the *Hubert* for Booth Line in 1955 — I had seen her on her Amazonian maiden voyage — she was a lovely little turbine steamer, a smaller version of the Blue Star South American liners. When the passenger trade to the Amazon and West Indies declined she transferred to Austasia Line, running from Singapore to New Guinea, Australia and Indonesia, via Malaysia. I flew to join her in Singapore. Her time in port was determined by cargo considerations rather than by need to keep to precise schedule which seemed to suit her passengers. She was the last passenger ship on the run, and many travelled in her for the sake of the voyage as much as for the transport she provided. Her home port was Singapore, though she was registered in London. Senior officers were British, the juniors Singaporeans — mostly Chinese with some Indians and Malays. The crew were all Chinese, most of whom lived in Singapore though many hailed originally from mainland China where they still had families. Our round voyage took about 12 weeks — Singapore, Penang and Port Swettenham (now renamed Port Kelang) in Malaysia, back to Singapore. Then to Port Moresby in New Guinea and Port Alma in Queensland, where we loaded a couple of deep tanks of tallow for Sydney, after which we called at Port Kembla, Melbourne and Hobart in the apple season, which lasted until July for the Singapore trade. We spent days — sometimes weeks — in each port, and went north again via Sydney, Brisbane, Port Moresby and Djakarta. Passengers embarked and disembarked at every port. Northbound cargoes were general and refrigerated; southbound mostly timber and rubber. She had an unusual arrangement of

135

Malaysia, **built as the** *Hubert* **in 1955 for the Booth Line**

general cargo lower holds *below* refrigerated tween and shelter decks — from her Booth Line days when Amazon logs filled the holds before she loaded West Indian fruit for Liverpool.

Loading was interesting, especially in Sydney where most of the big decisions were made. One day the cargo manager asked me if we could take 200 buckets for Djakarta. Certainly, were they plastic? No, metal buckets, he had been told. A minor item, they would be down next day. The following morning a convoy of lorries appeared carrying *dredger* buckets! On another occasion I was asked to load 20 gas bottles, which I took to be of the kind used for welding. They turned out to be large, heavy cylinders of cyanide gas, a cargo we could *not* accept.

Shortly after joining the ship my career almost ended. Welding repairs had been carried out down the forepeak tank and Chippy was on his way to inspect the work when I suddenly needed him elsewhere. I said I would inspect the welding and sauntered forward to the entrance, down a steel hatchway forward of the windlass. The heavy lid was hinged, and had to be hooked open in the vertical position to allow access. Thinking of other things I swung it open — and forgot to hook it back. I was smoking a cigarette, and was in fact doing all the things a first-tripper is enjoined *not* to do. Descending the ladder I steadied myself by grabbing the hand grip on the underside of the lid. There was a crash, blinding lights flashed, then all was darkness! My cigarette had shot out of my mouth and lay, glowing, in a coil of rope. My wrists were trapped under the lid and a warm liquid ran down my face. My mouth was full of pebbles. Teeth.

No one heard my shouts. I tried to raise the lid but it was too heavy. Rising panic overcame nausea and fear lent strength. Somehow I found myself out on the cool deck, and tottered along to the amidships accommodation, leaving a trail of blood behind me. My whites were striped with red like a barber's pole, my face one large bruise. The first person I met was the purser who promptly ordered a steward to phone for an ambulance, and thrust a large glass of scotch into my trembling hand. Although I knew whisky was not the thing for haemorrhages, it went down well, until I remembered the cigarette and told the people crowding round to view the remains. One raced forward to return with the good news that my cigarette was out. Then an ambulance drove up to the foot of the gangway. The attendant, a solemn Chinaman, looked at me intently.
'Are you Clistian?'
I suddenly felt he must be wondering what kind of priest to summon if I passed away on him. Shocked at the thought, I nodded. He smiled sadly.
'Pity,' he said. 'Better you become Jehova's Witness, like me!' At the hospital they stitched my head and sent me to Dr Lim the dentist — who measured me for new teeth.

Weeks later, as the ship neared Australia, I succumbed to rather severe headaches for which *The Ship Captain's Medical Guide* failed to reassure me. It deals with most things, from constructing a medical cabinet to dealing with a corpse, including short protestant and catholic services for the burial at sea. It even makes childbirth sound easy.
'Obviously written by a man,' commented my wife when she read it.
The doctor arranged for me to be X-rayed at the Bridge Street

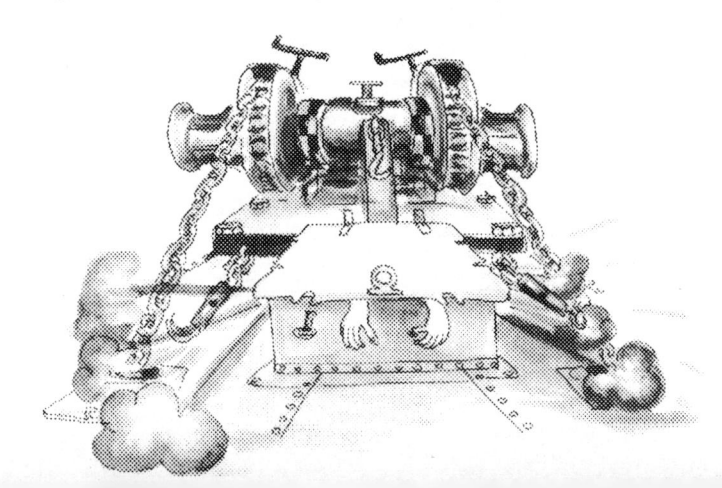

An artist's impression of the *Australasia*

Clinic, Port Melbourne. From a grey photographic plate my skull grinned — sound as a bell — and the headaches departed.

A few days later I was inspecting cargo in number five hold. Fifty-eight pound cubic bales of rubber, dusted with french chalk to prevent their sticking together, were pushed by wharfies from a high brow across the after end onto a large rope cargo net spread under the square of the hatch. As I stepped off the steel ladder into the hold, a bale bounced off the stow towards me, ricochetting like a tennis ball, and grinding my knee against the ladder. Back at Bridge Street Clinic the X-rays showed only bruising, but the radiographer recommended that I went home before accident number three!

Instead, I transferred to the *Australasia*, Austasia Line's other passenger ship, on the Fremantle to Singapore run, a round voyage of only three weeks. She was built in Belgium in 1950 as the *Baudouinville* for service to the Congo, and when a new ship of the same name was built she became the *Thyseville*. After the Belgians stopped passenger services to their newly independent colony she was sold to Booth Line and became the *Anselm* on the Liverpool —

West Indies — Amazon service. When this trade faded she became the *Iberia Star*, fifth ship on Blue Star's South American mail run. She went to Austasia Line in 1965 and soon became popular, especially with Australians taking long service leave. Both ships served as the passengers' hotels in port. The one week long run from Fremantle to Singapore made the *Australasia* an ideal carrier of fruit and vegetables for which the booming hotel industry provided a steady market.

One voyage we embarked a party of some 70 Salvation Army people in Fremantle, on a crusade to Singapore and back. News of their coming suggested that we would be smothered with wet blankets while bar sales zeroed. True, sales of alcohol dropped, but the more expensive soft drinks had never enjoyed better demand, and we could not have found ourselves more cheerful passengers! Their brass band played *Waltzing Matilda* as we sailed, with the Salvation Army flag fluttering bravely from the masthead. At sea they gave deck concerts daily while people sat in the sun on deckchairs listening with pleasure to Gilbert and Sullivan. Their young musicians had a pop group complete with psychedelic lighting and their young ladies did wonderful things with timbrels. During the day you came across groups having Bible readings in corners of the lounge, and for once I did not have to organise the passengers into endless darts matches.

After three voyages in the *Australasia* I returned to the *Malaysia*. Her passengers came in all colours and kinds, and most were delightful: elderly American couples travelled happily with Burmese, Siamese, Japanese, Chinese, Sikhs, Russians, and of course Australians and the British. I was amazed at the number of young couples in their late teens and early 20's who had walked from Britain, often with baby in a pram, via Turkey, Iran, Afghanistan, Pakistan, India, Burma, Thailand and Malaysia. In Singapore they discovered that to reach Australia they had to 'take the boat'. Full of determination and courage, they made light of their epic journey.

Five jovial lads in their early 20s joined one night in Brisbane, just before sailing time, carrying flagons of red wine, to disappear aft into the accommodation. Sailing from Brisbane was always spectacular. Coloured paper streamers stretched across the ever widening gap between ship and quay. Hippies danced. There were tears and flowers and three long blasts on the whistle as the steamer moved down river to the sea.

The bosun looked in to see me at six thirty next morning as was his wont. His greeting was succinct.

'No mooling lopes follard!'

"No mooling lopes forward?' I found it difficult, sometimes, not to mimic our Chinese.

'No lopes. Allee gone!'

Sure enough, most of the forward mooring ropes had vanished in the night. Furthermore, there were no mooling lopes aft, either. No chairs in second class lounge, no blooks in blook case. Allee gone! Probably floating far astern in Moreton Bay by this time.

We asked questions, but no-one knew anything. We had a shrewd idea but could no nothing in the absence of proof or confession. The prime suspects left us in Port Moresby as the police boarded by when the trail was cold. Next day as we steamed across a smooth sea towards Djakarta a young lady passenger asked the second mate what had happened to them.

'To whom?'

'To the boys who dumped the mooring ropes and chairs? Did they go to prison?'

'Nobody was arrested. We thought no one knew who did it!'

Young and pretty, she blushed and hung her head.

'I saw them push everything overboard when they were drunk. I was frightened to speak,' she burst into tears and the second mate could only take her in his arms, to comfort the poor thing.

In drydock in Singapore was a Hickory boat — the *Golden Ocean* of Hong Kong. Our third mate told me she had been a Booth boat, so I strolled along to see her. Under the paint at bow and stern could still be seen her old name — *Dominic*! She seemed much smaller than I remembered — but clean and in good condition. Both *Malaysia* and *Australasia* carried fourth officers so I was a daywork mate during the day — down holds and bilges in a boilersuit, or checking paint and gear. But in the evenings I was the chief officer, acquiring social polish in mess kit and cummerbund, listening to passengers' tales of their travels. It was fascinating — like a finishing school. Every senior mate should try it.

After eight months with Austasia Line I returned home, wondering what Mr Cox would have in store for me after my leave. 'The *Wellington Star*, old boy!', was the last appointment Mr Cox gave me. He retired the following year after more than 50 years with the company.

I was second mate of the same *Wellington Star* when promoted to mate in 1960, so took this as a favourable portent. She was loading in London for Pitcairn and New Zealand, and for the first time my wife could accompany me, while our three children were abandoned to kith and kin. We played grocer's delivery van to the Pitcairn Islanders — those hardy descendents of the Bounty Mutineers who still live on their rocky little island among the trade winds of the South Pacific. The seas were too rough for the boats to come alongside off Bounty Bay so, on the islanders' advice, we went to the lee of the land, off the south west corner. Cadets had already laid out the cargo in the shelter deck: four bags of flour for Mrs Betty Christian; soap powder and chocolate for Mrs Young; cooking oil and a washing machine for Mrs Brown; chocolate and biscuits for Mrs Clark; groceries for Mrs Warren. The men lowered the cargo into the boats on ropes while the magistrate, Purvis Young, paid the captain. The goods were carried freight-free but the cargo itself was paid for. Like their Tahitian ancestors of six generations before, the Pitcairners, in the words of Captain Bligh, are 'a delightful people with the most engaging dispositions.'

We arrived in Wellington in November and were told to sail from Auckland on December 24. Just two days of rain would have us in Auckland over Christmas! For once I was in no hurry to go home! From Wellington to Lyttelton, then to Port Chalmers which appeared to have changed little since February 15, 1882 when the first load of frozen lamb ever to leave New Zealand was shipped in the Albion Line's clipper ship *Dunedin*.

Approaching from the sea — where the chart shows depths of water sounded by Lt James Cook in *HMS Endeavour* — past the albatross gullery on Tairoa Head, the channel winds up Otago inlet between hills whose bright greenery is heightened by clumps of yellow gorse and broom, from ocean to the depths of country in less than half an hour. Soon you are off Port Chalmers, a stage set, where neat little buildings run along the waterfront from the black hole of the railway tunnel left to the grey and white stone spired church right, with the hills as backdrop. Port Chalmers is to Dunedin as Lyttelton is to Christchurch — Otago having been colonised by the Church of Scotland.

After Port Chalmers we carried on to New Plymouth, in Taranaki, a rich dairy region in North Island, at that time the largest cheese-exporting port in the world. Nowadays cheese is exported in cartons, but then it still came in cylindrical crates each holding two cheeses. We completed our loading in Auckland and sailed for Liverpool fully laden and with 12 passengers on December 24!

Next voyage the old *Welly Boot* took a full general cargo from London's Royal Docks to Fiji and New Zealand, and then paved the box boats' way to the east coast of North America by taking 11,000 tons of frozen beef, lamb, ice cream, chilled kiwi fruit, wool, casked tallow, milk powder, casein, sheepskins and grass seed — the.biggest cargo ever to leave New Zealand for America. Towards the end of loading we had to keep measuring the distance between loadline (the Plimsoll Mark) and the water so that I could calculate the amount we could still take — the remaining deadweight. This cargo was for Charleston, Norfolk, Philadelphia, New York, Boston and Montreal — where we loaded empty containers for London — another straw in the wind.

When in 1971 I finally quit the *Wellington Star* the company's fleet consisted almost entirely of ships like her. Box boats were building, true, but had yet to make their impact. I had been on leave three weeks when the marine superintendent rang. Could I join the *English Star* in Tilbury in three days time for a voyage to New Zealand? The *English* had always been one of my favourites — another voyage in her would be a pleasure — even though I *was* only halfway through my leave and halfway through decorating the living room. Father-in-law could finish the decorating and I could catch up on my leave another time, I decided.

The Marine Superintendent sounded amused when I said of course I would go.

Then he added, almost as an afterthought,

'As master, of course!'

Chapter 11
Command at last!
1971

ONCE THERE WAS a chief engineer and a captain who wished to impress a lady passenger. At dinner one evening they discussed not only who was the most important man in the ship but also the matter of succession.

'If you died, captain,' said the lady, fluttering her eyelashes prettily, 'would the chief engineer become captain?'

'He would not,' said the captain emphatically. 'The mate would.'

'And if the mate died?'

'The second mate would assume command, and if the second mate died then the third mate would become captain.'

The lady looked anxious, 'and if *he* died?'

'In such an unlikely case,' said the captain, fixing them both with a steely stare, 'The cadet would become captain!'

'There you are!' said the chief engineer, a twinkle in his eye, turning to the lady, 'I told you a cadet could do *his* job, didn't I?'

The *English Star* and I were old friends for I had been her third mate 15 years previously and her chief officer for two voyages in 1968. Not one of the company's biggest ships, she was, nevertheless, a large, six-hatch, 12-passenger cargo liner of what had become the classical type. I joined her as master one grey April afternoon in Tilbury Dock, ready to sail on the evening tide. The tailor kindly stitched the new braid onto the sleeves of my jacket. Cargo was loaded and hatches battened down; fuel had been checked and fresh water tanks were full. We were to carry no passengers this voyage, possibly because the *English Star* not only had a new master, but also a new chief engineer, a new refrigeration engineer, and a new radio officer; all on their first voyage in their new ranks. Some faces were familiar: three officers and several ratings had sailed with me before, and were probably wondering how I would shape up. Promotion improves some but has the opposite effect on others and, to a considerable degree, the master's attitude and ability determine whether his ship runs efficiently and happily.

I had been told years before that the full impact of attaining command comes only when you disembark your first pilot. Having cleared the Downs he wished me 'bon voyage,' stepped into his launch, and roared off towards the lights of Folkestone. I was Master under God. I hoped He would make allowances.

It was a fine, clear night as we rounded Beachy Head. The lights of several ships dotted the horizon, none likely to close us so there was no reason to remain on the bridge. I knew the second mate as a conscientious officer who would keep his watch properly, yet I felt strangely reluctant to retire for the night. The ship was in automatic steering, with the wheelman keeping a lookout in the bridge wing. The second mate sensed my unwillingness to go, and bustled round making cocoa. Thus relaxed I handed over, giving the standard night orders for the first time.

'Don't hesitate to call me. I'd far rather be woken for nothing than not be called when things go wrong.'

'Aye aye sir,' said the second mate cheerfully, and off I went to my bunk. Our Atlantic crossing was straightforward. The low, flat, rocky island of Sombrero guards one of the Caribbean's safest entrances, and as its tall framework lighthouse appeared on the horizon one sunny afternoon, right on time, I was seized with a ridiculous feeling of triumphant excitement, as though I had never made a landfall before.

From time to time senior officers would ask advice, their polite way of seeking approval of their intentions in the running of the ship. The purser, who had known me since I was third mate in the *Melbourne Star*, looked in to discuss paying the crew their weekly sub; did I think we should have a pub lunch on Saturday instead of a sit-down meal; and (the real cause for his visit), had I the latest regulations about overtime payments for the cook? The mate wondered if it would be a good idea to paint the vacant passenger cabins, and would I prefer the sailors to do it on overtime in the evenings, or the cadets during the day? The mate, bless his heart, was making me feel still involved in mate's work. It comes as quite a shock to realise, after so many years, that you are no longer responsible for such jobs and that you must allow the mate to work without your continuous advice. Provided he's doing what you want, of course! The chief engineer dropped in before lunchtime most days, to discuss the job and compare notes over a pink gin. His technical advice was always welcome, and his willingness to discuss engineering matters much appreciated. I was now seeing people from a new angle.

The ship's company seemed to have settled in happily by the time we arrived at Willemstad, Curacao, for bunkers. As we went alongside the quay 'port side to' we let go the starboard anchor and paid out chain to be used to haul off when we came to leave, as we would not be using a tug. Late that night a burly Dutch pilot came to guide us on our way. As the mooring ropes were let go, we hove on the starboard anchor and used our twin screws to advantage to turn the ship around off the berth, lining her up for the run down the narrow channel to the sea. We had been tied up at a quay just inside the Schottegat, a large lagoon where oil refineries and tankers scented the trade wind with petroleum. The channel, called in Dutch Sint Anna Baai, runs for three quarters of a mile between stony cliffs and through the little town. Halfway down the channel the mate telephoned from forward to say he could not get up the anchor which was trailing along the bottom on 15 fathoms of chain. I mentioned this possibly dangerous fact to the pilot who grinned cheerfully.

'Never mind, captain. Plenty deep water outside. I go now and wish you good night. Cheerio!'

There was no danger of our anchor snagging anything, but why it would not come up was a mystery: my first departure from a foreign port, too. I decided to head south to avoid coastal shipping, instead of turning west towards Panama. Once clear of traffic we stopped engines, and I walked forward with the chief engineer to find the mate and the chief electrician adjusting the windlass motor to make it heave harder. Obviously there was something on the end of the chain cable much heavier than our 75 cwt anchor. We tried heaving again when the ship had lost way. Fortunately the night was fine and the sea calm. The windlass took in the chain a couple of links, and grunted to a stop as the contacts grew hot. We tried ahead, then astern, to produce a pendulous swing of the chain to release whatever was on its end. We paid out the chain rapidly for a few fathoms then applied the brake suddenly, unsuccesfully. After half an hour of backing and filling in this fashion, suddenly a deep roar rumbled from under the forefoot, the ship leapt in the water, and the chain slackened. We'shone our torches over the bulwarks to watch the anchor rise. Neatly hitched to it was a 25ft length of six-inch steel bar which looked as though it had recently shed a large chunk of reinforced concrete. We must have picked up a piece of the Sint Anna Baai bridge, part of which had collapsed a few months previously. Eventually our catch was disentangled and without further incident we proceeded to Panama and across the Pacific to Cook Strait, which separates the north and south islands of New Zealand.

In New Plymouth I was to change ships with Captain Jack Calabrase, (third mate of the *Saxon Star* when I sailed in her as a cadet). He would take the *English Star* home while I spent the next six months or so in the *Caledonia Star*, after which she would probably be scrapped. Now almost 30 years old, she was the company's oldest ship — an appropriate command for the company's newest master. A ship abroad must never be masterless, and while we were in New Plymouth, North Island, the *Caledonia Star* was due in Bluff, South Island, so the gap was filled for a couple of days by the *English Star's* mate, Howard Cook, becoming Captain Cook for the occasion. After I had handed over officially to him in the shipping office and his name was on the ship's register, I flew to Invercargill, arriving at Bluff shortly ahead of my new ship. With some apprehension I watched her arrive, for she and nearly all her people were strangers to me. Though obviously well kept, she certainly showed her age as she approached through a grey curtain of drizzle.

Built at Greenock Dockyard as the *Empire Wisdom*, a twin-screw steam up and downer with scotch boilers burning coal, she resembled the prewar vessels of the Clan Line, who managed her from 1942 until 1944 when she was allocated to Blue Star Line. Renamed *Royal Star* she carried general cargo out and frozen produce home for the next 17 years, and visited some of the tinier ports of Magellan Strait and Patagonia. After a spell laid up in the Fal she was re-engined with twin screw MAN diesels in 1962 and renamed *Caledonia Star* to put her in the 'C' Class, the ships which ran from Britain to the west coast of North America. She sailed with the *Catalina Star*, *Colorado Star*, *California Star* and *Columbia Star* for another nine years, but by 1971 the west coast trade was becoming containerised. A new *California* and *Columbia Star* were being built, fully cellular box boats which would cut the three-and-a-half-month round voyage to eight weeks. So the old ship sailed from the UK to New Zealand for the last time, to work for the Crusader Line. She had already made two voyages to Japan when I joined her.

During the 1950s a consortium of British companies — Blue Star, Port Line, Shaw Savill and P and O (as represented by the New Zealand Shipping Company) — formed Crusader Line to develop trade from New Zealand around the Pacific basin to Japan, the west coast of North America, and the West Indies. Even 20 years before the EEC New Zealand realised that she had to widen her primary produce markets.

The new company's first ship was the *Crusader*, a beautiful little pale green reefer which carried on her butter-coloured funnel a device incorporating St George's shield and a crusader's sword. Two similar ships, *Saracen*, and *Knight Templar*, followed, all manned by Shaw Savill officers and Chinese crews. The trio was supplemented by ships from the parent companies from time to time and it was customary to paint such ships in Crusader colours. But perhaps the sheer size of the *Caledonia Star's* funnel dissuaded anyone from repainting it, so we became the only 'Blue Star' vessel trading to the Land of the Rising Sun. As a concession we flew the Crusader house flag.

Caledonia Star **at Bluff**

I had a month to settle in while we loaded in Bluff, and another fortnight in Lyttelton, Gisborne and Auckland, for the Crusader Line was run on gentlemanly lines. My new command retained many endearing features of her past life, including steam steering gear. Though her main engines were beautiful diesels only nine years old, many of her auxiliaries still ran on steam provided by her one remaining scotch boiler which had long been converted to oil-firing, although it retained its coal fire bars in the furnace grate. The baker's oven and galley stove burned coal, and her refrigeration machinery included two steam engines with enormous flywheels which were probably the last of their kind afloat under the British flag. Some refrigeration engineer of the past — obviously a man in love with his work — had christened these machines Grizelda and Esmeralda and made them varnished name boards.

I had never visited Japan before. An old aunt of mine who had been working in Hong Kong when the Japs invaded, spent the war in an internment camp so I had no intention of being more than coldly polite to her captors. First port was Naha in Okinawa whence we sailed up the Sea of Japan to the little port of Otaru, near Sapporo, where the next Olympic ski trials were to take place. Ashore I found it a picturesque backdrop for The Mikado, complete with little maids dressed for the part. I was made much of by the agents in this little Hokkaido port, as it seemed that my predecessors, Captains Pitcher and Calabrase, had made a good impression here.

I had expected Japan to be much more advanced: even in the cities the average citizen did not seem to enjoy a high standard of living and few even owned a car. City dwellers occupied tiny flats and in the smaller ports many lived in cramped wooden, unpainted houses with sliding doors, lacking piped water. The dockers worked no harder than those in Liverpool and London — and were as untidy a bunch of litter louts as I had seen anywhere. Our crew's first job whenever we left port was to clean up their rubbish, and we wondered what had inspired the Japanese reputation for cleanliness and neatness. From Otaru we made a swift dash through Tsugaru Strait aided by a four-knot current. Forging along at 15 knots we looked forward to a run ashore that night to see what Kushiro had to offer. Without warning there was a thundering crash, and the ship stopped dead in her tracks shuddering like a frightened horse. Funnel, masts and sampson posts vibrated for a terrifying 15 seconds. The noise stopped as suddenly as it had begun, and we sailed on serenely. Although in deep water it was as though we had run over a reef and I wondered if we had caught a derelict fishing vessel. Tanks and bilges were sounded at once, but we were taking no water, and the vessel seemed none the worse for her experience. The mystery was solved that evening by the agent, Mr Nishifuji.

'We had minor earth tremor today, nothing significant.'

With an average 1,500 such tremors a year in and around Japan ours was hardly worth mentioning!

After the formalities Mr Nishifuji asked if he could bring a few guests to see the ship the following morning, including his worship the mayor. This particular week, it seemed, was devoted each year to ships and the sea. The mayoral party would visit each vessel in turn — we were the only British ship — and then attend a special church service. I pointed out that the *Caledonia Star* had no suitable public rooms, so the party would have to be entertained in my dayroom. 'How many will come?' I asked, as the agent was leaving. 'Maybe 10, 12. You make speech. I translate. No problem. Thank you so much.' And with that he was gone.

The mate suggested dressing ship overall in honour of the occasion which, I knew from experience, meant hard work — getting out all the flags, bending them onto a line stretched over the ship from forward to aft via the mastheads in a colourful 'rainbow' display. I appreciated his suggestion.

'What will you talk about?' asked the mate, a little anxiously, as my disparaging views of Japan were well-known onboard by now. Well, the war was a long time in the past, I told him, and if the British ostracised everyone they had fought they'd do precious little talking.

'Quite,' said the mate, leaving hurriedly. But the point was well made; what *would* I say?

Ten to eleven saw me pacing the deck in my best whites, nervously rehearsing my greeting and speech. The mayoral party was due to arrive at 11 o'clock and the Japs have a name for punctuality. But the time came and went and by quarter past I was wondering if they had found another, more interesting, ship maybe one which could speak Japanese. Five minutes later a dense, laughing throng swept round the end of the wharfside shed, dozens of them, led by two pretty girls in pink, attended by press cameras. The mate brought them to my room where I greeted each with my Japanese

149

version of 'Good morning!' The prettier of the two girls, Miss Port of Kushiro, curtsied and presented me with a huge bouquet of flowers while her shyly smiling partner gave me a wood carving of a fisherman spearing a salmon. I was touched. Coffee appeared and the mayor made a short speech welcoming us to Kushiro whose people appreciated the cargo we had brought which helped the port to survive. He hoped we would enjoy our stay here, and trusted we would soon return in safety and happiness to be with our cherished families again. I was impressed by the lack of cant in this elderly gentleman's quiet voice.

In reply I told them that this was my first visit to Japan, and that I had come full of prejudice as a result of the war, that I had found my previously held dislikes were dispelled by the friendliness and kindness which I had been shown in their country. I added that we, too, were glad of the trade which caused our ship to be here, and hoped that it would increase to benefit us all, bringing with it not only greater prosperity but a better understanding between our two peoples. It was hardly original stuff, but it seemed to go down well as they gave me a standing ovation. After more coffee and pleasantries they departed for the next ship. Nishifuji returned that evening all smiles. Our visit, he said, had been the best of the lot. Of seven ships visited, only in the *Caledonia Star* had they been invited into the captain's 'own house.' Only I had made a speech and, without a doubt, we had the best show of flags. I felt we had done our little bit for Anglo-Japanese relations and the agent thought so too, it seemed, as he insisted on taking me at once on a Japanese pub-crawl. His director accompanied us (and signed all the bills.) We not only drank but ate also in each house, and I began to appreciate the considerable stamina needed to stay the pace at an international level. The director was a smartly-suited gentleman in his 60s, grey haired and dignified, who spoke barely accented English. Much later in the evening, he and I were propping up a bar exchanging life histories.

'You British amaze me, he told me. 'You never know when you are beaten, and you are progressive.'

I had thought it was the Japanese who were making the progress today, and said so.

'You have it over us all the time', he insisted. 'Your methods of industrial negotiation are highly advanced. You are prepared to go metric with your weights and measures; you even change your money. Whereas we Japanese are too damn hidebound!'

I found I was enjoying Japan after all. One expects the young to be less prejudiced, but even their elders seemed to respect the British, due perhaps to people like my old aunt, who had born the rigours of prison camp with dignity and even humour. Their Japanese guards, impressed by this reaction, talked about these uncrushable people at home.

Next day Nishifuji took me to lunch where, through the restaurant window, I watched a crowd of children in their smart blazers and white socks returning to school. Nishifuji was watching me.

'I know what you're thinking,' he said quietly. 'You're trying to equate the things we did during the war with the people you see here.' I had to nod.

'Prewar we Japanese lived feudally, especially in country districts. For instance, a landlord, a samurai, could take a village girl, married or single, and keep her as long as he wanted. If her husband or family objected, the landlord made sure they disappeared. But during the '30s Western ideas of democracy began to infiltrate our society, and the landlords realised that if these ideas gained hold, they would lose power, so they began to denigrate the white people. By the time war came we had been indoctrinated into believing that the white people were devils, to be destroyed like rats. It was, we were told, our mission to exterminate them.' When he saw the disbelief on my face he said soberly, 'It was all too easy. We were shown movies and photographs of English and Dutch punishing people with yellow and brown skins for small crimes by hangings and beatings. We thought you, then, quite as bad as you later came to think we were. Hence' — he raised his hands in a gesture of despair — 'our atrocities. Once they start, it is terribly easy for both sides to justify them.'

From Kushiro we spent several days in Tokyo, Yokohama, Nagoya and Kobe. In Yokohama one of our donkey greasers (now known as motormen) was admitted to a hospital run by American nuns. Each afternoon the agent's car took me up the long hill to visit the patient, and I generally walked back, picking a different route each time. Thus I discovered that while the crowded main streets of Yokohama are much the same as in any other city the back streets, a few yards away, revealed another world. Small, unpainted houses of wood with high peaked roofs and curling tiles crouched beside old warehouses and ancient temples. Cottage

151

industries opened directly onto the street, and I could look in without rudeness. In one I watched old ladies baling newspaper, with which the Japs seemed obsessed. Indeed, part of our cargo from New Zealand contained several tons of it. Elsewhere, coopers secured together the staves of wooden barrels not with iron hoops but with plaited rope; men made hammers, fitted handles onto axe heads; made dye in huge vats while a dense puce effluent ran into the harbour. Pollution was recognised and deplored, but little done to restrict it. Chimneys belched forth, and it was amusing (we thought) to see well-dressed city people wearing white smog masks in the streets, whether the air was smoggy or not.

The harbours were full of ships, for Japan, being a group of islands, depends upon its coastal trade to a much greater extent than Britain. Barges clustered around us in every port. The crew consisted of a young man and his wife, often with a baby strapped to her back, and it was common to see them nimbly shipping their barge's hatch covers while baby slept soundly. When they were ready to leave, father went below to start the engine while mother and baby took the wheel.

White flags with the green cross of safety flew everywhere, but, around the docks at any rate, flag waving and lip service seemed the extent of safety precautions. One morning we watched a waterborne procession making its way round Nagoya harbour, protesting against the American LASH ships. These mammoth vessels carry their container-filled Lighters Aboard Ship and need never go alongside, thus saving port dues. The ship's gantry crane hoists her lighters in and out while the ship lies at anchor. In theory the Lash ships are a dream of economy, dispensing with much of the port labour who consequently saw them as a threat to their livelihoods so that few such ships were allowed to work as intended because of local union pressure. Although labour savers they were inordinately heavy on fuel. The loss with all hands in the North Atlantic of Hapag Lloyd Lines' *Munchen* in December, 1978 showed just how vulnerable such ships were in heavy weather. Some years before this disaster an American second mate who had sailed in Lash ships told me how his ship was pitching heavily when a sea came aboard flooding the bridge, which was right forward. Suddenly he found himself waist deep in water, the scuppers too small to drain quickly. Had the water penetrated the wheelhouse steering console the vessel could have lost helm and broached, a situation which can lead to a ship capsizing very quickly.

Shortly before our visit the All Japan Seamen's Union went on strike which ended only when the owners transferred many of their ships to foreign flags and manned them with Koreans and Taiwanese. Union jobs disappeared overnight. This move also lessened the Japanese custom of ending a ship's name with the word 'Maru', as today at least a quarter of their merchant fleet sails under other flags. Even the Japs have difficulty in explaining the meaning of Maru: something between a temple, an inner belief, almost yet not quite a god. Applied to ships' names it was meant originally, to secure divine protection.

Japan's busy coastal waters provided an excellent training ground for an apprentice shipmaster like myself, particularly in the port approaches. Collisions occurred daily though not, I hasten to add, involving the *Caledonia Star*! The worst offenders were the vessels wearing the flags of convenience of Liberia and Panama.

Fishermen abounded. At night the sea would be covered to the horizon with their bobbing white lights, through which we picked our way with care. After a month around Japan it was a holiday to set off on the quiet run back to Auckland, even with the added excitement of evading a typhoon, as directed by Billy Nellist. We invariably began and ended our spell round the New Zealand coast at Auckland. Our second run north, it was said, would probably be our last before the ship was scrapped. A Wellington lady, Mrs Caddis, made us a 29 ft pennant, one foot for each year of the ship's life, which we flew from our foremast on departure from every port thereafter.

In Auckland we took aboard some show jumpers complete with their Japanese trainer, Kikki, who had been sent to buy three of the best for an establishment near Moji, in South Japan. Several of us had birthdays on the way north, and Kikki was surprised to find that in a British ship it is the birthday boy who buys the drinks. His own birthday arrived, and he insisted on being one of the boys. When he had 'a few onboard' his face became a bright coppery red, but he took the resultant cracks about the Rising Sun in good part. We had a farewell party for the ship herself in Osaka attended by all hands including, of course, Kikki, where we treated ourselves to a half pint pewter tankard each, inscribed 'Farewell *Caledonia Star*, Taiwan, 1971.'

This was the first ship I had been in where the crew as well as the officers had their own bar. Both ran well, without trouble, and I was pleasantly surprised to find that far from increasing drunkenness such bars abolished it. This was partly because it was accepted that the bar would be closed if trouble arose, but mainly demonstrated that if chaps are trusted they will generally behave. She was also the first ship I knew where people onboard had organised themselves into long-running competitions at scrabble, cribbage, dominoes, draughts, chess, and darts. The two teams, Officers and Gentlemen, took turns at providing hospitality. Indeed, the social life of the *Caledonia Star* was the most enlightened I had ever come across.

Finally I was ordered to Khaosiung, Taiwan, for breaking up. As Communist China had just been admitted to the United Nations and feelings ran high across Formosa Strait, I took the longer way round, east of the island, rather than risk getting caught in crossfire. The town was on a war footing: a harbour boom guarded by a destroyer, the surrounding hills bristling with rocket launchers directed at the mainland. After several days at anchor off the entrance a pilot came out, accompanied by two Customs officers who proceeded to throw the contents of our medicine chest into the sea — to prevent drug smuggling, they said. As the harbour boom closed behind us, and technicians dismantled our radio equipment, I realised that this was the end. The lagoon where ships are broken up is a spooky nautical graveyard where dozens of ships lie at crazy angles in tiers, waiting to be torn apart under the burner's torch and fed to the insatiable steel mills.

Far removed from most natural sources of iron ore, the Far East has long been interested in buying the world's scrap. A ship is sold at so many US dollars per ton of her light displacement. In other words, if the ship, without cargo, were to be weighed on a huge pair of scales, her price amounted to that weight of steel. All else is of little importance, even her brass and copper; and most of her woodwork is burned. Bonfires were dotted over a desolate no man's land between the lagoon and the distant, smoky chimneys of the steel mills. Here the people who broke up the ships lived in squalid shacks made from old timber and canvas. There were no quays. A ship would be run aground beside the bank, the next ship would go alongside her, and so on. The ships near us had long been abandoned by their crews and ours was the only one showing lights at night, a cheerful spark of life in the land of the dead. We were run, without ceremony, into the side of the *Texaco Kenya*, a conventional tanker built in 1952, where a man and boy were burning off the bridge deck and wheelhouse. When they had cut round, a wire rope was hooked on, and a derrick from a ship's mast standing on the bank, powered by old ships' winches nearby, swung the huge piece of ship onto a trailer which was then towed to the mill. Dismemberment went on all the time, accidents were common, and life was cheap. Fires broke out frequently in her cargo tanks and our crew became adept at extinguishing them before they spread to our ship. Nobody else seemed to care, but *we* were still interested in preserving what was ours until the time came to leave. We lived aboard for eight days while the financial details of the sale were concluded in London.

A Taiwan policeman took up residence in the pilot's cabin, adjacent to mine. One cold night I invited him in for a cup of tea. He could speak and read a little English, and soon noticed the *Daily Telegraph* world map on my dayroom bulkhead. His face clouded as he studied it.

'There is no Mongolia,' he assured me. The Mongolia on my map, he said, was part of China, of which his Taiwan leaders were the only legal government.

On the ninth day the agent gave me the coded telegram which advised that the deal had been concluded, instructing me to sign my ship over to her purchasers. We could then proceed home, our heavy baggage having left already by air freight. At my desk for the last time, I signed the necessary documents, closely watched by the agent, two Customs officers, and our friendly policeman. At the last signature the Customs officers began stripping my bunk, stuffing the pillow cases with sheets and blankets, and taking the curtains from the port holes on their way ashore. Such items were, it seemed, Customs' perks. I had been favoured this morning by a rare visit from the agency manager himself, who asked me eagerly, 'Have you please a screwdriver, Captain?'

A modest request, I thought, and gave him one from my desk drawer. To my amazement he bounded up to the wheelhouse, laughing like a schoolboy, and unscrewed our brassbound teak steering wheel, which he took ashore under his arm. The policeman, no longer friendly, ripped my map off the bulkhead and tore it into shreds.

Our mid-day meal was simmering on the galley stove but by this time we could not leave quickly enough, for scenes like those in my accommodation had been enacted all over the ship. As one sailor said, it was like seeing the corpse of a friend being robbed. I took down the Queen's picture and put it in my suit case. At least they would not have *her*! As we chugged away in the launch, a curl of smoke drifted up from the galley chimney, and I noticed that several of my hardbitten old shipmates had tears in their eyes.

Old ships on new trades

Chapter 12

1971-1973

THE *MELBOURNE STAR* in which I had been third mate in 1956, was unloading in Liverpool when I joined her in May, 1972. She carried her 24 years well, but as a ship ages her owners must balance potential earnings against the costs of keeping her in class. In the reefer trades this depends on world food demand; an upsurge in meat requirements by Russia or Iran, for example, may provide employment for the older, well-found ship. But no such reprieve was at hand for the *Melbourne Star* which I was to take to London, unload, and release to the Greeks for use as a floating cold store at Piraeus.

Leaving the Mersey on the evening tide, we rounded Land's End next morning. Shortly before midday I looked in on the chief engineer. Well over 60, Mr C K L Brown was more sprightly than many men half his age. He thoughtfully proffered me a pre-lunch gin.

'When do you want to arrive, Captain?' he asked.

'If we can reach the Royal Docks' entrance by dawn they'll probably take us in at once. Any later and it means anchoring until the next tide.'

He lit a cigarette. 'What speed do you need?'

'If you could make 20, it would be in the bag, provided we don't get fog of course.'

'I'll do what I can,' said Cyril.

Up the Channel I could feel her twin B and W's building up power, and the watchkeeping mate's positions pencilled on the chart showed that Cyril was certainly giving her the works. We overtook everything in sight, including a large passenger liner racing for Southampton.

We caught the tide, and the second mate handed me the chit with reverence.
'She's averaged 23, sir!'
Fred Carr, the dock pilot, overheard.
'Cyril here is he? He always said he'd get 23 knots out of this one, given the chance. Not bad for a swan song!'
I left her in the King George V Dock, London, and joined the *Queensland Star*, newly arrived in Cardiff with apples from Tasmania. One of a class of four, she was one of those lovely cargo liners of the 50s, built for the Australian trade, especially for the carriage of Queensland chilled beef, a trade which did not develop as hoped. But the ships were splendidly versatile and 25 years later two of them, the *Gladstone* and *Rockhampton Stars*, were still with us.

Apples unloaded, we moved across Alexandra Dock to a layby berth, making way for the newly arrived *Southland Star*, also in with apples. I was left for a while in charge of both ships. The *Queensland*'s name was being changed to *Brasilia Star* after the new capital. Container ships were already displacing the older vessels from the Australian trade but South America still offered employment, especially now that the four passenger ships on that service were to be scrapped. As my wife and two younger children were coming for the weekend and the *Southland Star* had more spacious accommodation, we took up residence there.

In the early hours of Sunday I awoke uneasily and went on deck. It had blown hard all night but both ships had been well secured to their quays. Through driving rain, however, I saw that our bow was 80 ft off the wharf! Modern mooring ropes, mostly synthetic, are flexible, which means that they can stretch like elastic bands until they flick themselves off the quayside bollards. Though our low stern was still alongside, all but one of the lines from our high forecastle had cast themselves off, stretching the last to its limit. The mate was already on deck with the few sailors left aboard over the weekend, and the bosun was climbing down the stern. Jumping onto the quay he seized the heaving line thrown from forward. Five of us, wrestling with the stiff ropes in the wild, wet darkness eventually hove her back alongside with the aid of our winches. The mate and I then kept watch from his cabin until dawn, as the wind slowly abated. One of the stewards had returned about 2 am, he told me, to find the ship blowing off the quay, mooring ropes twanging like harp strings. Shouting at the top of his voice above the gale he managed to alert the second cook. The night watchman was forward, trying to cope singlehanded with what had rapidly become a job for more than one man. The second cook called the mate, who called the sailors, as I awoke. (There had been no time to call me!) Had she broken adrift and blown across the dock, two Blue Star ships would have collided with each other whereupon I, as master of both, could soon have found myself master of neither! The children of course, were disappointed at missing the night's 'fun'.

A few days later another master came to the *Southland Star*, my family went home, and I took the *Brasilia Star* on her 'maiden voyage' to Buenos Aires— my first visit since I had been third mate 15 years earlier. A gale was blowing as we arrived off the mouth of the River Plate and I was instructed by radio to anchor near the Recalada lightship. A *pampero* had lowered the water in the estuary which precluded navigation, but after three days the wind abated enabling us to weigh anchor and embark a pilot, who informed me that the wreck of the *Tan Chi* had been blown into the centre of the dredged channel. We would have to go west of the deep channel, into the shallows to avoid her.

Our pilot, a middle-aged Argentinian, spoke good English in a mournful voice which his sombre clothes and drooping black moustache did nothing to enliven. As we began our run up the broad estuary the wind dropped and fog descended. Our 16 knots was too fast for safety and I warned the pilot to slow down. With a typical South American gesture he cocked his head to one side, smiled sadly, and raised his hands palms up.

'If we slow down, and touch bottom, we stick, and stop, and the tide is falling. If we maintain 16 knots, and touch bottom, we probably slide over into deeper water.'

The *Brasilia Star* **lowered her ensign as she passed the burned-out hull of the** *Royston Grange*

It was a nice choice so we kept going, watching the radar screen intently. Returning down the Plate to Montevideo after loading meat, we berthed ahead of the burned-out hulk of the *Royston Grange*. No paint remained on her rusted steelwork, her decks were hideously buckled, and her anchor chains hung in festoons around a gaping hole in her bow. Outward bound from Buenos Aires she had collided with the inbound tanker *Tan Chi*. There was a flash, an explosion, and a fire which raged through the *Royston Grange*, killing all onboard. The few survivors from the *Tan Chi* had no idea what caused the collision. The Plate is notorious for the cushioning effect of the sides of the dredged channel causing vessels to steer badly. We lowered our ensign as we passed, and the same thought gripped us all, 'there but for the grace of God go I.'

The South American run has the advantage of short, regular voyages, attractive to a married man, but I was not to remain on it. The *Brasilia Star* was bound for the Tyne to fit modern hatchcovers — and the *Montreal Star* was due in Vancouver requiring a new captain. After a few days, I was on a plane from Heathrow, together with the chief engineer, Paul Gleeson, who had been first-trip chief when I was first-trip master in the *English Star,* and the purser, Barry Byrne from Sydney, a shipmate from the *South Africa Star*. Our little flight party was completed by the electrician and a first-voyage cadet. We arrived onboard the *Montreal Star* in time for lunch next day, and sailed at 10 pm for San Francisco. No sooner had we rounded Cape Flattery than we ran into dense fog, the radar broke down, and the echo sounder failed. We were back to basic principles, as taught by the Brothers Nellist. Creeping

When the Barbadian crew brought their girl friends to board the
Montreal Star's **lifeboat it was the Bosun who saved the day and their reputation. It wasn't the girls who caused the trouble but their husbands seeking them**

along at four knots we blew a prolonged blast on our siren at intervals not exceeding two minutes, and kept a particularly sharp lookout. Visibility improved two days later as we approached the Golden Gate, and once over the arrival formalities it was time for the old man to catch up on his jetlag. The radar was repaired at our next port, Los Angeles, whence we took departure for Honolulu to load pineapples for New Zealand; from which it may be gathered that the *Montreal Star* was now on the North American service of Crusader Line.

She had been built nine years before in Sunderland at Bartram's, a now defunct yard which had launched ships since the days of collier brigs directly into the North Sea. They were then towed round to the Wear for fitting out. The *Montreal Star* and her several sisters were constructed there for the ECNA service — from Australia to the East Coast of North America which was now containerised. She had a Barbadian crew and British officers, the first time I had sailed with black men. Not only were they splendid seamen — many had grown up in the islands schooners — but they were gentlemen also. I liked their slow speech, reminiscent of more gracious days, and their courtesy, which ensured they were never short of girl friends in port. Seafaring in the *Montreal Star* was the kind lads dream about. Coral islands in the sun, or under a gibbous moon, white beaches, palms nodding in the trade wind. North from New Zealand we called at Levuka, once the capital of Fiji, now an idyllic backwater, so unpretentious that it does not even boast a picture postcard.

Levuka has two claims to history: the Fijian chiefs placed their islands under the protection of Queen Victoria here in 1875, and Prince Charles granted Fiji independence on the same spot 95 years later. In between, the German raider *Seeadler* (a sailing ship captured from the British) called here for provisions during the First World War. The inhabitants left town when they saw the Germans coming, but Count Felix von Luckner took his stores from the shop and left a note thanking the shopkeeper and promising payment after the war. It is now a treasured relic in the Levuka clubhouse.

Hurricanes occasionally sweep the Fiji Isles against which eventuality some of the wooden buildings are held down with ships' anchor chains, but for most of the year the weather is fine, the sea warm and calm, and the natives friendly. We loaded tuna fish in Levuka, from a recently built Japanese cold store, for Los

Angeles where it became 'Chicken o' the Sea'. It was caught by Japanese, Taiwanese and Koreans who wander across the South Pacific in search of their catch, using lines stretching for miles, with thousands of hand-baited hooks.

One evening we put on a ship's party for a dozen guests — the Japanese at the cold store and their wives, the agent, and the Customs officer. Such parties were held on the bridge deck, scrubbed until the planks gleamed white, sheltered by a spotless canvas awning, set about with coloured lights and national flags. We had no Rising Sun so the mate painted a large red disc on a clean white sheet. The party must have been a success because on our next visit, two months later, our guest list was more than 40.

We had just arrived in Levuka when there was a knock at my door. A young man entered whom I thought was from the Agent's office. In fact he was a member of the US Peace Corps working as a teacher in the nearby Queen Elizabeth High School. Would I allow him to work a passage to San Francisco for Christmas and then perhaps, bring him back next voyage for the spring term? I liked his novel approach, but the days of working a passage belonged to the past; international officialdom has seen to that. But we did have a vacant passenger cabin so I told him to return next morning, when I would be able to say yea or nay. To sign him on as a passenger-worker I needed company permission.

A telegram to our Wellington office brought a favourable reply — obviously the idea appealed to our general manager also — and next morning I took our recruit to the shipping office to be signed on the Articles as a supernumary at the nominal wage of a shilling per month. The shipping master, who was also the Customs officer, a courteous and pleasant Indian, took us into the low, wooden office by the harbour's edge. From a cupboard he took a huge green leather tome and opened it to the accompaniment of dust in little clouds. Levuka had been a busy port once. Framed faded sepia photographs showed the harbour packed with sailing ships. The wooden jetty at which our ship lay had been built at such an angle that a four-masted barque full of copra could use the prevailing trade wind to sail off to sea without use of a tug. But business of late had not been brisk. The last entry in the register of crew changes had been made in 1941.

Our passage-worker was keen and worked hard at the various jobs the mate gave him, starting at six thirty each morning with our bridge deck scrub. This kept us fit and also helped maintain the ship's appearance. The carpenter made us heavy 'bears' — longhandled scrubbing brushes — and the lamptrimmer mixed a powerful solution of detergent, caustic, and a few secret ingredients in a metal dustbin labelled 'Captain'. Normal bridge roles were reversed for this hour — while the ship steered herself in automatic, the sailor of the watch kept lookout and told us if anything hove into view. The mate, Tom Crookall, and I, together with the passage-worker, scrubbed the deck, hosed down, and dried off with the squeegee while the bosun and his men took on the boat deck: the resulting competition between officers and gentlemen gave us the cleanest decks afloat.

Between Honolulu and Cape Flattery we were overtaken by a south westerly storm, one of those which take time building up and seem as though they will last for ever, 'long foretold, long last!' Darkly lowering clouds enveloped us in frequent torrents of rain while a banshee wind tore loose anything not firmly secured, building up such a sea and swell astern that, as we rolled, we looked *up* from the bridge at the foaming crests parading past. She rode like a seagull, but I put a man on the wheel nevertheless. Had the automatic steering developed a fault under such conditions she could have broached to and rolled over like a toy boat in a bathtub. Planing along the crests, swooping into the deep furrows, rising again as the next awesome roller overtook us, it was exhilarating 'sailing'. Numerous birds sought refuge around our decks, to be fed on fish scraps by the cadets. The only birds remaining airborne were the albatross and Mother Carey's Chickens, those little stormy petrels which seem to delight in rough weather. A brown Hawaiian albatross, one of the very few of its kind to live north of the Line, wheeled around barely moving his enormous wings until he dived into our wake for galley refuse.

For days we drove north east towards Canada, with never a glimpse of the sun, moon or star. How fast we were going was difficult to decide. The engines gave us a good 18, but how much help the wind and current contributed could only be a guess, and how much our pitching offset this we could only estimate. If only we could get a sight! Satellite navigation systems, then, were things we read about in technical journals. The evening before our landfall a couple of stars peeped out at twilight, when the horizon was briefly visible between squalls. The mate and I had been waiting with sextants ready, silently praying for a quick chance to fix our position. He took one star, I another, and then we managed

163

to catch one more each before torrential rain blotted out everything around us. But four stars give a good fix and we were much nearer to the coast than we had believed possible. She *had* planed along, at 20 knots plus! An hour after dark Cape Flattery's light winked at us through the rain. We were on course.

As we swept into Juan de Fuca Strait the swell abated and when we embarked our pilot off Victoria the calm water and fresh scent of pinewoods helped us to forget the stormy seas outside, especially when we came to Vancouver, ablaze with Christmas lights. Our passage-worker arrived home in time and we spent Christmas Day in Tacoma, where we discovered that our Barbadian crew knew every carol in the book!

When we arrived back in Fiji we had to anchor for several days in Suva Harbour as the deepwater berth was occupied by the P & O cruise-liner, *Himalaya*. Our agent asked if we required a liberty boat, a matter which the chief, Paul Gleeson, and I, had already discussed. Liberty boats are expensive and we had two perfectly good motor lifeboats which would benefit from exercise. We would run our own boat — the chief and I — with the passage-worker as crew. So, we drew up a timetable and posted copies on the ship's noticeboards. Last boat back from the Golden Dragon 0230.

That evening we took the lads, much to their delight, to the stone steps beside the inter-island schooner berths. As promised, we were back at the steps on time. A merry throng of Barbadians came along the wharf accompanied by island girls who bounced into the boat with big grins, to our bosun's consternation.

'Ladies', he exclaimed. 'You can't board a ship at anchor. What *would* the neighbours think!'

Hoots of Barbadian laughter greeted this and the girls, still grinning, scrambled ashore. No doubt they would return when the ship berthed but that, as our American cousins say, 'was something else.' It's not the girls who cause the trouble — it's their husbands who come seeking them.

From Fiji we headed south to Auckland, where I watched a 12 ft sloop arrive one sunny morning, as though she had returned from a fortnight's inshore cruise. Only her steering vane indicated deep seas. Almost barrel-shaped with triple fin keels, painted light blue, the name *Sea Egg* suited her. That evening, by chance, our engineer officers met her owner, skipper and crew in a pub. John Riding, a tall, softly-spoken Englishman had sailed her from England and his current pressing problem was laundering clothes, so he was offered the use of our washing machine. Thereafter was much visiting between our two ships.

Paul and I dropped in one evening to see him aboard his *Sea Egg*, huddled among much larger yachts at Marsden Wharf. His bunk occupied the entire starboard side of the cabin; a couple of feet away the port side was filled with lockers. No distress flares or rockets, we noticed, which he confirmed cheerfully, saying that if he got into trouble he would not inconvenience others. He knew the risks, but did not believe the world owed him a living. His modesty and love of sailing impressed us. Sitting out on the cabin roof we yarned as dusk deepened. The simple act of fumbling in one's pocket for a cigarette caused the boat to rock, emphasising her tininess.

Next evening I happened to be on deck by our gangway when three men dressed in clean jeans and shirts came aboard, carrying the box of movie films which has become a *laisser-passer* to ships of all flags. Films are loaned from ship to ship for a night, enabling the naturally hospitable jolly jack to meet his counterparts from many lands, as well as see different movies. Taking the trio to be from the Hamburg ship astern I bade them good evening in German.

'No sir,' they grinned, 'we are Russians,' and pointed to the Soviet ship across the dock.

Never having met Russians before, I invited them to our officers' bar, a comfortable little room closely resembling an English country pub. Their eyes lit up as they entered, and yes, they would indeed like a drink please. 'No vodka; whisky please, if you have it!'

John *Sea Egg* Riding, having finished his dhobi, was present, and at first they seemed disconcerted by his fluent Russian. But they soon relaxed. Russian seamen, we had heard, are accompanied wherever they go ashore by a Party Member, and I had mentally allotted this role to the small dark one who suddenly dozed off, glass in hand. He spent the rest of the evening in a corner of the settee, dozing gently. At midnight our guests left, helping their shipmate down the gangway, looking worried. Next evening the two non-sleepers returned, bringing their doctor who spoke excellent English, to apologise for the man who fell asleep, and to thank me for not reporting him to their captain!

Their ship was from Leningrad, and we learned that the Soviet merchant navy, trading world-wide, is divided into regional 'companies': the Far East Line based in Vladivostok, the Black Sea Line from Odessa or Novorossiisk, and the Baltic company registered at Leningrad. Their ship was loading wool for Leningrad. They seemed delighted to be shown over the *Montreal Star* and were clearly astonished at our crew recreation room, where a swinging party was in progress. Strobe lighting, well stocked bar, music, girls — it was like a Barbadian night club, and a beaming black able seaman, immaculate as barman in white shirt and bow tie served them drinks on the house. The Russians looked at each other. Were these the downtrodden black colonials of British Imperialism? On their own ship not even the officers were allowed a bar! Aboard the Russian ship the following evening they treated us to a bottle of vodka and caviar, in the doctor's cabin, and conversation ranged widely. They were keenly interested in our views of world affairs, In Vietnam the war still raged. Was this not wicked? It was, we said, but so was the Soviet invasion of Czechoslovakia. Solemnly they agreed.

Their ship was modern and comfortable, and I was shown all over, including her radio room. Political slogans were on the bulkheads of every public room and alleyway, and photographs of the hierarchy frowned down at us. (They must have thought our ship very bare — no slogans, and our only portrait was that of the Queen in the saloon!) The Russian captain and his senior officers dined in an alcove off the officers' saloon, and the crew ate elsewhere. All in all, she seemed much more autocratic than my own ship. But, by the time we left Auckland, Anglo-Soviet relations were at a cordial level.

We saw John Riding frequently. He was always welcome aboard, and told us something of the practice and philosophy of small boat sailing. His greatest headache was finding room aboard *Sea Egg* for food and water. In rough weather off the Californian coast his boat had rolled over once, but she had righted herself, and he had survived to write a couple of books about his adventures. He now intended sailing to Australia, then on to England, to become the first man to do so in a boat so small. But somewhere in the stormy Tasman the *Sea Egg* foundered, and no trace of her was ever found. We mourned John's passing.

We sailed from Levuka at 1500 on a Wednesday, bound for Honolulu and Vancouver with cargo which included a small consignment of cased New Zealand wines carefully stowed amongst a much bigger consignment of onions in netting sacks. Heading north-east across the Koro Sea towards Nanuku Passage we retarded clocks 24 hours at midnight for the International Date Line. At 0200 the bosun, who suffered from insomnia, was pacing the afterdeck outside his cabin when he heard noises from below. Putting his ear to the deck he heard sounds, as of wooden cases being prised open — voices — laughter!

Going straight to the bridge he told the second mate keeping the middle watch, and was given the key to the ladder hatch, urged to call the lamptrimmer, and investigate, carefully. Opening number four hatch, the two Barbadians shouted down, 'Come out stowaway!' Out like a jack-in-the-box shot a young man, who made straight for the ship's side and would have been over and into the sea had not our lads restrained him. They brought him to the bridge, where I had been called. He was a young Fijian, slightly intoxicated and inclined to sullen silence until the bosun said sharply,

'You answer politely when the captain address you!'

In reply to my questions he told me that he wanted to seek work in America. Was he alone? No, two friends were still in that hold place, amongst the onions. The hatch was again unlocked and two more stowaways appeared, all three in their late teens. They had made a cosy little nest among the onions and stocked it with bottles of water, warm clothes, and food. They would not have starved, and may well have reached Honolulu undetected had they not found the wine. I paced the bridge, wondering what to do. If I took them to Honolulu they would be arrested and the ship fined. They would be sent back to Fiji, by air, under armed guard who would be on a return ticket and would stay at least one night in Fiji. All bills would be charged to the ship. On the other hand, to put back to Levuka would waste a day, and also several thousand pounds worth of fuel, wages and food. We would be a day late in Honolulu, which I knew was not crucial on this voyage. I turned

167

back, advising London, Wellington and Fiji by radio. The time was 0300.

Off the island the sea was calm and blue and the little town dozed in hot sunshine at the foot of the green, forest-covered hills. A boat came alongside our lowered gangway as we slowed down. When our three heroes were brought back on deck they failed to recognise their home from seaward. When invited to step down the gangway they thought we were casting them into the sea and resisted vigorously with wild, rolling eyes. When shown the boat and told they were going home in it, they were much relieved and left us in high humour.

Not having altered the clocks again, we were on our way towards Honolulu at exactly 1500 — 24 hours after our first departure, same day, same date.

Family Odyssey

Chapter 13

1973-1974

BLUE STAR LINE WIVES had accompanied their husbands on voyages for several years, but children had been permitted only to make short coastal trips. In 1973, to enable wives who were also mothers to make the occasional longer voyage, it was decided to allow children to go deep sea, and the Kinghorn family was the first to be so privileged.

My wife and I were delighted. Elder daughter Jennifer — deep into O level studies — was happy to stay at home with Granny; Michael, aged 12, cavorted around the house gleefully, but Susan, 10, was less enthusiastic at being separated from certain horses of her aquaintance — but she warmed to the idea after she had been assured that there *were* horses in New Zealand! We had only a fortnight to prepare for our voyage — which I estimated would take about three months. Both the children's head teachers were enthusiastic and readily gave leave of absence. Books were provided so that schoolwork could continue on voyage, and the children were instructed to commit everything they could to paper in the form of diaries and project books. (They still make interesting reading.)

We flew from Newcastle to Amsterdam on October 29 to pick up the ship. The children, flying for the first time, watched spellbound as familiar landmarks unfolded below — then the blue-grey sea, and finally the windmills and canals of Holland, to be seen at closer range from the bus to Rotterdam where we stood on the quayside and watched our ship come up river. I could still remember my excited trepidation on joining *my* first ship, so could appreciate something of our children's feelings as they clambered up the gangway. However, we found the *Tasmania Star* was warm and welcoming after the cold quayside wait, and she had that faint

The *Tasmania Star* carried the first Blue Star family ever to venture deep sea

pervasive smell of 'a real ship'.

A single-screw turbine vessel built in 1950 at Birkenhead, 12,604 gross tons, she was one of the company's largest. With accommodation for 12 passengers, there was plenty of deck space — two nine-hole golf courses, a tennis court and a quoits pitch. Above the fore end of the boat deck was the passenger deck where those who wished could enjoy the sunshine undisturbed by exuberant children. She was a fine ship but even the finest ship has limitations and we knew before we joined that our laundry facilities would be restricted to a couple of plastic buckets.

Next day we sailed for Le Havre (where to their parents' delight the children found that everyone did not speak English, and school French had to be used). In Antwerp the vessel had loaded Belgian crystal goblets; in Le Havre French wines. The dockers gained access to both and drank the best from the best. When I threatened to bring in the police I was told by the agent that if I did the whole port would strike. So much for French subtlety! Damage was noted and liability accepted by the stevedoring company. Had it not been, duty would have been charged in New Zealand on no-longer-existent cargo.

The children's first taste of heavy weather came crossing a

stormy Gulf of Lyons — as notorious as Biscay. Life improved at Genoa, especially on the day we went to Portofino by car. By late November the weather was still mild and sunny, most of the tourists had left, and we saw the picturesque little town at its best. Genoa itself was like nothing the children had seen — except in films — and the older parts of that ancient city could have been a backdrop for grand opera, especially in the evenings when narrow alleyways disappeared into black darkness between tall, washing-festooned tenements, beside which pools of yellow light spilled onto the cobbles from shop windows and quaint street lamps.

Some condenser tubes were leaking which our chief had to repair, resulting in more oily water than our sludge tank could accommodate. I asked the agent to send a sludge barge to take the surplus. This, he said, would be expensive, adding that if I were a Greek captain I would tell the chief to pump it into the harbour at night. I asked what if I were a Greek captain, and did this, and were caught? He laughed — a stiff fine, maybe prison. He hired a barge. Two minutes after pumping into the barge began, there was a bang and the pipe burst at the coupling, spraying oily water everywhere, including into the harbour. Fortunately, the harbourmaster saw the joke.

Below decks we carried steel in all shapes and sizes, with machinery, toys, chemicals, furniture, cement, paint — and the aforementioned Belgian glassware and French wine. Cased car parts and lorry chassis on the upper hatch covers were surrounded by serried ranks of bulldozers and yellow tractors. There was even a sports car on the boat deck, as at the last minute it could not be stowed below. Tarpaulined down, it was out of the way — cargo on the boat deck which restricts access to the lifeboats is unacceptable, of course. None of the cargo was in containers. By now we realised — after a month on the continent — that our 'three-month' voyage would be a little longer.

Tasmania Star's **deck cargo — before the box boats**

The Atlantic was calm and sunny — Funchal, Madeira's capital — like a travel poster as we steamed past, bound for St Lucia Passage into the Caribbean, and Willemstad for bunkers. In the Panama Canal we were delayed — most unusually — by fog, necessitating a tie-up at buoys, which enabled us to see the Canal both by day and by night, when we admired the subdued floodlighting along the banks and tingled to eerie 'Tarzan noises' from the jungle. The all-American Canal pilots were happy to explain the Canal's wonders and regarded our two wide-eyed little Geordies with amused interest.

As we began our haul across the Pacific, the first world fuel crisis hit the headlines, and I was radioed to conserve bunkers by reducing speed. Our 10 passengers would not arrive in New Zealand for Christmas after all, so as compensation we went through the Galapagos Channel and, later, stopped for a couple of hours off Pitcairn. I spoke by radio to the Pitcairners who came out to us in their longboats as dawn broke, lying alongside in the low Pacific swell, half a mile offshore. We took their mail to post in Auckland, bought stamps and wood carvings, and left with my

The Pitcairn Island schoolhouse with the cliff concealing Fletcher Christian's Cave where, in the early days, the mutineers would hide when a ship approached. The schoolmaster is always a New Zealander, picked from hundreds of applicants for a two year stint

dayroom strewn with pineapples, limes and grapefruit so sweet they could be eaten like oranges. To this day the Pitcairners are dependent on passing ships as their high, rocky island has no flat ground for an airstrip. Present population hovers around 60 and there are five family names; Christian and Young, Bounty mutineers' descendents: and the Warrens, Browns and Clarks whose ancestors came from America. They are a delightful and religious people, contentedly enjoying a commune now approaching its 200th anniversary.

We arrived in Auckland at the end of December, having crossed the Date Line on Christmas Eve, thus becoming the first people on earth that year to celebrate Christmas; as our calendar went from December 23 to Christmas Day. Due to circumstances beyond my control (and not, as darkly hinted, a specially arranged Kinghorn family benefit) we remained on the New Zealand coast for 94 days, until the end of March. The government's lifting of import restrictions resulted in a massive influx of shipping, coinciding with the height of the southern summer holiday season. Containerisation had arrived and the dock labour force was being run down while berths for conventional ships were under conversion and thus unavailable. Many years had passed since the ports were so busy. Fortunately for Blue Star Line we were on charter at a daily rate to another line with our outward cargo, so until this was discharged it was the old story of 'more days, more dollars!'

A month each in Auckland and Wellington, two weeks in Lyttelton, nine days in Bluff and two weeks in Timaru enabled us to see the wonders of Rangitoto Island, Rotorua's thermal region, the Waitomo caves, Queenstown, Akaroa, the tortuous mountain road alongside the Shotover River to the now non-existent gold rush town of Skipper's — as well as the Queen and Royal Family on walkabout in Wellington.

While the ship was in Bluff — population 500 including more character per cent that most other places — Michael learned to drive the harbour tug *Monowai*, and was rushed to hospital for an urgent appendix operation. Since we were to proceed to Timaru to complete loading, his mother stayed in an Invercargill motel for 10 days until he recovered. Had his appendicitis occurred at sea he would have died, as the operation proved complex and difficult, even to a skilled surgeon with full hospital facilities. As it was he made a good recovery and was able to rejoin the ship for her homeward run.

After three eventful months in New Zealand we were sad to leave. When, as so often happens, we left the sheltered waters of Foveaux Strait we hit a roaring Tasman gale. For a couple of days the children — seasick no longer — studied the elements, perceiving the difference between a 'rough sea' on the movie screen and the real thing, as we slowly made our way to Capetown, arriving on April 22 at daybreak. Sunshine crept down Table Mountain to bathe the city in dazzling light, breathtakingly beautiful, especially after three weeks at sea. As we neared our berth in Duncan Dock the *New Zealand Star* was leaving, the first ship we had seen since clearing the Australian Bight. In the 15 years since my last visit, the Tafelberg itself had not changed, but the thriving, prosperous city had grown upwards by at least five storeys.

When we sailed two days later, we found fog in the Benguela Current, off the west coast. One night a dozen or so small 'blips' appeared on the radar screen. Fishermen, I thought, and altered course to avoid them. Something strange here though! Echoes kept disappearing while others emerged clearly, from nowhere. The sea was calm so they could hardly have been small boats hidden by waves, and suddenly the fog took on a strong, fishy smell. Slaps on the water around us were accompanied by almost-human cries. Then, through swirling mist, we saw them: our 'fishermen' were a school of whales. Soon the weather improved and the ship's wood-and-canvas swimming pool enjoyed constant use. We saw the sun set with a green flash and the night skies twinkled with a million stars. The Plough, Orion and the Southern Cross were there together, while shivering patches of bioluminescence lit the waters with a weird beauty.

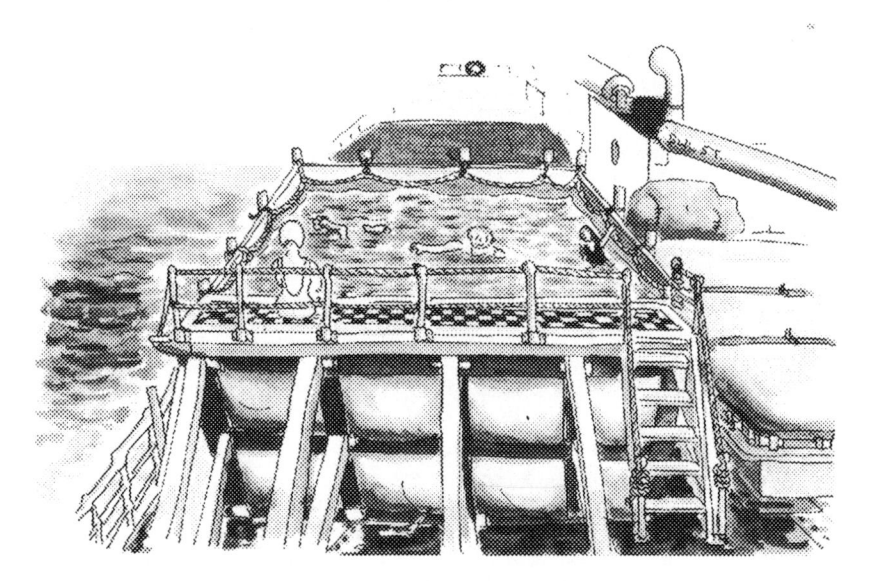

Six and a half months after leaving Newcastle we arrived, on May 14, 1974, in Liverpool, home to most of the crew. The sunny afternoon of our arrival became open day as wives and families trooped aboard in happy reunion. Next day *we* went home and the day after that the children returned to school. On the whole they had persevered well with schoolwork — *I* learned all about Henry VIII and his wives — and the Admiralty Pilot Books, invaluable sources of historical and geographical information, were read widely. We felt they had worked well under the circumstances and were certainly never bored. Nevertheless we were pleasantly surprised to find they had almost kept up with their classes in most subjects. If their French and German had fallen behind they had forged ahead in geography and general education. Six and a half months of almost exclusively adult company seemed to have done no harm, they had made many friends aboard ship and abroad, and in return had been made much of without, I think being spoiled in the process. Susan had ridden horses in New Zealand, father had had his most educational voyage ever, and mother discovered that sailing around the world can be fun, even in an orange plastic bucket.

Chapter 14

Adelaide's last voyage

1974-1975

ADELAIDE STAR'S KEEL was laid at John Brown's, Clydebank, in 1949, the first Blue Star liner to be built there since the 1920s, and the first of a new class of four big refrigerated ships for the trade between Europe and the Southern Dominions. She and the *Wellington Star* (1952) were twin-screw motorships while *Tasmania Star* (1950) and *Auckland Star* (1958) were single-screw turbine steamers from Cammell Laird's, Birkenhead. Outwardly and in the accommodation the four ships were near identical, but the *Adelaide*, with slightly more carrying capacity, was for many years the largest refrigerated ship in the world, with 602,991 cubic ft of reefer space, on a gross tonnage of 12,963. The *English* and *Scottish Stars*, both twin-screw motorships, which came from Fairfield in 1950, were similar but smaller, with six hatches instead of seven. These six were the last Blue Star liners to carry 12 passengers in the classic design introduced by the company during the 1930s. Passenger accommodation was arranged under the bridge in four double and four single cabins, each with private bathroom. Saloon, lounge and card room were on the boatdeck below. They were sea-kindly vessels and popular with passengers, crew and owners.

For 25 years the *Adelaide Star* plied from Britain to South and East Africa, then on to Australia and/or New Zealand, returning home via the Cape or Suez from the former and Panama from the latter. The shortest distance was chosen, using as interim bunker ports Tenerife, Aden or Curacao. A round voyage lasted about four and a half months — two per year including time taken for refits. She called at least once at Buenos Aires en route to New Zealand, and in 1969 took a Crusader Line cargo from New Zealand to Japan in the middle of a normal voyage. This occasional cross-trade trip in

Adelaide Star **at Capetown in her palmy days. How do you search a fully laden ship?**

the middle of an ordinary voyage made what was called a 'double-header'.

Her last trading voyage homeward was dogged by mechanical trouble. We sailed from Liverpool on November 1, 1974, with 6,000 tons of general cargo. While we were loading, a director of the cargo brokers asked if I went near Pitcairn Island and would I mind stopping there to deliver some cases of Churchill Centenary postage stamps. As the island lies across the great circle route from Panama to Auckland no diversion was involved, and cargo delivery is the best reason for a merchant ship to call anywhere — so of course I agreed. The director seemed relieved as their date of issue was to be November 30, the 100th anniversary of Churchill's birth, and no other ship could deliver in time.

The night we were due to leave Liverpool, police told me they had received a phone call warning that a bomb had been planted onboard. How do you search a fully-laden ship? To unload the cargo would have taken 10 days, so I hoped it was a hoax — some sailor's girl-friend trying to delay her lover boy's departure — and sailed on schedule. As we moved into the river, late at night, a mighty bang inside the funnel erupted a mini-volcano of orange sparks and flaming soot.

'There's your bomb, Sandy!' remarked Charles Morison, the pilot, laconically.

But it was merely the starboard engine demonstrating its personality, causing us to anchor in the river while the engineers toiled throughout the night to repair the damage. At Panama I sent word to Pitcairn, 'expect us in about 10 days.'

The weather was calm as we arrived-off, so the islanders experienced little difficulty in coming out to us, six cables offshore. Adamstown appears from the sea as a scattering of wooden houses among the trees, dominated by the schoolhouse below the high cliff which shelters Fletcher Christian's Cave, where the mutineers would hide at the sight of an approaching sail. I had told Tom Christian, Pitcairn's wireless operator, that ladies were welcome aboard as well as the men. (Ladies come only at the captain's invitation.) Two longboats ranged alongside, and up the pilot ladders came men and boys, ladies old and young, delighted to see fresh faces and old friends, with perhaps the chance to sell carvings, baskets, pictures, necklaces and other artifacts all beautifully made and unique to Pitcairn. Our arrival date, November 27, left ample time for the postmaster and his assistants to frank the first day covers which would be sent to philatelists world wide. Stamps contribute substantially to the island's liquidity.

Pitcairn has no resident doctor so the islanders manage with the services of a trained nurse who is usually the pastor's wife. But as an elderly lady was ill and a 13-year-old girl had stomach pains, they were glad to see our ship's Doctor Dutton, who went ashore in the first boat. The elderly lady was too infirm to visit the ship, but Yvonne Brown had a grumbling appendix and came with us and her father to Auckland, where it was removed. Yvonne, who had never before left the island, watched her home fade into the haze, tears rolling down her cheeks — until one of our young cadets came along for a chat. As we entered Auckland harbour eight days later, Yvonne pointed excitedly to cars, buses — even an aeroplane! Her parents hoped she would continue her education in New Zealand, but after her operation she could not get back to Pitcairn soon enough. Although many Pitcairners do now live in New Zealand — she preferred the island.

Our discharge and loading were almost as leisurely as in the *Tasmania Star* the previous year — once again it was the Christmas holiday season — but we were back off Pitcairn on February 23, 1975 — eight days out from Bluff — to embark a party of 13 islanders and four boats for the run to Henderson Island, 107 miles along the road to Panama. Officially they were collecting miro wood for carving; unofficially it was a week's working holiday, for when you live on an island as small as Pitcairn's two and a half miles by one, any change is as good as a rest! We swung the heavy longboats aboard with our 15-ton derrick and embarked our guests at midnight. Most dossed down in the lounge apart from Purvis Young, their leader, who napped on my dayroom settee. Next morning I awoke at six to find the blue Pacific had turned an unhealthy grey, with white horses chasing each other's tails across a rising southerly swell as the wind began to moan a lament. Suppose it became too rough to launch the boats? I called Purvis with a cup of tea and voiced my apprehension.

'Have no fear!' he boomed cheerfully, 'We have prayed for fine weather and the Lord will provide it, you will see!'

Which is precisely what He did for, as the sun rose, the clouds vanished and we rounded-to off the island on a calm, blue sea scarcely ruffled by the breeze. With the islanders' farewell songs 'Sweet Bye and Bye' and 'Goodby!' ringing in our ears, we cheered them, blew three long blasts on the whistle, and watched them chug off towards the gap in the reef and the palm-fringed beach beyond.

Henderson is low, uninhabited and devoid of water. Skeletons of long-lost shipwrecked mariners are to be found in caves there, one of which has a white cross at its entrance, erected by Pitcairners years ago with an American survey ship's assistance. Another cave contains an open pit full of human skeletons, all without heads — grim reminders of the South Seas' colourful past. 'Our' Pitcairners would make their way back home with the longboats down to the gunwales with the miro wood which no longer grows on their own island.

We arrived in Curacao with main engines seriously troubled, and for nine days lay alongside while our engineers, led by Peter Smith, the chief, worked round the clock in two shifts with minimal shore assistance. As often happens when the chips are down, the young bolshies worked as hard as the rest, revelling in their struggle of 'Man against the Mass'. En route to Liverpool, at 13 knots, fresh water ran out due to further engineering problems, fortunately with only two days to go, so we docked in Liverpool smelling delightfully, we were told. The date was April 1, but our superintendent was not fooling when he told me that the ship was to be scrapped.

When I returned to her from leave she was empty — her high, rusty sides and grimy paint combining with weed and barnacles above the waterline already giving an air of forlorn neglect. For her delivery voyage to South Korea the 62-man crew was cut to 34. We would proceed to Pusan at 13 knots to conserve fuel, so the run would take about seven weeks — round the Cape as Suez was still closed.

Just before we sailed the whistle jammed 'on' during testing, and for 20 minutes the old ship cried her heart out. We slipped down the Mersey in white moonlight, the lights of ships shedding long reflections on a sea of glass. Off the Bar the pilot cutter blew us three long blasts as she took Charles Morison back to Liverpool, now a low twinkle of lights far astern.

The weather remained clear round Anglesey, with Snowdon gleaming white above the lesser hills. Next day the sun clouded over into a pale yellow fuzz and the horizon grew indistinct. A cool easterly breeze reduced the damp south westerly airstream from the Atlantic with the inevitable result — fog! It was like being caught on a hilltop when the clouds come down. A cool breeze blew the grey swirls around us, blotting out sun and sky, forcing us to reduce speed dramatically in a world peopled by wraiths, mourned by the siren's wail. Below the engineers were on Stand By, ready at a moment's notice to alter speed or stop. The watchkeeping mate stared into the radar screen plotting the echoes of ships around us; the lookout man to port and I to starboard strained our eyes and ears while the wheelman concentrated on his course. Nonchalantly he flicked the teak, brassbound steering wheel over a couple of spokes, then back again, watching the ticking gyro compass card as though entranced. With nightfall fog seems to recede but this is mere illusion — the masthead lights still gleam like dull yellow balls of cotton wool. The wheelhouse, but for dim compass light, is in darkness. Occasionally a star can be seen overhead if the fog is shallow. On the bridge we take care not to slip on the wet, wooden deck.

The radar warns us that a ship on our starboard bow is on a steady bearing, closing at 10 knots. She shows as an orange spot on the dark, circular screen, ever nearing with each sweep of the scan. 'Hard a'starboard. Steer two six oh.'

The wheelman repeats my order and the ship swings. The echo, now on our port bow, clears us four miles off, but of her physical presence we see and hear nothing.

'Cluster of small echoes ahead sir, look like fishermen,' intones the mate, 'nearest five miles off.'

'Port easy, bring her back to one nine oh.'

'One nine oh she is, sir,'

A couple of minutes later the phantom fishers pass down our starboard side three miles away. Again, nothing is seen except the swirling clouds around us. Watches change and the night passes, but the fog remains. Dawn comes imperceptibly until masts and foredeck take on form and substance in varying shades of grey. Although tired, unshaven and unwashed, I cannot help admiring the dawn's pearly tints, the monochrome print of a colour film. Water swishing along the ship's sides, the muted beat of the engines and the siren's dismal warning are the only sounds, until the watches change with clumping feet and cheerful banter. The master remains on the bridge until the fog has gone.

We are crossing the western end of the English Channel now, heading south, and ships are fewer. Breakfast consists of coffee, a bacon and egg sandwich, more coffee, an apple. Lunch is a proper meal served on a tray by George, the white-coated steward, at the drop-table between the wheelhouse windows. By dinner-time the fog is becoming patchy and during an open spell I have a tray in my dayroom just off the bridge. One good thing about fog on this run, there is always something to look forward to; that it will surely go away! On passage to the Cape it *has* to clear sometime — maybe in five minutes, maybe the day after tomorrow. After the first 24 hours you get your second wind and weariness passes.

Eighty miles off Finisterre — Spain's north western corner — warmer air encourages optimism. The sky occasionally brightens where the sun should be, and the drifting wraiths are less opaque. The forecastle head sharpens under the sun's eyelashes and visibility opens to half a mile, possibly more. You never know unless you spot a ship whose distance off is known by radar. Visibility may extend a mile in one direction, 100 yards in another — half a mile here, three miles there, changing continually. But after darkness the masthead lights take shape. The mists drift away and a ship six miles off is sighted, her lights clearly visible. Just as the engineers are told, Full Away! the fog descends again, thick as ever!

In their brightly lit world of gleaming metal, amid the warm, comforting smells of hot oil, the engineers are probably calling someone a Jonah. But by 10 pm the fog has gone as though it had never been, the sky fills with stars and the lights of a solitary fisherman are visible, 10 miles off. The moon is rising.

'Full Away — South Africa here we come!'
With a sigh of relief the ship slides into normal routine. All that is necessary is to navigate, feed the inner man, and keep the ship clean and the engines running. We feel there's not much wrong with the ship that a lot of hard work (and much expense) could not remedy; in many ways she is in better condition than she was at this time last voyage. We bristle on seeing older ships *not* going to scrap. How dare they outlive us!

The mate, chief engineer, purser and I inspect the ship twice weekly: the food storerooms — emptier and emptier — and the accommodation. Berthing rearrangements for our reduced crew make life more comfortable and only one able seaman chooses to live aft in the old bosun's cabin — just to get the feel of being a bosun. Nevertheless we inspect all the accommodation to ensure that nothing untoward has occurred. Fuses have been drawn to avoid fire risk, and our torch beams cast grotesque shadows as our footsteps echo hollowly along deserted alleyways. Even the few remaining pin-ups pout forsakenly, missing the laughter of the lads who lived here and the kiwi birds who sometimes kept them company in port.

When a ship is sent to breakers she carries all her fittings and equipment, minus spares and extras. The portable swimming pool has gone to another ship; the cine-projector and films, and the Seafarers' Education Service Library, and most of the meteorological equipment are ashore but to compensate for lack of amenities all hands are paid a bonus for this voyage.

Albatrosses wheeled above as we neared the Cape; those who had ever sailed in the *Adelaide Star* and died were returning for a last look at their old ship.

'Albatrosses are reincarnations of dead seamen.'
'Those black ones are engineers in dirty boiler suits.'
'The white toffee-nosed ones must be the mates.'
'Those small ones are cadets and galley boys.'
'Those grand, proudly soaring royal albatrosses must have been captains . . .'
'Who are those bald-headed ones then?'

At Table Bay, we went alongside in the early hours of May 16, later to take aboard fresh fruit and vegetables, the few charts I had ordered and, main reason for our call, fresh water. After our last voyage I worried about being able to make the 25-day trip from the Cape to Korea without running short, but in the event we arrived with one day's supply — 17 tons — still in the tanks. Enough's a feast.

Tanks were topped up by six pm and we were off to the deafening salutes of tugs and pilot vessel who had heard we would 'no be back!'

Off the Cape of Good Hope we stopped both engines for repairs and the engineers slogged away with spanner and ingenuity late into the night after what had already been a hard day's work — to emerge with oil-blackened grins. The motors throbbed back to life.

The ship steered herself at sea with a man on standby in case of failure, bad weather or traffic. Since she is an old ship with no telephone to call the men to the bridge, by law we must keep three sailors in each watch. At sea in clear weather on a normal voyage two of these would be on daywork, but this voyage there are lookout duties only. For years the four-hour watch rota in British ships consisted of two hours wheel, then an hour on stand-by (usually in the messroom listening for the mate's whistle) followed by one hour's lookout. The first lookout stood the second two-hour trick at the wheel and the third man, the 'farmer', did the first hour's stand-by, followed by two hours lookout, then the last hour's stand-by, calling the next watch at one bell. (Why he's called the farmer is lost in the mists of antiquity!) This progressed so that every third watch you were farmer. Nowadays there is usually only one man per watch — two at most — and farmers, like peggies, are obsolete but however automated the ship, keeping lookout with a good pair of eyes is still paramount.

This was one of my hardest voyages. I was short staffed on an increasingly unreliable ship, yet overmanned with crew who had too little to do. I was unfamiliar with the South China Sea and had to navigate the full tricky length of it. Yet we had no cargo to care for, none to collect. All our efforts must be dedicated to delivering our old ship to her inevitable destruction.

Leaving the boisterous Indian Ocean astern we entered Sunda Strait, past volcanic Krakatoa's still smouldering remains, and thereafter enjoyed smooth waters all the way. Local sailing craft were picturesque by day, difficult to detect by night. We passed islands closely and continuously, skirting Borneo's northwest corner. Off Balabac Strait, Api Channel becomes Palawan Passage. Though 24 miles wide, this was rendered hazardous by land low and featureless, out of sight of eye and radar; and grey skies from which rain fell in frequent heavy showers. The Pilot Book warns of uncertain currents.

In recent years vessels have stranded either side . . . a large area westward is known to abound with dangers. Vessels are cautioned not to attempt to pass through this area.

It seems that every reef discovered in this 'dangerous ground' west of Palawan Passage is named after the unfortunate vessel wrecked upon it. There are Royal Captain Shoal and Half Moon Shoal, Bombay Shoal and Fiery Cross Reef, Mischief Reef and Sabina Shoal, Lord Auckland Shoal and Alicia Annie Reef. I could almost hear the crash as *Adelaide Star* added her name to the list, and awoke one night from nightmares which took us the wrong side of an island, heading for certain destruction.

A friendly Shell gas tanker, the *Gari,* overtook us on her regular run from Borneo to Japan, and offered to act as pilot.

'Lead kindly light,' we said, and followed the gas man gratefully, until we crossed latitude 12 degrees north, into the clearer seas of the Philippines.

On June 10 we arrived off Masan, to which I had been redirected, and where we were boarded by a Korean pilot, as the sun shooed away the morning mist, to take us 20 miles up a winding inlet, flanked by steep green hills. I asked the pilot, whose English was somewhat better than my Korean, if many ships were broken up at Masan?

'Oh yes,' he replied proudly. 'We now have four!'

When safely at anchor, I looked out over the town, asking about one of the tall, new white buildings.

'That,' he announced equally proudly 'Is an educational school.'

Masan, not much larger than a village, was once part of the Russian empire, I learn. Rows of trawlers lay tied together at anchor, forced out of commission by the recent fuel increases. Studying the Pilot Book (No. 43) again we learned with interest that tigers exist almost everywhere in Korea. Not often given to drollery, the Pilot continues that these tigers *are noted for their size, boldness and ferocity; they are hunted by the Koreans in winter, when the snow renders them somewhat helpless, but in summer the position is reversed, and numbers of the inhabitants fall a prey to them.*

Agents, purchasers and men from the breakers boarded us for discussions at which the agent interpreted. They wanted me further up the harbour which, as I pointed out, would put us aground at low tide, and my orders were to keep afloat. When the sale was complete, I said, I would take the ship wherever they wished. After a few idle days a coded telegram from London told me that the money had been received, and that I could now hand over the vessel to the purchaser's agent who could not then be found. Our agent and I eventually ran him to earth in a teahouse, whereupon he ordered green tea in little china bowls for us. Papers were produced, studied, and signed. My ship was no longer mine. She would be melted down and rolled into steel plate for new shipyards. So, in one form or another, the *Adelaide Star* may be at sea yet!

Friday the 13th of June dawned bright and clear with promise of another hot day. All hands turned to bright and early with cases packed. The chief, in going-home suit, took the controls himself, despatching the other engineers on deck to watch us enter. To my fury the steering wheel was missing, and I berated our Korean watchmen, showing them the little heap of brass sawdust below where it had been sawn off. They shuffled uncomfortably until the able seaman who was to steer us the last mile in cheerfully assured me that he could use the little wheel on the electric auxiliary pedestal. With pilot embarked we crept in touching bottom occasionally as we went. Small fires broke out first in the port engine, then in the starboard to be extinguished promptly by our chief. As we came to the last resting place, with two anchors down and sternlines ashore, the chief phoned the bridge to say he regretted he could give no more movements. But no more were needed. We had made it!

A launch came to take us ashore. Suitcases were piled into a rope net on deck, ready to be swung into the boat, along with grips, a few canvas kitbags, and a canvas parcel neatly stitched, which bore a strong resemblance to a shrouded steering wheel and which I queried. The seaman who had cheerfully steered us in looked sheepish and explained that he was taking it home for his sister's pub in Lancaster. Did I mind? My own views on the matter remained undeclared. The agent, whose watchmen still smarted under my admonishments, pounced upon the parcel: Apparently steering wheels are *agent's* perks! He requested I accompany him to the office which was off a narrow, dusty street where the air was enriched by sewage dribbling through open drains. I was brought tea by a very pretty secretary before they gave me the news; there was no flight available before Tuesday. And this was Friday! I thumped the desk — the expense of this would take away any profit on the sale of the ship! I exaggerated of course, but the mind boggled at the prospect of keeping track of everybody for three nights in Korea! They would have to do better. They said impossible. I urged them to try.

Meanwhile, back at the quayside, transport had arrived; two small carts each pulled by a moth-eaten horse. One of the sailors tried to befriend the first animal and was promptly bitten in the chest. By this time the lads were in carnival mood and the spectacle of two small carts piled high with luggage, topped off and surrounded by singing sailors, one blood-spattered, caused a stir in town with children following the procession to the office. Undismayed our agent sent the bitten sailor for an anti-tetanus jab and bought him a new shirt, while announcing to cheers that all would feed at the best hotel in town. I made no mention of any prolonged stay here. Lunch on a Hilton rooftop was superb: crisp linen, sparkling glass and silver and banks of flowers made for a lucullan meal, as we gazed across the harbour at our old ship. Back in the office after lunch the agent was all smiles.

'Flight arranged tomorrow!'

At Pusan airport an end of term spirit manifested itself, causing a worried airport official to visit me.'You are Captain Singhorn?'

'Kinghorn.'

'In charge of party?'

I nodded.

'This way please. Airplort manager wish to speak!'

Airport manager was very smart in dinner suit and black bow tie.

'Captain,' he said sternly, 'I think your men are somewhat intoxicated.'

He was right of course, and International Flight Regulations stipulate that if any member of a party is under the influence of drink or drugs none may board their plane. So I told the manager of our long, hard voyage to Korea in our dearly beloved ship, which only yesterday we had deliverd to shipbreakers; how our grief was overcome by the kindness of his fellow Koreans, and how my men were now so happy to be in his country. It was this, I said, which accounted for their delightfully high spirits. Snatches of 'Maggie, Maggie May' drifted into the office.

'Captain,' he said seriously, 'I think your crew have more spirits than high spirits!'

He saw us off, probably feeling that the sooner he was rid of this lot the better, regulations or no regulations.

In Tokyo we had an eight-hour wait during which I busied myself finalising the acounts. I could see a crowd gathering at the far end of the airport lounge and — mildly interested — went to see. American tourists were crowding round three of my sailors, clapping, urging them to sing again.

'Give us *I belong to Glasgow* again, Mac. Gee, you guys sure can sing!'

I drifted away. The long night wore on. In the small hours, by which time the airport lounge was festooned with sleeping sailormen, our call came to a BOAC jumbo jet. I was given a quiet seat in a corner to finish the accounts while the lads spread themselves around, delighted to be among fellow Britons once more. Community singing, they felt, was in order. It would help to lighten the journey. Alas, many fellow Britons did not share their enthusiasm. It was not that our lads were offensive, but seafaring vocabulary does not always appeal to those unfamiliar with it. Complaints!

The lifejackets routine was deemed hilarious, encores were demanded and stewardesses looked flustered as I drifted off to sleep to the gentle accompaniment of *Cats on the Rooftops*. Daylight came and stayed with us as we landed in wind-swept, snow-scattered Anchorage, Alaska and made our way into the lounge while our plane changed crew and took bunkers.

There a very prim and proper BOAC lady informed me that my crew were drunk, that passengers had complained. She read me the international regulations. I apologised. The crew apologised. We promised to be good boys. She was not amused. The doors at Anchorage were not the kind which open at your approach. So when an absolutely gorgeous blonde air hostess from the new flight crew approached, her hands full of papers and clipboards, her face clouded as she realised she could not open the door to get out. Forthwith, one of my tough, hardbitten sailors — a wee lad from Glasgow with longish hair who was noted for his ever-readiness to fight — shot out of his seat and opened the door, bowing as she swept out smiling warmly. Ten minutes later we, too, were aboard, and had scarcely taken off when the chief steward came looking for me.

'Captain Kinghorn?'
'The captain would like to see you sir, on the flight deck.'
Here we go again! Up the spiral staircase, through the first class lounge. At least I was going to see the flight deck!

The captain, a steely-haired, steely-eyed New Zealander, fresh and clean cut in his crisp white shirt looked me up and down, tired, unshaven, unclean — more like the skipper of a Panama tramp than the ex-captain of an ex-British cargo liner!
'Are you having a pleasant trip, captain?'
No mention of international regulations.
I replied guardedly thus far the trip had been very absorbing. He laughed.
'I'll bet it has!' And he asked all about it. Slowly I realised this dear chap was *not* going to criticise my crew. I began to feel better — less the trampship skipper, more the British Captain.
'As you'll know, I'm not allowed to drink on duty, but I'm sure you could do with one?'
He ushered me into the first class bar, where the gorgeous blonde hostess smiled sweetly as she poured an enormous whisky.
'Captain,' she sighed, 'I think your crew are wonderful!'

Chapter 15

Last of an era

1976-1977

AFTER THE ADELAIDE STAR I had my baptism in Box Boats. The 24,212 ton ACT 5 is engaged on a round-the-world-service, an entirely different life and not half as bad as I had imagined. From Liverpool to Fremantle at 22 knots in 22 days, via the Cape!

This confirmed my long-held belief that the only job in a box boat was the master's. The large number of ports visited within his tour of duty and the rapid turn around means that the master experiences more ship-handling than he does in a conventional ship, a part of the job I enjoy. But once port formalities are dealt with, and sleep caught up on (not much time for sleep at sea when calling at five ports in five days in fog) the master might just get ashore for a while. Because cargo is usually worked around the clock and the mates never break watches, *they* have little respite. On cargo watch, they and the refrigeration engineer must ensure that the boxes are loaded and unloaded according to a plan, made ashore, that the boxes are put in the right way round, are connected to the cold air intakes if refrigerated, and that any damage caused by stevedores is noted. What the officers usually don't know, is what the boxes contain. They know they are 'chilled', 'frozen' or 'general', but that is far less satisfying than seeing the cargo itself. Many boxes are hired rather than owned by the shipping company and their owners' colours make for a bright show, but it's all external. Nor do the engineers stop, as there are many jobs which can only be done when in port. What was a leisurely week's maintenance and survey is now done in 24 hours. The purser has all the local port paperwork to keep track of as the ship moves rapidly round the coast, store-taking only when it does not interfere with cargo work. But it is amazing how easily people adapt to the pace.

191

Captain Kinghorn's first command of a box boat — ACT 5 seen passing the Sydney Opera House. A better life than imagined

It was with no great regret that I took up my next appointment, the *Auckland Star*, in Liverpool. Some shipping companies keep their container men in container ships and their conventional men in conventional ships, but Blue Star Line — wisely in my opinion — ring the changes to keep all on their toes, able to daddy any ship which comes their way. The *Auckland Star* was the last of the big, 12-passenger, seven-hatch ships the Company had built. A product of Cammell Laird's yard at Birkenhead, like her twin sister *Tasmania Star*, she had single-screw steam turbine propulsion. At 11,482 tons gross, 572 ft long, she was large for her type. Two leisurely 'old fashioned' voyages followed, with full, non-containerised cargoes, from the Bristol Channel port of Avonmouth via Western Samoa and Fiji to Australia and New Zealand. On our second voyage we loaded frozen meat and butter in New Zealand for Bulgaria and Russia, my first excursion behind the Iron Curtain.

Having loaded at Lyttelton, Mount Maunganui and Napier, we

sailed one sunny Sunday morning, laden to our marks and had barely cleared the breakwater when the VHF crackled into life. We had left our 17-year old deck boy behind, the harbour-master told me! As we were only half an hour out — no great time when you are off half way round the world — I turned back. Not only did I not want to lose our lad, but the paper work surrounding such escapades is daunting! The ship had been 13 days in Napier, long enough for young love to blossom and ripen, and his sweetheart had come to see him off. Embracing behind a hut on the wharf,

The author's first excursion behind the iron curtain as Master of the *Auckland Star*. **The minefield was not marked by buoys**

time had stood still for them, if not for us, and to their dismay they had seen the ship steam out of the harbour! He was happy to be bought back onboard by pilot cutter, preferring the banter of his shipmates to the penalties for desertion, and thanked me profusely for returning for him.

After Fremantle for fresh water we crossed the Indian Ocean to Aden, which I had not visited since the British pulled out, still sitting like a giant brown cinder at the edge of a grey-blue sea. Soon after our arrival that night the Port Health officer insisted that all had to be innoculated against cholera. Our purser pointed out that nobody was going ashore, most had turned in anyway, and that we had called only for bunkers. Our immense Yemeni Arab official was unimpressed.

'Everyone must have choleras!' he repeated thickly.

Hopefully the purser offered him a large whisky, which he knocked back in one gulp, placing his glass down to indicate a strong belief in his inability-to-fly-on-one-wing-theory. The glass was refilled. The purser said he would find the crew, to receive their choleras. In turn, the Port Health officer said he had the necessary injections in his little bag which was not, of course, too little to take 200 Bensons and a bottle of whisky. Leaving an open bottle on the cabin table, the purser left the room, to return 15 minutes later having told me what he was doing. When he returned to his room the whisky level was well down, and Port Health was sitting with a contented smile on his glossy face, hands folded demurely across a colossal paunch.

Would he like to take a bottle when he left, asked the purser kindly?

The Port Health officer blinked.

'Two bottles,' he said.
'What about the cholera certificates? asked the purser.
The Port Health officer dived into his bag and pulled out a sheaf of blank certificates, already stamped and signed.
'You fill in their names,' he leered, 'and one for the road!'
It was not so much a request as an order.
Rather unsteadily, Port Health finally left and we saw him no more. We promptly tore up the worthless certificates.

Once upon a time Aden bumboats hung around the ships like wasps round jam, selling all manner of souvenirs, and latterly transistors and Japanese battery toys. But now — no bumboats; and no fresh fruit or vegetables either. Private enterprise, it seems, is not now encouraged in the People's Republic of South Yemen. In the early morning sunshine we saw that the harbour was full of ships lying mostly, as in days of old, to buoys, busily working cargo into barges. The quays were piled higgeldy-piggeldy with boxes, bales, crates and cartons of import cargo in confused heaps, and with sacks of cement lying on top of cartons of TV sets while tractors with flat tyres lay at chaotic angles; a right stevedore's nightmare! Our Russian pilot followed my eyes, and explained that much of that cargo had been there for months.

'They're all the same, these people,' he said disparagingly. 'They couldn't organise a cup of coffee in a coffee shop! This lot is free aid from overseas, but between laziness and corruption they can't distribute it.'

When we reached the Suez Canal, which I had not seen since 1968 (four months aboard the *Scottish Star*) a tired Egyptian pilot who anchored us efficiently late that night in Suez Bay had been working since early morning.

'Not enough pilots,' he said tersely, as he swung us neatly into our appointed place between two ships.

'Won't employ any more. Slow astern. They say they can't afford to! Let go the port anchor.'

Next day another overworked but equally pleasant and efficient pilot took us through to Ismailia, where he handed over to another. All pilots are now Egyptian, most with British Master's Certificates obtained at South Shields Marine School, so we had no language problems! Signs of the recent war included the battered ruin of what had once been a fine, modern hospital on the west bank. The Great Bitter Lake, where I had spent my time in the *Scottish*, was full of anchored ships waiting for the southbound convoy to pass. Towards the western shore was the long-abandoned *African Glen*, sole survivor of the Great Bitter Lake Association, now sitting on the bottom, upright, her deck just above the water. While we were at anchor I was delighted to see the Hapag Line *Munsterland* come in, to anchor near us. She had been one of our Bitter Lake favourites, manned by a splendid captain and crew although there was no one now in her who had shared the great incarceration. She was on her last voyage before being sold to the Chinese.

From the Suez Canal we made across the eastern Mediterranean towards the Dardanelles where pilotage is compulsory through the narrow Bosphorus to the Black Sea. Our Turkish pilot made his oblations to Mecca at the appointed times — in the privacy of my room when I realised he was a devout Muslim — and while he made his brief disappearances I did the piloting, feeling that under the circumstances we were probably in Very Safe Hands. We lowered our ensign to the British, French and Turkish cemeteries as we steamed by — Istanbul still resembled an illustration from the Arabian Nights as the last rays of twilight flashed on minaret and dome, a floodlit castle looking like the stage setting for Camelot as we ghosted past. Two Turkish gunboats criss-crossed round us in the darkness and, suddenly, we were alone on a silent Black Sea with a rising crescent moon low in the east casting its reflection before us.

Next morning at Bourgas we delivered the first New Zealand butter to Bulgaria — the start of a new trade, we hoped, as the EEC now showed such little interest in New Zealand's dairy produce. Our charts revealed that the coast was still sown with mine fields; not unswept old ones but new ones, aimed against the Turks with whom the Bulgars have quarrelled interminably. The approach channel through the minefield was unbuoyed, but the day was fine and we were able to use land marks to make an approach. We anchored in the appointed spot whereupon a rather agitated agent came by launch to question me closely about our draft. Could I possibly reduce it, he asked?

Alas, no, not without pumping out fuel or water. I had been told to arrive at this draft, and here we were. Ashore, I noticed a large bulk carrier alongside what was probably the only deep water berth in the port. It was summer, late June. The air was warm and the trees were in full leaf and bloom. Most buildings had the faded, slightly dilapidated air and pastel colours of Brazil and Argentina. A dominant Soviet war memorial accentuated by red and white slogans advised the Bulgars to strive continually for socialism, etcetera. There was no commercial advertising and little food on display in the shops, but outwardly the people seemed cheerful enough.

Agent and harbour master ordered us to proceed at once up coast to Varna. According to my mine-infested chart we would have to go round three sides of a square to reach Varna — but I had watched ships proceeding direct, apparently through the minefields themselves. With oil fuel rising in cost all the time you become conscious of saving miles where possible. I asked the harbour master, smart in khaki drills with four gold bands on his epaulettes, if I could go direct. 'If you head out on this course for two miles, and turn to port when this headland bears so much (he pencilled a figure in the chart's margin), you will be all right. That part is clear.'
'Marked by buoys?' I asked, to which he grinned and shook his head.
'You will be safe, I promise.'

Once alongside in Varna, work of discharging our butter cargo began. Like Bourgas, Varna was a pleasant little town, a holiday resort, rich in history — but its foodshops, too, resembled Old Mother Hubbard's cupboard. The *Auckland Star's* crew numbered 68, eight less than her original complement when she was built in 1958, but still a lot of mouths to feed. The purser had made a shopping list and the local providore arrived. It was impossible to find *that* amount of fruit and vegetables, he apologised. But this was high summer in one of the most fertile parts of Europe! The providore shamefully hung his head. No longer, it seemed; there had been bad weather, the farmers would not work the farms properly. He would take the purser by van to see what they could find. In the shops they drew blanks, but in the so called Free Market, where farmers sell their own produce in a way which does not comply with idealogical principles of socialism, they fared better. From this stall, a few heads of lettuce (the stallholder's total stock.) From the next, some beetroot and a little cabbage. Here, a few heads of tired looking celery; there, a few tomatoes. The best of the crop, everybody said, was exported. Where to? They looked over their shoulders, and answered — Russia!

A soldier, posted at the foot of the gangway to inspect our passes before proceeding ashore, was an amiable fellow in a comic opera uniform in which the old royal crown had been replaced by a red star. Aboard was Van, a New Zealand engineer of Dutch ancestry. He played the bagpipes and was allowed to practise onboard between five and six pm each day, when nobody would be trying to sleep. One afternoon, Van partook liberally of the excellent local wine, before returning to the ship for his practise He decided that as we were alongside he would treat the locals to a performance and tuned up at the top of the gangway, whence he descended slowly to the majestic strains of the *Flowers of the Forest.* As he paused for breath at the foot of the gangway our astonished Bulgarian soldier asked for his pass. Van had forgotten it, anyway he wasn't going ASHORE — he was just going to play his bagpipes on the quay. The guard did not understand and kept saying, 'Pass, pass; you must have pass.'

Van assumed he had said, 'you may pass,' and inflated with a great droning sound which drowned further speech, began a spirited version of *Scotland the Brave* and stepped ashore. The guard watched in disbelief as Van marched slowly up and down the wooden quay, solemnly piping his heart out, to the obvious delight of the crew of a nearby Chinese ship.

This vessel became a conversation point between me and the agent next day. The mate wished to paint our ship's side before we sailed for home, and I had asked the agent on our arrival if we might do this. At Napier, the ship always surges alongside the quay, which takes off the paint on the port side — and on the long run homeward the bare metal rusts. It is *essential* that you paint the port side again between Napier and home! (Or used to be.)

'No,' she said primly, 'this may cause pollution. We have no tides in the Black Sea to carry your pollution away. We do not allow ships to paint overside here!'

Fair enough. Prohibiting overside painting is too common these days around the world, even in tidal ports — and anyway I liked the agent, a homely young-middle-aged lady who ran her office efficiently. She and another lady did all the thinking while the donkey work, typing and the making of tea and coffee, was done by a callow youth of 17. That was the total staff.

The morning after Van's bagpipe performance I was taking my pre-breakfast turn on the bridge when I noticed a line of Mao-suited Chinamen walk down their gangway carrying drums of paint and rollers on bamboo poles. They began to paint their ship's side, grey above the waterline, green below. They worked well, did a good job, and had just finished and trooped back aboard when our agent arrived at a quarter to noon (the time agents arrive the world over). I met her on deck, outside my room.
'We respect your rules, Vera,' I said. 'But that Chinese ship has been painted this morning, as you can see!'
Vera looked doubtful.
'Either,' I said, 'she has broken the law or you have one law for them and another for us, and if you have it's racial discrimination. In direct contravention of the Helsinki Agreement, too!'
I was unsure of my ground here, but the Agreement was in the news so I felt I was being topical.
'That Chinese captain,' Vera fumed, 'shall be shot!'
'Shot?' I echoed, horrified.
'Well,' she conceded, 'prison, with hard labour!'
'Good heavens Vera, you have harsh laws here!'
All I had been hoping was that she would allow *us* to paint overside also!
'I shall certainly speak to him, anyway!' she said, adding with a wicked wink, 'maybe!' and with that she swept me into my dayroom for her lunchtime coca-cola.

Before leaving Varna I was given radio permission to enter Soviet waters, what is known as 'pratique', which must be obtained at every port a ship visits. It is usually granted by port health authorities when satisfied that a ship is free of disease and not vermin infested. This granting of *radio* pratique smacked of efficiency. We arrived off Novorossiisk shortly before midnight and I was looking for the red light under the white light which signifies a pilot cutter the world over, when a blinding searchlight was suddenly switched on at the lighthouse and beamed upon us; our introduction to Soviet Russia, where searchlights, we found, still loom large in local security. This particular searchlight seemed only to read our name as it switched off as suddenly as it had come

199

on, leaving us in pitch darkness.

We were alongside by daybreak, when an army descended upon us. Some were in military uniform — Customs — some were port health, others were white-coated biologists to take samples of our frozen lamb cargo. The agent was a rather intimidating lady who kept close rein on her lively sense of humour. I was asked to sign numerous documents, far more than are usually required, and had to declare that I had nothing to sell or exchange or otherwise dispose of other than the ship's cargo, possessed no pornographic literature, would not attempt to dispose of any monies other than Soviet roubles except in special tourist shops. I was not to dump garbage or paint the ship overside. The crew were to be back onboard by midnight every night, though I as captain could stay out all night if I so wished (thus enabling me to bail my men out of jail when they got into trouble!) I also had to sign a pledge that no food, drink, or anything else would be offered to the guards protecting the ship. A uniformed port official accompanied each man to his cabin to search for contraband and unsuitable magazines which were given to me to lock up until the ship sailed. Not only was a Red Army soldier placed at the foot of the gangway with a telephone and a little aluminium tray on a stand in which to keep the passbooks, but others were posted on the quay beside our mooring ropes. They were unarmed, spoke to no one but their reliefs, and must have been bored to tears.

Later a train of refrigerated railway wagons was shunted alongside complete with an accommodation car, its gallery hung with washing and around which children played. Smoke curled upwards from its little chimney, a house on wheels. When we asked where the meat was to be taken, people looked disinterested and replied, 'Moscow probably.'

Dockside cranes unloaded the cargo in canvas slings, each slingload stopping before it reached its truck to be weighed and sample slices carved by the biologists. Then it was manhandled into the wagons. Work proceeded steadily but at no great rate, and there seemed to be people everywhere. The dockers themselves were men, but the tally clerks were women, some quite young girls. The work was labour-intensive, and down the holds those dockers not actually heaving the meat played cards. Even they had to present passes before coming aboard and collect them as they went ashore. This show of security, however, did not prevent a good deal of pilfering. Not only did cuts of meat mysteriously disappear (as happens in ports the world over) but our storerooms were broken into, raw eggs and tins of coca-cola pilfered, and the eggshells and empty cans strewn around the holds. Several cabins were burgled and when I complained the police were called in. The local constable, very smart in white and gold peaked cap with red star prominent, white jacket with gold buttons and black trousers, tried to be helpful but the stolen transistors were never recovered. I felt that the penalties were so severe that nobody would ever be caught.

Provided we presented our passbooks to the gangway guard, we were allowed ashore without let or hindrance. We could take and use cameras and wander around as we pleased. As a break from the oppressive air of Russia I loved to stroll round the old parts of the town in casual dress. Old ladies in black sat in rocking chairs outside their cottage doors in the evening sunshine and smiled at me kindly as I passed; a safety valve to an arid backcloth of stupid regulations and a shortage of food for the crew. At the dock gates girls in white coats carrying huge pistols in holsters shyly asked us for 'chiglets'. American ships came here frequently with wheat from the USA (to the former breadbasket of Europe!) Their sailors were well liked and often gave the pistol-packing-mommas packets of chewing gum — chiglets. All night three searchlights played their beams erratically round the port, from watchtowers manned by soldiers with machine guns. The beam of a search light would creep revealingly around the harbour to fall upon a seaman walking back to his ship, pass on, and then jerk back, playing cat and mouse with him to the gangway.

Upon arrival in Novorossiisk we were introduced to the International Seamen's Club, the Russian equivalent to our own Missions to Seamen, where we went most nights. Housed in an old building near the dock gate, the 'Mish', as the Russians called it, was run mainly by well-educated young ladies whose main job was to interpret. Jobs for well-educated girls in Russia are not plentiful, and on leaving their polytechnic or university they are given two work options. The state pays for their education, so the state allocates them jobs, for a while anyway. With their feminine pleasantness and kindness they did much to mitigate the harsh reality of Russia. I liked the Russians if not their system.

During the nightshift discharge of our meat, work would suddenly stop at one hold and begin at another when a railway truck was full. Rather than move the train it was simpler to shift to a hold opposite an empty truck. As a partially empty hold must be

201

covered to allow refrigeration to resume without drawing in warm air that particular hold had to be covered each time work ceased. The old *Auckland Star* had beams and plug hatches so rather than ship these, a canvas or plastic tenasco sheet was drawn across and lashed in place with rope tails, heavy and slippery work as ice was everywhere. At first the card-playing Russian dockers made no move to help our second mate; this was ship's work, not theirs. After covering up a couple of times on his own, he turned a baleful glare upon the card-playing proletariat, and eventually exploded. His subtle innuendoes were lost, but the tone of his abuse sank in. They grinned sheepishly and began to help. Before the night was out *he* had *them* doing the work while he supervised, which speeded up discharge enormously.

Occasionally I was called upon to write letters to the authorities aplogising for my crew's behaviour which, outside Russia, would have given no offence. We had a good crew of decent lads, not a tearaway among them. But one night they met some American sailors from a nearby grain ship, and hospitably invited them aboard for a drink. The guard at the foot of the gangway unsmilingly denied the Americans access.

'But just a minute, tovarich, this is *our* ship and these are *our* friends. Who d'you think *you* are to say they can't come aboard?'

All the guard could say was 'nyet!'

One of the lads, full of resource (and probably local liquor, as he knew he was about to commit a dreadful crime) came aboard himself, and reappeared several minutes later with a couple of cans of beer which he thrust into the guard's tray.

'Here comrade, have one yourself, and cheer up!'

Hands were raised in horror. Bribery! I received an official deputation from the authorities in the early hours forbidding my crew to go ashore again.

My letter next morning seemed to right matters but similar trivial incidents over the 12 days we were there — jolly jack against the grim face of authority — together with the nightly 'searchlight tattoo', became strangely depressing. Although Russia was an interesting experience, none of us was sorry to leave. Coming through the Dardanelles was like stepping back into reality, and we breathed more easily; especially, in my own case, when we reached Malta, where my wife joined for the remainder of the voyage, the last 'old fashioned' voyage — with general cargo out and refrigerated cargo homeward — I was to make.

An era ended, fortunately the Company carried on.

Chapter 16

Survival

WITH THE EXCEPTION of the steamship *ACT 5* and the motorship *Southland Star* (now converted to a box boat) the ships described in this book have all gone, most for scrap which helped to pay for new vessels. Some ended their lives more dramatically. HMS *Conway*, the oldest by more than a century, was wrecked under tow in the Menai Straits in 1953 en route towards Birkenhead for what would have been her first drydocking since 1939. A towline parted and the tide swept her onto rocks from which she never refloated. I have been told by one who was there that the monstrous sound of her great timbers cracking as she settled and broke her back was deafening. Fortunately, no one was even injured. *Conway* lasted another 20 years as a shore-establishment but by the mid-70s two years' pre-sea training was a luxury. The *Conway*, and later the *Worcester*, died mainly because the demand for cadets had dwindled with the shrinking merchant navy. Today's cadets receive a two-week induction and are then fed sandwich courses which are not the meals they used to be. But it is no bad thing that cadet training now emphasises working on ships at sea. The Nellist approach to examinations was ideal provided it was accompanied by adequate sea time, but a disproportionate amount of theory against practice is not in the interests of good seamanship or ship operation.

The *Saxon Star* was sold in 1961 to D L Street of Newport and became the no-longer-refrigerated tramp *Redbrook*, still under the British flag. After four years' colourful career she passed to Greeks as the *E Evangelia* and was wrecked on October 19, 1968 in the Black Sea where she became a total loss.

The *Dominic*, as the *Golden Ocean*, foundered off the Andaman Islands in the Bay of Bengal in 1971. When I was in her in 1955 a welded seam opened up for a couple of feet below the waterline in the engine room, where a timely cement box effected a watertight temporary repair. Had a similar crack opened in a less obvious place — a hold for instance — the ship could easily have foundered earlier.

The heavy-lift *Australia Star* was chartered to Norwegians for whom she sailed — manned by Blue Star personnel — as the *Concordia Gulf*. In 1974 she was sold to the Italian Costa Line, and as the *Cortina* is still with them. Her place in Blue Star Line was taken by smaller ro-ro ships which are more suitable for today's heavy lifting.

The *Wellington Star* went in the mid-70s to the Middle East Express Line and became a sheep carrier called *Hawke Bay*, transporting both the quick and the dead — live sheep above, frozen mutton below. The *Malaysia* went to the same company becoming the *Khalij Express* ('Khalij' being Arabic for 'Gulf') and carries 20,000 at a time on the hoof. By sailing under the Saudi flag she obtains remarkably cheap bunkers and is probably earning more money than she ever did when her passengers were two-footed.

The live-sheep trade is mainly between Adelaide and Fremantle and Bandar Abbas (Iran), Kuwait and Libya. To the Iranians the Gulf is the Persian Gulf. To Iraq, Kuwait, Saudi, Qatar, Bahrain, the Emirates and Oman, it is the Arabian Gulf. It is a growing market for the primary produce of Australia and New Zealand which the EEC chooses to exclude.

From Australia, live sheep are carried to the Middle East and slaughtered on arrival. In New Zealand — the extra five days at sea makes the difference — the sheep are slaughtered before shipment, strictly according to Muslim tradition. This new trade from New Zealand and Australia to the Gulf and India was pioneered by Blue Star Line with two purpose-built container ships — *Australia Star* and *New Zealand Star*, the latter being my privilege to take new from the stocks on her early voyages. Those two ships combine the best of containerisation with conventional shipping. They have cranes to work their cargo much of whose organisation is left to the ship, thus providing job satisfaction; their rapid progress port to port makes them viable cargo carriers today and hopefully tomorrow. The Gulf Trade from the Antipodes is supported now by modern conventional cargo ships carrying sheepmeats in bulk (rather than containers).

The old trades are mostly operated with box boats which are not only bigger, but spend so little time in port that they can make more voyages per year and thus earn more freight. The tendency to carry more cargo faster in bigger ships which began when sail gave way to steam has accelerated and probably will continue. There will never be as many ships as there were — a sad fact of life for the shipbuilding and repairing industries. The container revolution of the '70s flooded the market with well-found conventional ships at give-away prices. Many of these — from North European flags — were bought by the Chinese, who run them on trades where low wages enable totally subsidised ships to operate as though no competition existed. Some old ships passed to the Greeks, many more to the flags of convenience of Liberia, Panama and Cyprus. The only certain factor about vessels under those flags is that their owners are not Liberian, Panamanian or Cypriot. Some, indeed, are chartered back to their old or associated companies. Many more operate the low-freight bulk trades — running with minimal cost and maintenance until either they drop to pieces, sink, or are scrapped when the next survey falls due — whichever comes first.

In 10 years time, perhaps less, most of the ships displaced by the container revolution will have gone. What then? Shipowning can

From now on the *New Zealand Star* and her like dominate the world's waterways

still be profitable if costs can be kept low enough. The answer seems to lie — for all but the most particular owners — in the standard ship, built to a successful design at a lower price than a custom-built vessel. There is nothing new in this idea: probably the best remembered is the Liberty ship of World War 2. The Americans, the Russians and their satellites, and the Japanese have built standards ever since. One of the most successful types is Austin Pickersgill's SD 14, a remarkably versatile and economical general cargo vessel suitable for world wide trading, now seen under many flags as well as our own.

Shipowning cannot be compared with any other business, and some of the saddest sea stories of recent times are those of once-proud private companies which went public and died as a result. Their ownership became too remote, dedicated to instant profits, ignoring the fact that shipowning is highly personal, requiring infinite skill, patience — and investment. The companies which survive, and prosper, are those remaining in private hands, whose owners are not afraid to make decisions which may not bring immediate gains but which can become long-term successes. The weather, global politics, and luck play their parts. A potato famine in Northern Europe might provide cargoes from Canada for the astute shipowner with ships available. An upturn in demand for frozen meat by Russia or Iran, or butter by Bulgaria, may increase trade from New Zealand. But a ship trapped by someone else's sudden war can be a financial disaster. Shipowning is not for the faint-hearted.

The Falklands War has underlined the importance of having a merchant navy which can respond rapidly to crisis: it has shown that the present decline in British ownership must be reversed if we are to survive. I travelled to the Falklands in October 1982 — four months after the conflict ended in Argentina's surrender at Port Stanley — as passenger from Ascension Island in the *Norland*, a North Sea ferry whose normal run was between Hull and Rotterdam. This versatile ship, 12,998 tons gross, proved ideal for her work as a troopship. Converted in a few days she left Portsmouth on April 26, 1982 with 2 Para aboard — and was the first vessel into San Carlos Water to land her troops on May 21. On May 23-24 she survived air attacks without being damaged and was at South Georgia by May 29. On June 3 she again defied Argentine air strikes at 'Bomb alley' to land the Gurkhas. On June 11 she deposited 1,046 Argentine prisoners of war at Montevideo and on

June 23 repatriated a further 2,047 to Puerto Madryn in Argentina. In July she landed the Queen's Highlanders in the Falklands and was the longest-serving ship of the original task force. Without her, and the other supporting merchantmen — Cunard's *Atlantic Conveyor* paid the ultimate price, sunk with her master and 11 of her crew — the war could not have been fought effectively.

My own command, the *Avelona Star*, a modern reefer ship, sailed from Portsmouth in June under the command of Captain H K Dyer, to operate as a 'floating supermarket' to the Task Force.

A major reason for the decline of British shipping is that successive British Governments have refused to make the kind of concessions to British shipowners which foreigners take for granted. We do not want hand-outs but a sensible national policy of granting investment allowances would go a long way to help us compete with the world on the terms which the rest of the world lay down for themselves. Lavish aid to third world nations enables them to build fleets of merchant vessels which proceed to run our own off the seas in the trades which *we* pioneered. With low-paid crews, subsidised by their governments, they can of course offer lower freight rates than can British ships. If you want your cargo carried cheaply you put it in the cheapest carrier and risk the chime of the Lutine Bell. The British shipowner is under increasing pressure to 'flag his ships out' under a flag of convenience, with cheap crews and lower overheads. Whether this is efficient long term is debateable, especially if, as is likely, Liberia and Panama demand that their own seamen be employed in their own flag vessels. This could soon lead to further requirements, that a ship must be *commanded* by a person of her flag nationality — as applies already in most shipowning countries including our own. But cheapness is not always best, and in the long term we can still consider ourselves among the best.

We can still build superb ships, operate them well and safely, and carry the world's cargoes as they should be carried. Our survival as a trading nation still depends on the British Merchant Navy. But wasn't it ever so?

Index

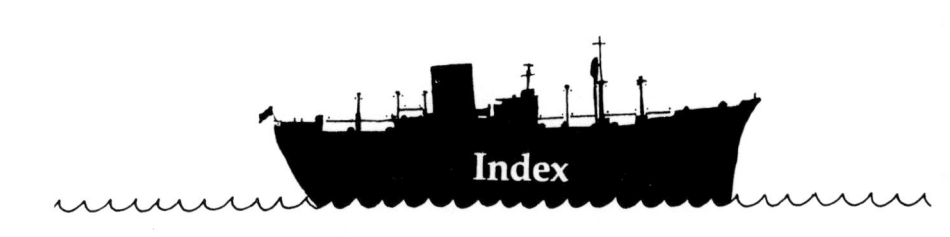

A

Achilles HMS (cruiser) 28
ACT 5 SS (container ship) 191, 203
Adamstown (Pitcairn Island) 179
Adelaide 66, 111, 113, 204
Adelaide Star, MV 177, 183, 185, 186, 191
Aden 38, 109, 125, 177, 194, 195
Afric MV 120, 121, 122
African Glen SS 128, 129, 196
Agalampus MV 127, 130, 132, 133
Agapenor MV 127
Ajax HMS (cruiser) 28
Akaroa 174
Albion Line 141
Alca SS 26
Alcatraz Penitentiary 32
Aldridge, Captain Giles 107, 109
Alexandria 130
Alma Doepel (hulk) 97
Altmark (German supply ship) 28
Amazon, River 47, 48, 50, 51, 53, 54, 135, 136, 139
Ambrose Light Ship NY 54
America SS 54
Amsterdam 169
Anchorage, Alaska 188
Anglesey, Marquis of, 18
Anselm MV 138
Antwerp 59, 63, 75, 76, 78, 98, 170
Api Channel 184
Archibald Russell (4-masted barque) 16, 19
Argentina Star SS 63
Argentinean Reefer MV 96
Armstrong's, Ship & Engine Works 15
Askew, Captain W H 123
Atlantic Conveyor SS 207
Auckland 79, 80, 95, 99, 141, 148, 153, 165, 166, 172, 173, 174, 178, 179
Auckland Star MV (War loss) 78
Auckland Star (2) SS 177, 192, 197, 202
Austasia Line 135, 138, 139, 140
Australasia MV 138, 139, 140
Australia Star (1) MV 78
Australia Star (2) MV 117, 118, 120, 204
Australia Star (3) MV 204
Avelona Star MV 12, 207
Avonmouth 192

B

Balabac Strait 184
Bandar Abbas (Iran) 204
Bangor (N. Wales) 18
Baron Line 44
Barrow-in-Furness 118
Barry, Glam 31
Baudoinville MV 138
Beauty Point 37
Beira 34, 35, 36, 82
Belem 48, 50, 53, 54, 59
Belfast 34, 36, 77
Belfast HMS (cruiser) 101
Ben Line 24, 86
Bibby Line 99
Birkenhead 170, 177, 192, 203
Blackwater, Essex 123
Blenheim 96
Bligh, Captain 141
Blue Funnel Line 16, 69
Blue Riband of the Atlantic 54
Blue Star Line 23, 45, 47, 61, 69, 77, 87, 97, 98, 103, 104, 107, 117, 122, 127, 134, 135, 139, 146, 147, 159, 169, 174, 177, 192, 204
Bluff NZ 146, 148, 174, 179
Boca 28, 64
Boleslaw Beirut MV 128
Bolton Castle SS 87
Booth Line 47, 49, 50, 56, 61, 135, 136, 138, 140
Bosphorus 196

209

Boston, Mass 142
Bounty Mutiny 141
Bourgas 196, 197
Bradford 99
Brasil Star SS 61, 62, 63
Brasilia Star MV 158, 159, 160
Bremen 68
Brest 64
Bridge Street Clinic, Port Melbourne 137, 138
Brisbane 37, 97, 98, 99, 100, 111, 121, 135, 139
Brisbane Star MV 78
British India Steam Navigation Co 24, 44, 69
Brocklebank Line 24
Brooke-Smith, Commander John 22
Brooklyn 55, 56, 57
Brown, Mr C K L, Chief Engineer 157, 158
Brown Family, (Pitcairn Island) 141, 173
Brown, Miss Yvonne 179
Buenos Aires 28, 29, 30, 64, 68, 159, 160, 177
Burns Philp & Co Ltd, 94
Byrne, Barry (Purser) 160

Columbia Star (1) MV 24, 25, 30, 31, 34, 146
Columbia Star (2) MV 147
Concordia Gulf MV 204
Condors (German aircraft) 41
Conway HMS (Ex HMS *Nile*) 18, 20, 22, 23, 28, 29, 34, 36, 203
Cook, Captain Howard 146
Cook, Captain James 141
Cortina MV 204
Cossack HMS 28
Costa Line 204
Cox, W E 61, 65, 67, 68, 71, 75, 103, 125, 135, 140
Cristobal 32, 33
Crookall, Tom 163
Crusader MV 147
Crusader Line 147, 148, 161, 177
Cuidad de Barcelona MV 26
Cunard Steamship Company 6
Cunard White Star Line 20
Curacao 32, 80, 177, 180
Cutty Sark (clipper ship) 18

C

Cabadelo 58
Caernarvon 21
Cairns 83
Cairo 125, 126
Calabrase, Captain J 146, 148
Caledonia Star MV 146, 147, 149, 150, 153, 154
California Star (1) MV (War loss) 23
California Star (2) MV 123, 146
California Star (3) MV 147
Cambria (Thames sailing barge) 99
Canadian Star MV (war loss) 23
Capetown 34, 66, 174
Cardiff 75, 158
Carlisle 75
Carlson, Captain Kurt 31
Carr, Fred (Pilot) 25, 26, 158
Cartaret NJ 55
Catalina Star MV 146
Charles Racine (wreck) 36
Charleston, South Carolina 142
Chesapeake Bay 57
Cheshire MV 99, 100, 101, 102
Christchurch, NZ 95, 141
Christian, Family (Pitcairn Island) 141, 173
Christian, Tom 179
City of Birkenhead SS 95
Clan Line 24, 69, 86, 146
Clarke Family (Pitcairn Island) 141, 173
Clyde, River 34, 86
Colchester 123
Colorado Star MV 146
Columbia River 32

D

Dampier, King Bay 119
Danube Navigation Company 128
Dardanelles 115, 116, 196, 202
Dawson, Mr (Pilot) 26
Deseado 30
Dickers, Captain S A M 47
Distressed British Seaman 82, 83
Djakaria 135, 136, 140
Djakarta MV 128, 132
Dominic MV 48, 49, 59, 61, 140, 203
Dominion Monarch MV 95
¡*Doric Star* MV 28
Dunedin 141
Dunedin (sailing ship) 141
Dunedin Star (1) MV (war loss) 78
Dunedin Star (2) SS 86, 87, 88, 89, 90, 105
Dunkirk 70, 98, 100, 102
Durban 34
Dutton, Dr 179
Dyer, Captain H K 12, 207

E

E Evangelia MV 203
East London 34
Echo (schooner) 96, 97
Edinburgh 75
Edinburgh HMS (cruiser) 15
Edinburgh Channel 26
Elbe River 103, 107
Ellaroo SS 95
Ellerman Line 24, 99

210

Elswick 15
Empire Clarendon MV 75
Empire Star (war loss) MV 78
Empire Strength MV 34
Empire Wisdom SS 146
Endeavour HMS 141
English Star MV 67, 68, 123, 125, 134, 142, 143, 146, 160, 177
Erikson, Gustav (ship owner) 16, 35
Esquimalt 31, 32
Exeter HMS (cruiser) 28

F

Fal, River 123, 146
Falkland Islands 11, 14, 206
Falmouth 31
Farrell Lines 128
Federal Lines 24, 69, 77
Fenara (Egypt) 125
Flint, Islet 82, 92
Flying Enterprise SS 31
Folkestone 144
Fortaleza 51, 52, 54
Foy Boats 15
Fremantle 69, 110, 111, 120, 138, 139, 191, 194, 204
Funchal 172

G

Galtieri, (Ex-President, Argentina) 14
Gan, Island 121
Gareloch 123
Gari MV (tanker) 185
Garibaldi (ketch) 23
Gateshead 76
Gatun (tug) 92
Geelong 98, 99
General Average 108
Genoa 171
Gibraltar 101
Gisbourne 148
Gladstone, Queensland 37
Gladstone Star MV 158
Glasgow 75, 76, 86, 188
Gleeson, Paul (Chief Engineer) 160, 164, 165
Glen Line 24
Goddard, Captain T M 19
Golden Ocean MV 140, 203
Graf Spee (German warship) 28
Gravesend 26, 106
Great Bitter Lake Association (GBLA) 127, 129, 196
Greenock 86, 146

H

Hamburg 68, 98, 99, 103, 118, 165

Hamburg America Line 127
Hansa Line, Bremen 118
Hapag Line 152, 196
Harris, J F (Cadet) 36
Harrison Line 89
Harwood, Commodore 28
Hatton, Captain M G 18, 20
Hawke Bay MV 204
Hebburn-upon-Tyne 67
Henderson Island 179, 180
Hickory Stream MV 49
Hilary RMS 50
Himalaya SS 164
Hobart 37, 97, 98, 99, 135
Hong Kong 95, 140, 148
Honolulu 161, 163, 167, 168
Hubert SS 135
Hudson (barque) 27
Hull 117, 206

I

Iberia Star 139
Ilheus 64
Imperial Star (1) (war loss) MV 78
Imperial Star (2) MV 65, 68, 75
International Seamen's Club (USSR) 201
International Postal Union 131
Invercargill 146, 174
Ismailia 101, 195
Istanbul 115, 116, 196

J

Jangadas (Brasilian fishing craft) 51
John Graham (steam dredger) 97

K

Karamea MV 80, 81
Kavo Yerakis MV 134
Keels (Tyne barges) 15
Khalij Express SS 204
Khaosiung 154
Killara MV 127
Kill Van Kull 55
Knight Templar MV 147
Kobe 151
Krakatoa (Volcano) 184
Kushiro 148, 150, 151

L

La Guira 49
Langsdorf, Captain 28
Larnder, Peter (Cadet) 25, 26, 27, 28, 31, 33

211

Las Palmas 64
Lautoka 94
Lawhill (4-masted barque) 16, 35
Le Havre 170
Lednice MV 128, 133
Leningrad 166
Lenna (ketch) 97
Levuka 161, 162, 167
Liberty ships 206
Linthouse 87
Lisbon 64
Liverpool 26, 36, 59, 68, 75, 79, 86, 98, 99, 100, 107, 108, 112, 114, 115, 120, 136, 138, 142, 148, 157, 175, 178, 180, 181, 191
London 24, 27, 38, 52, 62, 63, 68, 71, 76, 78, 79, 84, 93, 94, 95, 97, 98, 99, 100, 107, 119, 123, 130, 135, 141, 142, 148, 155, 157, 168, 186
Los Angeles 33, 161, 162
Lourenço Marques (Now Maputo) 34, 35, 78
Luckner, Count Felix Von 161
Lutine Bell 207
Lyttelton 79, 95, 96, 141, 148, 174, 192

M

Maatsuyker Lighthouse 37, 38
MacAskill, Joe 89, 94
Magdalena SS 27
Malacca Strait 101
Malaysia SS 135, 139, 140, 204
Malta 77, 85, 202
Manaus 53, 56
Manhattan 55
Marjorie (hulk) 35
Masan 185
May Queen (ketch) 97
Mbengga Passage 94
McDonald, Mr (Pilot) 94
McKenzie, Compton (Author) 89
Mecca 196
Melampus MV 127
Melbourne 35, 36, 66, 82, 83, 110, 111, 114, 121, 135
Melbourne Star (1) MV (war loss) 78
Melbourne Star (2) MV 65, 66, 68, 75, 144, 157
Mercantile Marine Service Association (MMSA) 18
Merchant Navy Training Board 33
Mersey, River 18, 157, 181
Messageries Maritimes (French shipping line) 127
Middle East Express Line 204
Middlesborough 119
Missions to Seamen 34, 132, 201
Mobile Alabama 104
Moji 153

Moller Line (Hong Kong) 87
Mona Passage 34
Monowai (tug) 174
Montevideo 28, 64, 160, 206
Montreal 142
Montreal Star MV 160, 161, 166
Morison, Charles (Pilot) 178, 181
Moscow 200
Moshulu (4-masted barque) 16
Mount Maunganui 192
Moyana (ketch) 18
Munchen SS (Lash ship) 152
Munsterland MV 125, 127, 129, 132, 133, 196

N

Nagoya 151, 152
Naha 148
Nandi Waters 94
Nanuku Passage 167
Napier 192, 193, 198
Nasser, (President of Egypt) 101
Navem Hembury SS 52
Navula Passage 94
Nellist Brothers 43, 44, 45, 59, 91, 153, 160, 203
Nellist's Nautical School 39, 40, 41, 42, 43, 44, 68, 86, 96
Nelson, New Zealand 96, 97
New Plymouth 141, 146
New York 54, 55, 142
New Zealand Shipping Company 24, 69, 77, 147
New Zealand Star (1) MV 78
New Zealand Star (2) MV 174
New Zealand Star (3) MV (container ship) 204
Newcastle, NSW 98, 99
Newcastle-upon-Tyne 39, 75, 76, 119, 169, 175
Newport, Mon 31, 107, 108, 203
Newport News 57
Nicklin, Mr Frank (Queensland Premier) 100
Nippara MV 127
Nippon MV 127, 129
Nishifuji, Mr (agent) 149, 150, 151
Nordwind MV 127, 132, 133
Norfolk, Va 57, 142
Norland MV (North Sea ferry) 11, 206
North Shields 71
Novorossiisk 166, 199, 201

O

Odessa 166
O'Malley, Joe 37, 38
Osaka 153
Otaru 148
Outward Bound Sea School, Aberdovey 23

P

P & O Line 6, 20, 24, 69, 147, 164

212

Palawan Passage 184, 185
Pamir (4-masted barque) 16, 35, 68
Panama Canal 14, 32, 33, 77, 80, 81, 91, 92, 104, 145, 146, 172, 177, 179
Pangbourne 18
Para, River 50
Passat (4-masted barque) 16, 35, 68
Penang 135
Philadelphia 142
Piraeus 134, 157
Pitcairn Island 141, 172, 178, 179, 180
Pitcher, Captain William 82, 148
Plas Newydd (N. Wales) 18
Plate, River 64, 68, 159, 160
Polish Ocean Lines 128
Politician SS 89
Polly Woodside (3-masted barque) 36
Pommern (4-masted barque) 16
Port Alma 135
Port Chalmers 141
Port Dinorwic 21
Port Elizabeth 34
Port Invercargill MV 127, 129, 130
Port Kembla 35, 113, 135
Port Line 6, 24, 45, 69, 77, 127, 147
Port Moresby 135, 140
Port Said 101, 108, 128
Port Stanley 11, 206
Port Swettenham (Now Port Kelang) 135
Port William 11, 12
Portland, Or 32
Portofino 171
Portsmouth 206, 207
Prague Spring 133
Puerto Madryn 207
Pusan 181, 187
Pyrmont 99

Q

Queen Mary RMS 86
Queensland Star MV 158
Queenstown NZ 174

R

Rangitoto 174
Rathlin Island (hulk) 35
Raul Soares SS 53
Recalada Light Ship 159
Recife, Pernambuco 57, 58, 68
Redbrook MV 203
Result (3-masted schooner) 31
Rhodesia Star SS 104
Rhodes 108
Riding, John (yachtsman) 165, 166, 167
Rio de Janeiro 27, 64
Rio Grande (Tierra del Fuego) 29
Roberts, Captain G G (RD RNR) 48, 49, 58, 59, 60
Rochester 99

Rockhampton Star MV 158
Rock ferry 18
Rollicker (tug) 12
Rona (hulk) 35
Rondo (Norwegian yacht) 83
Ropner Line 44
Rosario 68
Rosneath Patch (Clyde) 86
Rotorua NZ 174
Rotterdam 59, 169, 206
Rotterdam Lloyd Line 82
Royal Docks, London 24, 47, 62, 80, 88, 142, 157, 158
Royal Interocean Line 82
Royal Mail Line 20, 24, 27, 45
Royal Navy 90
Royal Star SS 146
Royston Grange SS 160
Runciman Line 44
Runic MV 99

S

Sacramento, River 33
Salford Docks, Manchester 34
St Lucia Channel 172
San Carlos Water 12, 206
San Francisco 32, 33, 160, 162
San Sebastian Bay (Tierra del Fuego) 29
Santa Cruz (Tenerife) 25, 26, 66, 177
Santos 27, 28, 64, 68
Sao Luiz do Maranho 51
Sapporo 148
Saracen MV 147
Saxon Star MV 34, 36, 37, 66, 146, 203
Schelde, River 59
Scotswood-upon-Tyne 15
Scott, Captain Robert F, RN 96
Scottish Star MV 67, 68, 125, 127, 130, 131, 133, 177, 195
SD 14 (Standard type of ship) 206
Sea Egg (yacht) 165, 166, 167
Seafarers' Education Service Library 183
Seattle (Wash) 32
Seeadler (German raider) 161
Senator (hulk) 53
Shandon (hulk) 35
Shaw Savill Line 6, 24, 69, 77, 80, 94, 95, 99, 120, 121, 147
Shields 15
Ship Captain's Medical Guide 120, 137
Shotover, River 174
Sindh MV 127, 130, 133
Singapore 100, 135, 138, 139, 140
Skippers, NZ 174
Skoots 31
Smith, Peter (Chief Engineer) 180
Soderblom, Charlie (Lamptrimmer) 27, 28
Sombrero Passage 144
South Africa Star SS 103, 104, 117, 118, 160
South Shields Marine School 39, 40, 44, 86, 195

213

Southampton 18, 157
Southend, Essex 86
Southern Cross SS 94
Southland Star MV 158, 159, 203
Spanish windlass 91
Stapleton, N.J. 55
Staten Island, N.J. 54
Staten Island (US Coastguard icebreaker) 96
Stena Inspector MV 12
Stockton, Calif 33
Straat Malacca MV 95
Street, D. L. (ship owner) 203
Suez 77, 84, 88, 120, 128, 177
Suez Canal 101, 104, 123, 125, 181, 195, 196
Sunderland 117, 118, 161
Suva 93, 94, 95, 164
Sydney, N.S.W. 36, 77, 98, 99, 111, 112, 114, 115, 121, 135, 136, 160
Sydney Star MV 75, 76, 77, 78, 81, 86, 90

T

Table Bay 183
Tacoma, Washington 104, 164
Tallinn 106
Tan Chi (tanker) 159, 160
Tasmania Star SS 47, 95, 169, 177, 179, 192
Texaco Kenya (tanker) 155
Thames Sailing Barges 24
Thompson, Captain 'Asdic' 103
Thursday Island 100
Thyseville MV 138
Tilbury 65, 142, 143
Timaru 79, 174
Timaru Star MV 75
Tokyo 151, 188
Townsville 83
Transatlantic Line 127
Trinder Anderson Line 86
Turmoil (tug) 31
Turton, Jim (Bosun) 106
Tyne Flappers (paddle tugs) 15
Tyne Improvement Commission 15
Tyne, River 15, 68, 76, 80, 160
Tynemouth 19

U

Union Castle Line 20, 24, 123
United States SS 54
Union Steamship Company of New Zealand 11
Uruguay Star SS 47, 63, 65

V

Van Asbeck, Dolph (Engineer) 198, 199
Vancouver 32, 160, 164, 167
Vancouver Star SS 67
Varna 197, 199
Vassil Levsky MV 128
Victoria, VI 164
Viking (4-masted barque) 16
Vinnen, Cadet (aboard *Pamir*) 68
Vladivostok 166

W

Wakeford, Captain 'Wally' 18
Warren family (Pitcairn Island) 141, 173
Warsash (sea school) 18, 25
Warspite (ketch) 23
Wear, River 161
Wellington, NZ 96, 98, 141, 153, 162, 168, 174
Wellington Star (1) MV (War loss) 78
Wellington Star (2) MV 86, 140, 142, 177, 204
West Point SS (US troopship) 54
Whisky Galore (book and film) 89
Whitley, Ted (Cadet) 34, 36
Willemstad 50, 91, 145, 172
Wilmington, Calif 49
Wolf Rock Lighthouse 59
Worcester HMS (sea school) 18, 203

Y

Yarra, River 35
Yeoward Brothers 26
Yokohama 151
Young family (Pitcairn Island) 141, 173, 180
Young, Purvis 180